MORE HOURS IN MY DAY

Emilie Barnes
Sheri Torelli

HARVEST HOUSE PUBLISHERS

EUGENE, OREGON

MORE HOURS IN MY DAY

Copyright © 2008 by Harvest House Publishers, Inc.
Published by Harvest House Publishers
Eugene, Oregon 97402
www.harvesthousepublishers.com

Library of Congress Cataloging-in-Publication Data

Barnes, Emilie
More hours in my day/Emilie Barnes.
    p. cm.
  ISBN-13: 978-0-7369-2253-1
  ISBN-10: 0-7369-2253-9
  Rev. ed. of: More hours in my day. 1982.
  Includes bibliographical references.
  1. Time management—Religious aspect—Christianity. 2. Women—Time management.
3. Home economics. 4. Women—Conduct of life. 5. Women—Religious life. I. Barnes, Emilie.
More hours in my day. II. Torelli, Sheri. III. Title.
  BV4598.5.B371994
  640—dc2094-6866

                                                                2008002357

Contents

Our Stories

Emilie's Story

God Works Everything Out

You created my inmost being; you knit me together
in my mother's womb. I praise you because I am
fearfully and wonderfully made.

PSALM 139:13-14 NIV

Irene was a Jewish girl, the oldest of five children, born in Brooklyn, New York. When she was a teenager, her mother died giving birth to a baby girl. Irene's Papa, a gifted tailor, died a few years later, leaving the teenager to raise her brothers and sisters. Jobs and money were in California, so the young family headed for Hollywood to make a life for themselves.

As a young adult, Irene designed and sewed tennis dresses for movie stars in the early 1920s. She worked hard to support herself and her brothers and sisters. When she was 29, she met Otto Klein, a 40-year-old chef for Paramount Studios. They married in 1930.

Irene wanted children, but Otto wouldn't hear of it. As a German Jew and a veteran of World War I, Otto had barely escaped the war with his life. He wasn't about to bring children into such an angry world. Twice Irene became pregnant, and twice he forced her into abortions. When she became pregnant a third time, Irene refused to terminate the pregnancy. In July 1934, a beautiful son, Edmund

Francis, was born. Four years later, on April 12, 1938, Emilie Marie was born. Otto adored his baby daughter, but his young son became the victim of a father filled with hatred from abuse he'd suffered as a child.

Otto was a creative and artistic man. As an orphan in Vienna he was placed in the royal palace as a kitchen helper. His exceptional ability eventually gained him training by the finest chefs in Europe, and he became an expert Viennese chef. He escaped war-torn Europe, traveling first to New York and then to Hollywood. He became a chef to movie stars, including Clark Gable, Mickey Rooney, Lana Turner, Greta Garbo, Mario Lanza, Douglas Fairbanks, Judy Garland, and many more. Yet deep inside this successful man was a little boy still hurting from the loss of his parents.

Otto turned to alcohol to escape his pain, eventually jeopardizing his career and his family. His drinking fueled his angry perfectionism, resulting in violent outbursts at the shortcomings of his coworkers, wife, and children.

Irene's fear for her safety and that of her children smothered her fun-loving, sanguine temperament. Edmund stored his anger for his abusive father, releasing it later in rebellion. And Emilie—that's me—became a very bashful, quiet child.

I have only a few happy memories of my father. When I was nine years old we moved to Long Beach, California, where Daddy managed a restaurant called Ormando's. He would take me on walks along the beach, and we would fish off the pier. He gave me a beautiful blue bicycle on my tenth birthday.

Daddy lost his job at Ormando's due to his temper and drinking. My brother, Edmund, who was almost 14 at the time, began his years of rebellion. Then Daddy became very ill. He refused to listen to his doctors. Instead he got mad at them and demanded that they make him well.

Because of my father, the emotional thermometer in our home was almost always on high. It was my job to try to keep peace, and

I was able to cool Daddy's temper at times. He adored me and never abused me. But I hurt inside because of what he did to my mother and brother. I suffered from nightmares, and I often wished Daddy would die so we would be free of his hot temper.

Daddy didn't let Mama cook very often because she didn't meet his gourmet standards, but she was also great in the kitchen. Her corned beef cabbage rolls and other Jewish meals are a delicious memory. Occasionally Mama and Daddy would prepare a meal together, and I would sit on the drainboard watching and learning. Those were happy times for me—probably because Daddy wasn't drinking on those days.

The summer after my eleventh birthday Daddy died, and we were released from his bondage. I cried as I looked toward heaven and wondered about the afterlife, but I quickly pushed those thoughts out of my mind. Mama was now a single parent with two children to care for. Being unemployed and uninsured, Daddy had left us with hospital and doctor bills.

My aunt and uncle kept us afloat financially and helped my mother open a small dress shop in Long Beach. We lived behind the store in a three-room apartment—kitchen, living room, and one bedroom. It was perfect for our needs. We gave Edmund the bedroom, and Mama and I slept together in a Murphy bed in the living room. Mama gave me the responsibility of caring for those three rooms while she ran the dress shop. I painted the whole apartment myself, even though I'd never painted in my life. I decorated the walls and, with help from Mama, made curtains, tablecloths, and chair covers. I planted flowers in our window box and kept the bathroom and kitchen spotless. Under Mama's direction I prepared meals and washed the laundry.

Mama was a Proverbs 31 woman and didn't even know it. She was a hard worker, often working at the shop late into the night. She watched for bargains in order to make our money go further. Together we transformed our simple apartment into a haven of peace.

My brother shattered our peaceful home, making it a home filled with stress and worry. His teachers called, the principal called, and then Edmund was kicked out of school. Several times the police called Mama in the early morning hours, telling her that Edmund was in jail. Mama and I would get up, wait for the city bus, and travel to the police station to bail him out. Poor Mama was heartbroken over her son. Finally Edmund enlisted in the Marines. A few years later he married.

Mama was able to work us out of debt, so we moved to a larger apartment away from the store. By this time I was in complete control of our apartment—washing, ironing, and planning meals. I was also going to school, working in our dress shop, and traveling with Mama to the garment district in Los Angeles once a month to buy dresses. My mother trained me well.

During the years following Daddy's death, we became active in a local Jewish temple. On Wednesdays, after public school, I attended Hebrew school taught by the rabbi. At 15 I was confirmed at the temple, and my family was proud of their little Jewish girl. But my confirmation didn't bring peace to my heart, and I still didn't have the answers to my questions about life after death.

At age 16 I attended a modeling class at the Wilma Hastings Modeling School. It was there I met Esther, the most talented, beautiful, and natural model in our class. Esther later went to New York and became a supermodel, appearing on the cover of several fashion magazines.

Esther stayed with me a week that summer. We went to the beach, worked in the dress shop, and played "fashion show." One evening we went to the movies, and there we met Bill Barnes. Bill wanted to date Esther, but Esther and I had an agreement that we would only double date. Esther told Bill he would have to find a date for her girlfriend (me!). Bill's identical twin, Bob, owed him a favor, so Bob became my blind date.

I was immediately attracted to Bob. His deep tan, faded denim pants, white shirt, and saddle shoes made quite an impression. He was a mature college student, athletic and strong. He opened doors for me, displayed gracious manners, and carried himself with an air of gentleness. There was something very different about him.

Esther and I had been experimenting with cigarettes and planned to smoke in front of these college men to show them how mature we were. When Esther offered me a cigarette I heard a voice inside me say, "Don't do it!" So I refused, and was I ever glad! Later we discovered that Bill and Bob didn't smoke.

I was shy, bashful, and very quiet during our blind date. I figured that if I didn't talk a lot I wouldn't say the wrong thing and reveal my age. I didn't want to blow it with this handsome, gentle man.

I was absolutely shocked when Bob called me for a real date. On the day of our date I cleaned the house, baked cookies, washed and set my hair, polished my nails, and washed and ironed clothes. I created atmosphere by lighting candles and boiling cinnamon sticks on the stove to give the apartment a homey aroma. I wanted everything to be perfect—even the things he wouldn't see when he came to pick me up.

Being the homemaker of the century, I won the heart of my man—except for one area. I was Jewish, and Bob was a committed Christian. Mama really liked Bob, a clean-cut gentleman, but my aunts and uncles were outraged that Mama allowed me to date a Gentile—and worse yet, a dyed-in-the-wool Baptist. "You are making a big mistake, Irene," they told Mama. "He'll never amount to anything. He's not good enough for our Emilie. They'll have a miserable life. She's too young, so send him away. Better yet, send her away."

Even though I didn't know it at the time, God was in control. By the time I was 16 my relationship with Bob was growing deep and serious. Bob's family was praying for me during those dating months as Bob patiently read the Scriptures to me, took me to church, directed me to messages by Billy Graham, and introduced me to his Christian friends. One verse that pierced my heart was John 14:6: "Jesus answered, 'I am the way and the truth and the life. No one comes to the Father except through me'" (NIV). I asked myself, *Is Jesus the Messiah our people are waiting for?*

Then I read Romans 6:23: "The wages of sin is death, but the gift of God is eternal life in Christ Jesus our Lord" (NIV). *Eternal life—is that the answer to my questions about life after death? Can I have life forever and ever by believing in Jesus Christ and receiving Him into my heart? Is dying merely a change of address from earth to heaven?*

Bob gently guided me to the family of God. One night, in the quietness of my room, I knelt, opened the door of my heart, and invited the Lord Jesus—Messiah Yeshua—into my life. I asked Him to change me and give me a heart ready to serve Him. I asked Him to take control of me and guide me on a path that would please Him.

Having cleared the only hurdle between us, I wanted to marry Bob Barnes and build a healthy, happy, spiritual home free from abuse and anger—a home with harmony, love, and the fragrance of Jesus. I knew we could have that kind of home even though the path might be rocky at times. Bob and I were committed to the common goal of serving the Lord and serving each other. We could survive as a couple with God's help.

The criticism from my family grew strong, especially after Bob and I announced our engagement. My aunt and uncle offered to send me to one of the best finishing schools in Europe, buy me a car and a wardrobe, and provide an unlimited expense account if I would not marry Bob. But my heart now belonged to God and to Bob. I'd already received the greatest gift—God's Son, Messiah Jesus—with no strings attached. I told my aunt and uncle that I loved them, but I was going to marry Bob and establish a Christian home.

In September 1955, Bob (age 22) and I (age 17) were married. Yes, my relatives' hearts were broken. Family pressure was heavy on Mama, who had to sign legal papers so I could marry at my young age. I thank God that I was not disowned or "buried" as some Jews are when they marry outside the faith. My family didn't think our marriage would last more than a few months, but we had a loving God guiding our hearts and lives.

Shortly after our wedding I began my senior year of high school and Bob began his first year of teaching. I wasn't much older than his students. Bob helped me with term papers, signed my report cards, and attended senior activities with me. I received the home-maker of the year award, starred in the senior play, and served as student body secretary. I was the only married student at Long Beach Poly High School.

After graduation I kept house, worked in the dress shop, and later took a job with a bank. I wanted a family, but Bob felt we should wait until we could afford a house and he was secure in his school district. Three years later our daughter, Jennifer Christine, was born.

Just a few months after Jennifer arrived we became parents to three more children. My brother Edmund's wife left for the market one day and never returned, walking out on her husband and three pre-school children. Edmund became very depressed and was unable to care for his children. Bob and I felt they needed love and stability, so we asked Edmund if he would let us take them into our home. We soon became legal guardians for Tawney, Keri, and Kevin.

Are you a morning person or a night person? Your efficiency and success may increase if you arrange your tasks around the natural rhythms of your body. Schedule top-priority projects during your peak hours and routine work during your low times.

Mothering four children under the age of four was an exhausting job. I cooked, baked, cleaned, washed, ironed, and did everything I could to create a loving home for our family. I made all the children's clothes, plus my own. Whenever Bob wasn't refereeing football or basketball games he was home by four, which was a great help. I was happy that my childhood responsibilities had equipped me with the tools I needed—another proof that God works all things together for His purposes.

A few weeks after Edmund's children came, I discovered I was pregnant. I was so sick that it was difficult to carry on with our four children. One day I took them into the backyard, spread a blanket on the grass, and then passed out from exhaustion. Thankfully the children were okay when I awoke.

Another day three-year-old Keri got into some paint cans in our neighbor's garage. I found her covered head to toe in red oil-based paint. After stripping her clothes and cleaning her with paint remover and a warm bath, I put us both down for a nap. Fifteen minutes later she was back into the paint again.

In May 1960, Bradley Joe was born, giving us five children under five years of age—and I was only 21. My mother was still running the dress shop so she was unable to help me. Bob was a great help, but he had a profession, night classes, and a part-time refereeing job. So raising the children was my baby in more ways than one. I survived the next few years until Edmund remarried. His new wife had two children, and Edmund's children moved back into his home. We've seen Edmund's first wife only once in more than 37 years, and she's never contacted her children.

By this time Mama's business had faltered, and she filed for bankruptcy. She lost what little she had and slipped into a deep depression. She was in her early sixties with no home, no job, and no future. We invited Mama to live with us until she could reorganize her life. Mama's visit turned out to be another step in the path of God's plan. Being in our home, she attended church with us. The Spirit of God touched her heart. In 1964 Mama invited the Messiah into her life! John 14:14 says: "If you ask me for anything in my name, I will do it" (GNT). I'm trusting our Lord for the salvation of each of my family members.

Bob and I continued to raise our family, and we learned much together. We were committed to God, family, love, goals, and raising responsible adults. I worked at being industrious, creative, and very organized in our family life, which gave me more hours in my day.

At 29 I became the first chairwoman of the Newport Beach Christian Women's Club. That year I was asked to speak to more than 800 women at a conference in Palm Springs. I was scared to death. But the response to my testimony overwhelmed me. Other chairwomen asked me to speak at their meetings. Rose Tiffany, a longtime Christian friend who supported me in prayer that day, answered, "She'll come," and started booking dates. Since that time I've spoken to hundreds of Christian Women's Clubs.

In 1971 we moved from Newport Beach to Riverside, California. I was 33 years old. Our years in Newport Beach had given us some very close friends and church relationships. We'd grown spiritually so much at Mariners Church that it was hard to begin again. By this time Mama had moved into a senior citizens' building. She attended Bible studies, met others her age, and grew through the great teaching she received.

Our move to Riverside wasn't easy because I was homesick for our friends. It was during this time that I met Florence Littauer. We had much in common as speakers, and our husbands encouraged us to create a seminar for women. In the spring of 1973, Florence and I taught our first "Feminar" to a handful of women. God was paving the way for our future ministries. Soon Florence founded C.L.A.S.S. (Christian Leaders and Speakers' Seminar), and Bob and I founded "More Hours in My Day" time-management seminars. Florence and I were just two ordinary women open to God's leading, with two supportive, encouraging husbands cheering us on.

In 1997 More Hours in My Day was meeting the needs of a lot of women across North America. Bob and I were traveling, speaking, and selling organization tools in many different denominational churches. This schedule was physically tiring, but we enjoyed every minute of it. It was so exciting to see women come and get encouragement for their homes and families. At this time I began to feel very fatigued and found it difficult to write and speak. By early 1998

I had lost 30 pounds, and I came home tired each weekend. It took me three days to rebound.

My Bob and our daughter, Jenny, sat me down one Monday and said, "Mom, you have to go to our family doctor and find out what's happening with you." My blood work showed distress signals. The doctor said, "You need to see an oncologist right away." The next day I was at a local oncologist's office, and he confirmed that I was in the early stages of chronic lymphatic leukemia. He felt we should monitor it for now; there was no need for aggressive treatment.

I wasn't progressing as I felt I should and sought a second opinion from a specialist at the Hoag Cancer Center in Newport Beach. At Hoag, Dr. Barth diagnosed me with non-Hodgkin's lymphoma. I had a tumor the size of a football in my stomach! He immediately started me on chemotherapy, which burned away the tumor. We became very proactive in my treatment from that point on.

After 31 years in Riverside, we sold our beautiful "Barnes' Barn" and moved to Newport Beach to be close to my doctors. I had to cancel all speaking engagements for the next year. Then I went into remission, and my hair began to grow back curly and gray. Two months later the disease flared up, and I started another round of chemo to fight the new onslaught. It became evident that even the newest and strongest chemo could not keep me in long-term remission.

In May 2000, with much prayer, Bob and I journeyed to Seattle, Washington, for a bone-marrow transplant at the Fred Hutchinson Cancer Research Center. A 23-year-old Canadian gentleman, who was a perfect match for me, unselfishly donated his healthy bone marrow. On the night of June 6 and the morning of June 7, I had a successful bone-marrow transfusion. I had to stay on heavy immune suppressant medication for at least two years so my body wouldn't reject my new bone marrow. It's been quite a few years now, and I am in full remission with no signs of the disease in my body.

Life is so fragile and uncertain, but God's plans are always better than our own. All those relationships of the past became our support system during my healing process. People have been so great, offering prayer and encouragement! Never throw away your old friends.

I've finally returned to a very limited speaking schedule. And my Bob and I continue to write books. We've had more than 65 published and feel so blessed that God has allowed us to help men and women and boys and girls through our writing ministry. We praise God for His faithfulness to us. One of our favorite verses is found in Psalm 16:5: "You, LORD, are all I have, and you give me all I need; my future is in your hands" (GNT).

Through all these trials, the organization skills and practical knowledge I'd developed helped keep our home running smoothly.

Before my cancer, my friend and colleague Sheri Torelli started working with me on More Hours in My Day seminars and products. After my diagnosis she really stepped in and kept the business going, staying with my principles and techniques and adding her own special touches.

Today we work together helping women all over the country get organized and improve their home and family lives. Although I'm semi-retired now, I'm delighted that God brought Sheri into my life so I can pass much of the torch of More Hours in My Day into her capable hands.

As we share the practical, time-tested principles in this book, I know they'll help you get organized and reduce your stress. The plan works!

Sheri's Story

How I Got Out of a Mess

Have you ever been awakened in the middle of the night, your heart pounding and you feel so unsettled you don't know what to do? That happened to me. What caused my anxiety and stress was simply that I was a complete mess due to the overwhelming disorganized condition of my home. The clutter and mess had finally taken its toll.

I suffered from "Sentimental Pack Rat Disease with Perfectionist Tendencies." Although this is not a recognized disease, it is nonetheless very real to those afflicted. I was drowning in hopeless clutter and disorganization. And my perfection tendencies made it almost impossible to get anything accomplished. That's how I learned a principle I teach in seminars today: "Perfectionism yields to procrastination, which yields to paralysis." I had no plan, no goals, no hope. I was a young wife and mother, and I desperately needed help.

I was raised in a Christian home by a mother who believed that cleanliness was next to godliness. I knew clean; I even liked clean. However, I was born without the "O" chromosome, the organizational gene. I never learned to be organized in my time management or the clutter in my home. Can you relate? Are you missing that same gene? Keep reading!

I met Emilie in 1981 at a seminar she was conducting at my

church. I didn't go to the seminar to get organized. I only wanted more hours in my day, and the seminar flyer promised just that. I didn't plan to get organized or to get a handle on my clutter, which at this stage had become so overwhelming I experienced night sweats and nausea. I figured more time is what I needed, and the large sign in our church foyer compelled me to sign up. As a "sentimental pack rat" I had no desire whatever to attend a class on organization because I knew what would happen. I was sure the first thing the teacher would tell us is, "You have to throw away your stuff." And I didn't want to do that. My stuff was very important to me, and I was completely unwilling to let it go. But I signed up and showed up.

As Emilie began teaching I sensed a difference in the way she shared that I hadn't experienced before. She taught with such a heart for us who were attending the seminar. She was genuinely concerned that we understand that organization was attainable and possible and the key to less stress. Her sweet spirit was delightful, and I found myself taking in everything she said. She spoke simply and lovingly and told us that as makers of our homes we needed to recognize the tremendous contribution we make to our families.

She also told of our need to see clutter in a new light. Stuff is only stuff, and most of it is completely unnecessary. At first I was skeptical...very skeptical. My "stuff" was very necessary. That's why I carried it with me from one room to another, from the house to the garage, from one house to the next. When she pointed out that most of us didn't even know what stuff we had, I knew she was right. I realized I had no idea what was in many of the boxes stacked in my house and garage.

Emilie shared her philosophy: "If you haven't used an item in a year, you need to give it away or throw it away." This was almost more than I could absorb. What if I needed it someday? What if the kids or my husband needed something? What if, what if, what if? As a pack rat I could justify everything I owned (once I knew what I had).

But I listened to what Emilie had to say. I took in her ideas, suggestions, and tips. It didn't happen overnight, but the principles I learned and began to implement started making a difference in my home. My husband, Tim, began to notice, and even the kids saw the difference. I became a more serene and confident person. I began to have more peaceful days because I discovered Emilie was right—I really was the one who set the tone in my home.

What I failed to realize the morning I met Emilie was that our meeting was not a coincidence, but a divine encounter. After Emilie and I became friends, I still told her she had to give me two weeks notice before she came to my house. No dropping in for a quick chat and a cup of tea because I had to have time to make my home presentable enough to allow her through the door. I was so sure she would make mental notes of what was wrong with my house and what I needed to change.

> Ask yourself, "What's the best use of my time and energy right now?" If that's not what you're doing, switch to a higher priority. What you're doing might be good, but is it the best?

Of course Emilie wasn't taking notes—my lack of organization was still a source of guilt and anxiety for me. As I became more involved with Emilie and had the opportunity to work with her, I finally realized how much God orchestrated my attendance at her seminar that day so many years ago. I found more and more ideas that helped me get control over my life and my home. The results and benefits have been truly life-altering. Today my home is clutter free and filled with peace and serenity. And I'm delighted to say that I can relax and enjoy the wonderful gifts God has given me—a beautiful, peaceful home; a wonderful husband; and two great kids. And my family is much happier too!

Are you like I was? Wanting desperately to provide a place of comfort and peace and safety but having no idea how to bring it about? Or maybe you are somewhat organized but desire some help to take it to the next level. Or maybe you want more hours in your day. There's an old saying, "If momma ain't happy, ain't nobody happy." It's so true. We women do set the temperature in our homes. We are the ones who determine home sweet home. Is your home a place of comfort and peace? Do family members and friends come in after a long day at school and work to relax—to sit back and enjoy each other in safety and comfort? Isn't this what you want for your home? Well, I have some great news for you: There is hope! There is light at the end of the tunnel. There is a way out of the clutter and mess. If I can do it, so can you!

The time-tested, proven ideas for getting your home in shape—and keeping it that way—in this updated and revised edition of *More Hours in My Day* will bring hope and healing, some direction and guidance, and practical solutions to the problems of disorganization and clutter. Implementing the simple and practical suggestions will ease your stress and get you started on a new way of life. Yes, it is a process...and you're taking the first step by reading this book. So let's get started!

We serve a God of order, not chaos. But
He doesn't expect perfection from us.
He just wants to see growth and honest effort.

PART ONE

Organization Basics

1

Me, Get Organized?

God created man in his own image,
in the image of God he created him;
male and female he created them.

GENESIS 1:27 NIV

O ver the years we've received countless phone calls, letters, and emails from women who want to know how to better manage their time. Some need only a bit of encouragement and a couple of ideas that will save them time and help organize their homes. Others need a complete overhaul and, in desperation, call us for hope and help. Either through coaxing from their husbands, children, friends, or clergy, they have realized they can be more effective if they could somehow get organized.

That word *organized* means many things to many people. For some it might be putting their papers in colored file folders and for others it means putting all their seasonings in alphabetical order. For some it means a clean house, and for others it means being able to quickly retrieve papers that have been stored. Webster defines *organized* as "to form parts into a functioning whole." That's pretty simply stated. The opposite of organized can be defined as *dismantle*. And many times *dismantled* is exactly what seems to define our homes and our personal lives. As women, wives, and moms, we're the primary makers of our homes; we have "authority" over our homes.

Authority doesn't mean power; it simply means responsibility and accountability. In our society, women have generally been given authority over what happens and doesn't happen in the places we call home. At the end of the day we are responsible for what is accomplished and what is left undone.

We don't profess to have all the answers for organization and time management, but we've found the following to be basic requirements when a person wants to become more efficient. By saving a few minutes here and there, you will have more time in your day or week to spend on your priorities.

❏ *Start with you.* What causes you to be disorganized? We find that organized people have a calmness and serenity about them that disorganized people don't have. Search yourself to see what is causing all that confusion. See if you can't get rid of that internal clutter before you move on. In some cases you may need to meet with your clergy or a counselor who can help you unravel the causes of this disorganization. (We didn't say it was going to be easy to get organized!)

❏ *Keep it simple.* There are many programs available, but choose one that's simple. You don't want to spend all your time updating charts and graphs. When Emilie began teaching organization and then writing about organization, there were few available resources. Today resources are available in books, magazines, and on the Internet. By taking some valuable time to research what works best for you and your style of cleaning and organizing, you can find the system best for you.

❏ *Make sure everything has a designated place.* One of our sayings is "Don't put it down, put it away." Another is "Don't pile it, file it." If there isn't a place for stuff to go, it's going to get piled. That's one thing you want to avoid. I (Sheri) promised my husband, Tim, that every time I am ready to make a purchase, I take the time to decide if I have a place at home for it. If there is, I feel free to buy the item. But if there isn't a place, I wait for another time. Another good motto to adopt is "For every new item purchased, something else has to go." This keeps you in the habit of rotating and eliminating items you no longer need or want.

❏ *Store like items together.* My (Emilie) husband, Bob, has his gardening supplies and tools together. I keep my laundry items in one place, my bill-paying tools in one area, my prayer basket and its tools together, my cups/saucers, drinking glasses, and dinnerware all in their general area. I (Sheri) keep my scrapbooking materials together near my rubber stamping supplies. My husband, Tim, keeps all his photography books and equipment in one area. We never have to look far to find exactly what we need. The less time you spend searching for an item, the more time you have to do projects and activities. Keep everything together in one place.

❏ *Even though you are neat, you may not be organized.* We suggest that women use notebook organizers. Choose a style that fits your personality. You might create your organizer using computer software designed for that purpose. There are two things to remember when using a planner: 1) write it down, and 2) read it. It doesn't do much good if you write a birthday date or appointment on your calendar and then forget it because you didn't read your calendar. Write *and* read. Another rule for organizers: Buy what you will use. Don't purchase a Franklin Planner if Post-it Notes work better for you. Don't purchase an electronic planner if technology isn't your forte.

❏ *Get rid of all items you don't use.* Read chapter 15, "Total Mess to Total Rest" in this book. It gives you great suggestions for getting rid of all the unused *stuff* that has accumulated over the months and years. As a side benefit you'll be blessing others with your unwanted items.

❏ *Invest in the proper tools.* To be organized you need tools: boxes, bins, hooks, racks, and containers. Watch for bargains and sales at your favorite stores.

❏ *Involve the whole family.* Delegate jobs and responsibilities to other members of the family. My Bob (Emilie) takes care of all the repairs at our house. When something is broken, he is Mr. Fix-It. My Tim (Sheri) takes care of all the gardening and yard work at our house. When our children were young, we delegated jobs that were appropriate for their ages and development. All parents want to raise responsible adult children. That will only happen when they're given responsibility. Depending upon the ages of your children, you will need to tailor-make their chore list. Also, change off frequently so they don't get bored. Don't do something yourself that another member of the family can do. Delegating will save many minutes and hours in your day. And people who are involved in decision-making, planning, and carrying out have a vested interest in the success of the venture. Don't hesitate to delegate!

> When delegating jobs to children, write the chores on slips of paper and place in a basket. Let each child pick two or three chores and add them to the family chore list. That way you aren't assigning the jobs, they are.

❏ *Keep master lists.* Use a three-ring binder, 3 x 5 index cards, and journals to keep track of your possessions and tasks. You may think you'll never forget that you loaned that CD to Brad or that video to Christine, but you will. Write it down and keep the list in a place where you won't overlook it. And make sure to keep it in the same place all the time. That way you'll never have to search for it.

❏ *Reevaluate your system regularly.* Nothing is written in concrete. See how other people do things, read books to gather ideas, and continually evaluate your system. Change what's not working.

❏ *Use labels and signs.* If containers, bins, drawers, and shelves aren't labeled, the entire family won't be able to spot where things go. We have also used color-coding to identify items belonging to various members of the family: blue for Bevan, red for Chad, and purple for Christine. Keep the color system consistent throughout the home. Even small children can identify colors.

We use fine-point paint pens and permanent markers to label clothes, glass and plastic jars, and wooden items. (Don't use water-based pens—the writing won't last very long.) You can also purchase a label maker, which makes the job neater and easier. Also, writing your children's names on their belongings helps get those items returned if they're lost.

Where should you start? Start with these suggestions. Get them under control, and then you can move to more specific areas. The important thing is to get started. Once you get going, your progress and the resulting order will excite and motivate you to keep going.

2

Women—The Heart of Homes

Some will use gold or silver or
precious stones in building on the foundation;
others will use wood or grass or straw.

1 CORINTHIANS 3:12 GNT

Whether you are single, married, with children or without, or blending two families into one, in today's world we're seeing a return to a more traditional home. We're looking at the past and seeing what we can do to improve. Becoming the women God uniquely created, yes, we're going back to tradition—but we will do it in a new way. We'll take on the mystique of the feminine woman—being a lady for whom men will open doors, want to romance, long to be with—the woman who is beautiful inside with the charm that desires and is desired.

How are we going to accomplish this? By evaluating and changing where we place our values and by building a strong foundation of faith in God's Word.

Women, we are the glue that holds our homes and families together. We set the thermostat in our homes. Is your goal to be at home? But you still need to help with finances? Okay, set that goal: "I'd like to be at home full-time within six months or one year."

When setting goals, always determine a time or date when you want to reach your target. Can you do something from home that will add income to your family and still allow you to stay home? We've both had successful, home-based businesses for many years. We contributed to our family incomes and were at home to raise our kids. Will you work at a career but still want to create an enjoyable, livable home? We can help you do that too.

The Home's Heartbeat

You are the heart of your home. Do you create a sense of peace and serenity—a place to relax and refresh, and regroup? Emilie's mother was a beautiful example of how the woman is the heartbeat of her home. She was a single mom and had to work to support her family, but she knew how to balance all that was required of her and still be there to meet the needs of her two children. The "heart" in the home is created by teaching, delegating, and being there whenever possible. We can be there for our families even if we must work outside our homes, even if we're single parents, even if we're blending two families into one.

You are responsible for causing your own effects in life. Tackle the toughest, most challenging assignments in your life first, understanding that gratification will come after you've started the job.

What can we do to become the makers of our homes and the heartbeats therein? Begin by looking at the 8,760 hours we have each year and reducing the stress in our lives that is caused by disorganization. If we sleep an average of 8 hours per day, that equals 2,920 hours a year. Working outside the home uses another 2,000 hours. That leaves 2,700 hours of time to wash, iron, plan and prepare food, and clean. During this time we also attend Little League, soccer games, music recitals, doctor appointments, concerts, events, and more. We help with homework, volunteer, and watch television.

Approximately 37 hours a week is what it takes to accomplish our domestic chores. If we work outside our homes, how can we get it all done? There is little time left for personal time—or for positive interactions with our family members. What is the answer? It's in the remainder of this book! You can go from "Total Mess to Total Rest" in only 15 minutes a day.

Our survival lies in three areas:

1. *Delegation*—Women, we can't do it alone. Supermom is a myth. Call a family meeting and share your need for help and how members can pitch in. Prepare ahead of time a list of areas in which they can help. Every parent—single, step, or otherwise—wants to raise responsible adult children. The only way to do this is to give them responsibility, being careful to give them what they can handle for their ages.

2. *Dialogue*—Continue to share how you're doing, and allow your family to share with you. As busy as we all are, it's important to communicate our feelings concerning teachers, schoolwork, homework, yard work, friends, and (especially) God. Call family meetings often to discuss what is working and what isn't. If you're single, meet with your friends and family often and share how you're doing.

3. *Interaction*—There is much we can teach our children as we work side by side. When the children join us in baking cookies, preparing meals, mowing the lawn, washing cars, cleaning bathrooms, changing linens, raking leaves, and shoveling snow, we are creating a team. You'll be amazed at what you'll find out about your children and their feelings as you work together. You're present with them—available for them to dump on and share with. In turn, they learn how to work, and many times your conversations will turn to spiritual matters.

Women, we are the remodelers and the harmonizers of our homes. We are a country of broken homes, broken hearts, and broken health. Staying married today is such a challenge! To keep the flame of love alive takes creative work. Several things need to happen:

1. *We must be willing to surrender our egos to the needs of the other person.* Ephesians 5:21 (NIV) says, "Submit to one another out of reverence for Christ." Putting your spouse first, doing things that elevate him and show him respect will come back tenfold.

2. *Pay attention to the other people.* Make your spouse and children feel special and unique, honoring and treating them as you want to be treated.

3. *See your husband as the leader God calls him to be.* You married him and saw his many fine qualities. Be willing to follow his leadership even if you are smarter, wiser, or more organized. Be his helpmate, encourager, and supporter through difficult times. Give your input, but let him make the final decisions. Remember, he is held accountable and responsible for the family. Let your children see how much you respect and admire your mate. Harmonious couples give security to children.

> When delegating chores to your husband, remember to let him do the job his own way. Praise him for a job well done, and thank him for helping. He'll be much more willing to help in the future.

4. *Help your husband feel good about himself.* Build your man up in his eyes, your eyes, and in the eyes of the world. Let him know he will always be your hero. Take every opportunity to compliment your husband. Admire his masculinity. Praise his accomplishments. Everyone needs to feel loved, needed, and important.

5. *Shower your family with love.* First Corinthians 13:4-8 (NASB) says, "Love is patient, love is kind and is not jealous; love does not brag and is not arrogant, does not act unbecomingly; it does not seek its own, is not provoked, does not take into account a wrong suffered, does not rejoice in unrighteousness, but

rejoices with the truth; bears all things, believes all things, hopes all things, endures all things. Love never fails."

Don't waste time arguing day and night. A smart woman will love, love, love. It takes years to learn patience, to bite your tongue, and to consistently overlook faults. Husbands and children are not always easy to love, but neither are we sometimes. In the end love wins out—always! By working toward harmony in the home, we come out winners every time. Here are three keys to making a loving home:

❏ *Submit to Christ and His leadership.* Give Him your family, yourself, and your failures. We can never change our mates or other people, but God can.

❏ *Commit to God.* Give God your attitudes, your behavior, your stresses, your work, your career, and every other area.

❏ *Receive or rededicate yourself to Christ.* Be an active part of the family of God, and then allow God to work in your family. Begin living your life with purpose. My (Sheri) personal life verses are Proverbs 31:28-29 (NLT): "Her children stand and bless her. Her husband praises her. 'There are many virtuous and capable women in the world, but you surpass them all.'"

Family Mission Statements and Goals

The plans of the diligent lead to profit.

PROVERBS 21:5 NIV

As Bob and I (Emilie) traveled all over the United States and Canada, we found that a majority of individuals, couples, and families had never taken the time to develop a written statement of purpose for their lives.[1] But if we don't know what our purpose, goals, values, and priorities are in life, we'll not be able to effectively manage our lives, homes, and families. Charles J. Givens stated, "The difference between those who accomplish their dreams and those who only dream of accomplishing them is planning and control."[2]

Another great planning quote I (Sheri) discovered many years ago and use often when teaching organizational seminars is "To fail to plan is to plan to fail." This is really true.

When Tim and I (Sheri) were first dating, one of the most attractive attributes he possessed was his ability to plan and set goals. He already had a plan for the next 10 years. I wasn't sure what I was doing the next 10 minutes. Even at the young age of 18, Tim was very diligent in his planning and goal setting and had learned how to execute those plans. Because of his excellent strategies, he purchased his first home at age 19. Over the years I've also become a person who plans and sets goals. Setting goals doesn't mean losing my spontaneity, but it does help me see some of my dreams become realities. It was hard, but over the years, with practice, it's become easier.

Many people don't want to take the time or effort to develop sound strategies to be successful in life. They "go with the flow," letting life control them rather than them controlling life. These people often end up angry, cynical, frustrated, and disappointed. On the other hand, people who plan and set goals tend to be satisfied, joyful, and successful. They radiate happiness and contentment.

Develop a Mission Statement

Your *purpose* or *mission* in life is why you do what you do. Your *goals* are action steps that can be measured and will help you reach your dreams. Your *planning* identifies a to-do list for implementing goals and dreams. *Scheduling* helps you put time limits on the accomplishments—one year, three years, five years. *Projects* help you visualize what actions will help you develop a master plan to accomplish your purpose or mission in life.

"The greatest thing in the world is not so much where we start as in what direction we're moving."

OLIVER WENDELL HOLMES

Let's begin with a purpose or mission statement. When we think of success, the foundation and basic building block is writing down what we want to accomplish.

Surprisingly, there are only 25 or so major values in life, and different combinations of these values result in the differences in people's actions. By identifying and prioritizing our current values, we can:

❑ *Set our goals* to enable us to spend more of our lives and money doing and experiencing those things that are most important to us.

❑ *Eliminate values conflict* by making sure no values pull us in opposite directions.

❑ *Create an environment of mutual support* in our personal relationships by realizing that two people do not need the same values to create a successful relationship, but they must support each other's values emotionally and financially.[3]

Bob and I (Emilie) have chosen a verse of Scripture for our purpose or mission: "Seek first His kingdom and His righteousness, and all these things will be added to you" (Matthew 6:33 NASB). All our life decisions are tested by this verse of Scripture. Will a particular decision pass this litmus test? If it doesn't, we don't do it.

Tim and I (Sheri) have chosen our mission statement from the Bible as well: "Always try to do good to each other and to all people" (1 Thessalonians 5:15 NLT). We believe that by helping others we are doing what Jesus did while here on earth. We are carrying on for Him and doing what He has commanded us to do. We are confident we'll find purpose and success by loving and helping others.

Emilie and I encourage you and your husband to write out what you want to accomplish in life. This statement will be your guiding force for establishing goals. Remember, this statement is general in nature and isn't meant to be strictly measurable. Writing your mission statement will help keep you on your chosen path in your decision making and goal setting. You may change your mission statement or purpose at any time. It is not set in concrete; it is merely a base for planning a meaningful life.

Goals: A Dream with a Deadline

Goals prod us into action. They are a means to an end. A well-stated goal has three qualities:

❑ It states *quantity* (be specific).

❏ It gives a *deadline* (start and completion dates).

❏ It is *written out* (though not set in stone).

"I want to lose 15 pounds by July 1" or "I want to read through the Bible this year by December 31" are brief goals. Bob Barnes often says, "Goals are dreams with a deadline." Goals are specific objectives you've decided to work toward by investing your time, money, and energy. A goal can be accomplished very quickly or it may take a lifetime. Only choose goals that are in keeping with your value system and that help you meet your purposes in life.

Each year between Christmas and the first part of January Bob and I (Emilie) take a trip someplace where we can kick back, recreate, and plan for the year ahead. Tim and I (Sheri) do the same thing. You may not be able to get away for an entire weekend, but you can set aside an evening for a nice dinner, conversation, and planning.

Once your goals have been determined, be committed to them. Work together to achieve them. Your level of commitment to any goal determines how you will handle interferences along the way. Remember that these goals aren't set in concrete; they can be changed or altered as needed or desired.

Putting your goals in writing makes them accessible. Somehow the physical activity of writing them out gives greater credibility to their value and your commitment. Don't just write them down and file them away. Keep them where you can refer to them from time to time—in the front of your Bible, hanging in the hall, on your desk. Sometimes you may need to modify a goal, and sometimes you'll want to confirm that you are on target and move on. You may have set a wonderful goal, but you must consider other people, costs, added education needed, time away from home, and so forth. Be somewhat realistic. Not all goals are possible for today. Some are "A" priority (urgent); some are "B" priority ("maybe items"); some are "C" priority (no time, money, or energy given to this right now). Some B and C items may become A's, but not today. To help you, we've included some goal forms at the end of this chapter.

Another necessary part of your written family mission statement and goals is a place for you to jot down the steps to achieving them. Think through the various steps necessary and write them down. Put down the dates you make changes to your goals so you can remember and track what's happening. When you reach a goal, date it, mark it completed, and celebrate!

Success doesn't come by luck or accident; it comes because individuals dream, set goals, and then schedule, plan, and accomplish. They work diligently on making those dreams come true. When it comes to life issues, you must have a plan so your daily decisions will support your overall purpose and dreams. Each decision you make, even the seemingly insignificant, determines where you will be tomorrow. Be future-thinking in most of your choices.

Whether you're married, have children, or are single, write a Family Mission Statement. This will really go a long way in helping make decisions about where you're going and what you want to do.

Our composite of lifetime goals helps define who we are and where we want to go. This way we actively participate in life instead of letting life control us. Setting goals and making decisions to support them isn't always easy, but the difference is worth the effort! We've been given 24 hours or 1440 minutes or 86,400 seconds in each day. Those who get the most out of life are those who make wise decisions based upon what life means to them. Live with purpose!

Family Life Goals

Theme Verse: _____

_____

My purpose or mission in life is: _____

_____

1. **Spiritual goals**

   a. *To read the book of John* _____

   b. _____

   When?

   a. *By May 1* _____

   b. _____

2. **Physical goals**

   a. *To weigh   pounds* _____

   b. _____

   When?

   a. *July 1* _____

   b. _____

3. **Family goals**

   a. _____

   b. _____

   When?

   a. _____

   b. _____

4. **Financial goals**

   a. _____

   b. _____

   When?

   a. _____

   b. _____

5. **Professional goals**   a._____

                            b._____

                            When?

                            a._____

                            b._____

6. **Mental goals**   a._____

                            b._____

                            When?

                            a._____

                            b._____

7. **Social goals**   a._____

                            b._____

                            When?

                            a._____

                            b._____

8. **Community service goals** a._____

                            b._____

                            When?

                            a._____

                            b._____

The most important foundation of this form is stating your purpose or mission in life. From this statement comes the value for all other planning. Make sure your goals are consistent with your statement. If not, drop the goal or change your statement. Your statement and goals must be consistent with each other.[4]

4

Organized from the Inside Out

Always keep on praying. No matter what happens,
always be thankful, for this is God's will for you
who belong to Christ Jesus.

1 THESSALONIANS 5:17-18 TLB

Do you look around your home, room, or office and want to throw up your hands in disgust and say, "It's no use. I'll never get it together!" We can help! With a few simple tools you can be organized. When I (Sheri) met Emilie, I was hopelessly disorganized. She gave me many tools to use that made my life easier. These concepts can make the difference between a stressless, organized, functioning home and one that is in chaos. I call them "Commandments for Organization."

1. *Break the big jobs down into manageable tasks.* This may be a very difficult thing to do in the beginning for those of you who are "practicing perfectionists." This was a tough area for me (Sheri) because I always wanted to do the job perfectly and all at once, but since this isn't a perfect world, I wasn't able to do it perfectly. So instead of getting a small task completed, I wouldn't do anything. My home was a disaster. This was the rule that changed how I functioned at home, allowing me to go from "total mess to total rest."

2. *Do the worst job first.* Once you complete what you consider the most difficult job on your to-do list, everything else will seem much more doable. Get the worst out of the way, and you'll be more relaxed as you take on the less overwhelming tasks.

3. *Don't put it down, put it away.* This seems too simple, but you will amaze yourself at the time you save by following this rule. If you tried to figure out how much time you waste picking up and moving the same objects from place to place and room to room, you would understand the magnitude of this simple tenet of organization. And this is such a great thing to teach your children. Start when they're young and be diligent and consistent. They will catch on quickly, and your workload will decrease.

4. *Invest in a timer.* This will be one of the best purchases you ever make. Again this may seem simple, but in the long run you will have more time if you use a timer to keep you on task. I like to consider myself "spontaneous" when in reality I am just very easily distracted. I start out on a project but very quickly become distracted by something else—a phone call, finding something out of place and stopping to return it, etc., and soon I will completely forget what I was doing in the first place. A timer keeps me on track. Timers will also help us get more jobs completed because many times we won't start a project because we assume it will take more time than it actually does. (See chapter 16, "Miracles in Minutes.") Working against the timer keeps us on task and motivates us to work quickly. Try it and see what a difference it makes for your home organization. As you get small tasks completed, you'll feel a sense of accomplishment, which will encourage you to tackle another project. This is a great way to make a game out of picking up toys, books, games, or tidying rooms with your children. Set the timer and the first child to complete his or her chore gets a small prize. Get creative and let the children learn the benefits of a clean and organized room.

The old saying "everything has a place and everything is in its place" is a very helpful mind exercise and quickly became one of Emilie's principles of organization. Many times the reason we don't put something away is because it really doesn't have a "home." A main reason we end up with too much clutter is because we purchase items but have nowhere to store them.

So let's get organized! First, you need four tools:

❏ a to-do list
❏ calendars
❏ a telephone/address list
❏ a simple filing system

These four tools can drastically change your life from feeling confused to feeling organized. These are the basic tools for a new beginning.

A To-Do List

Write To-Do at the top of a piece of paper. Then write down all the things you need to do today. As you accomplish each item, you'll get so much pleasure crossing it off. At the end of each day review your list and start a new page. Update by adding new goals or adjusting ones that weren't completed. At the end of the week consolidate your several pages for the week and start again on Monday with a fresh page. As you get more experienced with this list, you can rank items by importance.

Why does a half-hour job often take twice as long as you thought it would? Probably because you estimated only the actual working time and didn't take into account the preparation—getting out and putting away tools, for instance.

The first is #1, the next is #2, and at the bottom of the page is #3. You can use letters of the alphabet to rank items, as well as "yes," "no," and "maybe." These added techniques help you maximize your time. Do what works best for you.

You don't need to buy a planner. Only get what you will really use. It makes no sense to purchase an expensive planner if it stays in a drawer. Don't buy a BlackBerry or other electronic planner if you'll never turn it on. Post-it Notes are easy to use and easy to throw away when jobs are completed.

Another helpful tip as you begin working from a to-do list is to make your list the night before. This way you wake up ready to take on the day.

Remember, a to-do list isn't permanent. You might need to adjust or change your list, but at least you have a plan in mind.

Calendars

There are three main types of calendars. The first one is a two-page, month-at-a-glance calendar. At one glance you get a good overview of the month. Details aren't written here, but you can jot down broad descriptions of engagements with the time involved: meetings, lunches, dinners, speaking engagements, and medical appointments.

The second type of calendar shows a week on a two-page format. This usually includes a small calendar of the month and room for notes for each day.

The third type of calendar has a page for each day. On this day-at-a-glance calendar you get more detailed and write what you will be doing for each hour or half hour. Be careful that you don't over-load your calendar and jam your appointments too close together.

As a guideline, if you've been somewhere before and know where you're going, allow 1¼ times the amount of time you think the appointment will take. If the meeting will last one hour, block out one hour and 15 minutes on your calendar. If you've never been to where the appointment is, allow 1½ times the amount of time you think it will take. If you estimate the meeting will last one hour, block out one hour and 30 minutes on your calendar.

Don't forget to schedule time for you each day. This doesn't need to be a large block of time, just make sure you do something that will help refresh your spirit. You will be a better wife, mother, friend, and coworker if you take some time for yourself.

By implementing a monthly or weekly calendar and a page-a-day calendar, you'll really make a big impact on your quest for organization.

A Telephone/Address List

First consider what will work best for you. A traditional telephone/address book doesn't give much room for details or broad categories. Whatever you choose will become your personal telephone and address book. You might want to list certain numbers under broad headings such as schools, attorneys, dentists, doctors, plumbers, carpenters, and restaurants. These will help when you don't know or can't remember a specific person's name or organization.

If you have a client or customer listed, you might want to jot down personal data about the person to review before going to your next meeting. This information helps you identify your customer. Items to note might be names of spouse and children, sports interests, favorite foods, and favorite vacation spots. This enables you to add a personal touch to your exchange, and the client will be impressed that you remembered all that information!

Use a pencil when writing down addresses and telephone numbers in case they change.

And remember to buy what works best for your lifestyle and personality. A Rolodex address system is easy to color-code and update.

A Simple Filing System

"Don't pile it, file it." This principle will really tidy your area up. Go to your local stationery store and purchase four dozen

$8\frac{1}{2}$ x 14 (legal size) colored and manila file folders. I (Sheri) recommend colored file folders for family members and manila folders for regular files. The legal size folders are more functional—they can accommodate longer-sized papers.

On these folders write simple headings: Sales Tax, Auto, Insurance, School Papers, Maps, Warranties, Taxes, Checks, and so forth. Arrange them alphabetically. Then take all those loose papers you find around your home and put them in the proper places. If you have a metal file drawer to house these folders, that's great. If not, pick up a cardboard storage box in the office supplies section at a store. Later you can invest in a better file cabinet.

As a family, sit down and create colored file folders for each member. As age allows, let the children choose their own colors and decorate their folders. Place mail, notes, or items of interest from magazines in the appropriate family member's folder.

Don't you already feel some relief by just reading about these four aids? It takes 21 consecutive days to acquire a new habit, so…On your mark! Get set! *Go!*

Your To-Do List

Which one of you, when he wants to build a tower,
does not first sit down and calculate the cost to see
if he has enough to complete it? Otherwise, when
he has laid a foundation and is not able to finish,
all who observe it begin to ridicule him.

LUKE 14:28-29 NASB

Many people are paralyzed because of their inability to make a decision and get their gearshift into drive.[1] One of the ways we are ineffective in our lives is by the great time-waster called *procrastination*. In adults, procrastination generally signals some kind of internal conflict. After we've made the decision to do something, a part of us holds us back. Why? The reasons could be almost anything, but some are:

- ❏ We feel overwhelmed.
- ❏ We overestimate the amount of time needed.
- ❏ We would rather be doing something else.
- ❏ We think if we wait long enough, the task will go away.
- ❏ We fear failure.
- ❏ We fear success.
- ❏ We enjoy the last-minute adrenaline rush.

Ways to Stop Procrastinating

❑ Make a "Call, Do, See" list. Use the last five to seven minutes of each day to jot down several activities that need to be done tomorrow (see sample list at the end of this chapter).

❑ Keep a log of how long various projects take.

Studies show that the success rate for people who write down their goals is about 90 times greater than for those who don't.

❑ Work with the time available, breaking the task into small bites or "instant tasks." You'll get a lot of satisfaction completing these small tasks. And at least *something* is getting done. See chapter 16, "Miracles in Minutes," for more ideas on this concept.

❑ Say no to "lesser" projects.

❑ Do things as they come to you.

❑ Ask yourself, "Is there a simpler way?"

❑ Eliminate distractions.

❑ Make it easy to work by grouping like things together.

❑ Reward yourself for getting started.

❑ Tell someone what your deadline is.

❑ Expect problems; things don't always go as expected.

❑ Delegate.

❑ Start today!

To Do

Date: 5-14

Call:

1 Ben's Plumbing
   555-4221
2 Insurance – Car
   555-4702
3 Lamb School
   Jenny's Teacher
4 555-9990
5 Pastor Cook
   555-0233

Do:

1 Take clothes
   to cleaners
2 Car pool driver
   this week
3 Take dinner
   to Merrihews
4 Visit Mrs. Jones
   at hospital
5

See:

1 That Chad gets
   homework done
2 Hubby for
   lunch
3 Barbara D.
   at ballgame
4 That Christine's
   dress is hemmed
5 Focus on the Family
   on T.V. @ 8:00 P.M.

6

Daily Scheduling and Time Management

*She gets up before dawn to prepare
breakfast for her household and plans
the day's work for her servant girls.*

PROVERBS 31:15

When Emilie was growing up she learned about organization and planning. But I (Sheri) had to learn the hard way—after I became an adult and had already established bad habits. By implementing the principles and practical ideas Emilie shared with me, I finally got a handle on the disorganization of my home. What a relief! And today I share those principles with the women who attend More Hours in My Day seminars, which I took over when Emilie semi-retired.

So how can we take care of our children and our husbands and still keep our priorities in order and glorify the Lord? It's difficult, there's no doubt about it. But there are steps we can take to make it easier. Let's look at what God says about having more hours in the day and also how to be the women He wants us to be.

The Night Worker

Let's start with our daily routine. Proverbs 31:17-18 tells us that the virtuous woman is energetic, watches for bargains, and works far into the night. Some of you are saying, "I've got a 24-hour job." You do, absolutely. If you have children at home, you *are* working 24 hours a day. Some of you were probably up three or four times last night with a sick baby. There's no doubt God knows what He's talking about when He says you work far into the night, especially if you work outside the home too. Your time is short at home, but being organized will help free you from guilt feelings about a messy house.

So let's start with the night before our workday. In More Hours in My Day seminars we teach the incredible benefits of doing as many things as possible the night before to ease your hectic morning hours when you're getting everyone to their respective places.

The Laundry Game

One of the ways to start organizing is to gather your laundry and sort it. (A lot of these things you'll be able to teach your children to do. We encourage you to do that.) Take a piece of fabric (a remnant or whatever—something with many colors) and make a laundry bag about 20 inches wide by 36 inches high. Also make a dark-colored bag and a white bag. You might want to use king-sized pillowcases with shoelaces strung through the top. You can also use plastic laundry baskets tied with coordinating fabric.

Now gather your little ones and announce, "Okay, we're going to play a game. The game is called Sort the Laundry." Then get out your colorful laundry bag and say, "This is the bag where all the dirty clothes that have a lot of colors go. Now find something in this dirty clothes pile that has a lot of colors." So they run over and pick something up, and you say, "Right! Now put it in the multi-colored laundry bag." So they put it in there.

Then take the dark bag (navy blue or dark brown) and tell them, "This is where all the dark-colored clothes go. This bag is for blue jeans, brown T-shirts, navy-blue socks, and so forth. Now run over and find something that's dark-colored." You see, you're playing a game with them. They do it, and you say, "Great! That's absolutely right!" Then you take the all-white bag and say, "Now this is where the white dirty clothes go—white T-shirts, white socks, white underwear. They go into the white laundry bag."

Now you're going to give them a little test. You say, "Okay, now find me something that's colored." They run over, pick it up, and put it in the right bag. And then, "Find something that's white." And they put it into the proper bag. What you're doing now is teaching children as young as four years old how to sort the laundry. When they're six and seven and ten, do you ever have to teach them again? No, you've already taught them. By the time your children are in middle school, they can be completely responsible for their own laundry—sorting, washing, drying, folding, and ironing. Clothes begin to be important to kids about that age, so it's a great time to make them in charge of their clothes. If they don't wash something, they have to wear it dirty or wear something else. They'll catch on fast. And it really will give you more time for other important tasks.

Bags and More Bags

Another option that really works well is to make individual laundry bags for each of the kids to hang in their rooms behind doors or in closets. Make individual bags that are very colorful and match your kids' rooms. A tall plastic trash can works well too, preferably one with a lid. This is where they put their own dirty clothes. Then whoever's job it was for the week to sort the laundry can go around, collect everybody's laundry bag, and sort these clothes into the three large laundry bags that are now by your washing machine, in the garage, on the service porch, in the basement, or wherever you happen to have your laundry area.

One lady had a great idea if you have the room. Buy three plastic trash cans in different colors, and put them in the garage. Label them white clothes, dark clothes, and colored clothes. Your kids can sort the clothes by playing a basketball game with the clothes, trying to hit the right containers.

Daily Work Planner Chart

Date: March 23-29

	Mom	Dad	#1 Child	#2 Child	#3 Child	#4 Child	#5 Child
Saturday		– Clean out the garage – McDonalds – 6 p.m.					Feed dog →
Sunday		Church—Family					
Monday	Laundry (Katie)		Clean bedroom			Fold clothes	Feed dog →
Tuesday	Ironing (Mom)	Set out trash (Tom)	Rake leaves	Rake leaves	Rake leaves		
Wednesday	Housework		Vacuum house			Dust w/Mom	
Thursday		Wash car (Peggy)		Help wash car			
Friday	Laundry	Set out trash	Mow lawn (Dad)	Sweep walks (Henry)	Water plants (Lily)		

The Daily Work Planner Chart

Now take a good look at the Daily Work Planner Chart. Take all the chores for the week, write them on individual pieces of paper, and put them in a basket. Then go around one by one and have the children pick a chore. Make it like a little game. Whatever they choose is the chore they have to do for the week. Then mark the chores on the Daily Work Planner Chart.

Your kids have chosen their own chores, so they can't say, "Golly, how come I have to do this one again?" They *chose* it, so they have to live with it for a week. Notice that Mom and Dad are listed on the chart too! This shows the kids that we're working *together* as a family. At the end of the day, when they've checked their charts and have done their chores as best they can, you can put a little happy face or a star on the chart. Stickers and rubber stamps are great also. At the end of the week check the chart and say, "You know, our family did a fantastic job this week. As a family we're going to have a picnic at the park (or go bicycling, or have an evening movie night with popcorn, or do something else that's fun) because we've really worked well together in accomplishing everything." Do you see what that's doing? It's uniting your family.

Setting the Table

Another chore that can be delegated is setting the breakfast table the night before. A five-year-old can learn to do this. It amazed us when teenagers would come over and they didn't know how to set a table. They didn't know the proper place for the knife, fork, and spoon. This wasn't their fault—it was because Mom and Dad never took the time to teach them. As the five-year-old sets the table the night before you can say, "Okay, Timmy, do whatever you want. You can use Mom's good china, or you can use paper plates, or you can have candlelight, or you can put your favorite teddy bear on the table as a centerpiece."

Too many times we put the good china on the table only when

company comes and at Christmas. Who are the most important people in our lives? Our families! So why not use the good china for those people who mean the very most to us? If a plate or saucer gets broken here and there, it gets broken. We would rather have our families enjoy the nicer things and use them and live with them than have them in a china cabinet where they can't be enjoyed. So let your children have the freedom to use the good china and teach them how to set the table.

The Weekly Calendar

Get out your Weekly Calendar. List those things that are happening this week in your family. Terra has to be at the dentist, Nicholas has football practice, and Elizabeth has Brownies. Then you can quickly look through the calendar and see when you're going to be needed to chauffeur kids, provide treats for classes, go shopping, and so forth. (See sample on next page.) You can be calm because you know where you're needed and where your children have to be. Check the Weekly Calendar over and fill it out the night before so you'll know what's happening the next day. Also, fill in your work schedule if you work outside your home. Then your family can see at a glance what's going on.

The First Job of the Day

We women often have to get up early because, even though we have modern appliances, we still don't seem to have enough time. Why? Because we're not using time effectively and efficiently. We need to get our homes organized and ready for the day, and for some of us that may mean getting up at five o'clock. If I asked you if you made your bed today, how would you answer? In our seminars about one-third of the women admit to not making their beds. How long does it take to make a bed? About two minutes—that's the average time. So what's two minutes out of a whole day to make a bed?

Weekly Calendar

	Monday	Tuesday	Wednesday	Thursday	Friday	Saturday	Sunday
Morning		Take treats to Jenny's school					Children's church—take guitar
Noon			Lunch with Susie			Bob golfing with Joe	
Night	Birthday party for Christine		church		Pick up Brad after football practice		Dinner with Mom & Dad

Before I met Emilie, I (Sheri) was one of those women who didn't make my bed most mornings. I figured I would just get in it again at night, so why bother. Emilie helped me see that when I complete that small job that takes less than two minutes, I feel a great sense of accomplishment that spurs me on to other things of even greater value. I love walking by the door and seeing the bed made. It didn't take long before making the bed became a habit.

The Bed Lesson

I (Emilie) asked my son after his second year in college, "Brad, do you make your bed at school?" He replied, "Mom, I'm the only one in my house who makes his bed." And I know why he does it. Once when he was about eight years old he hadn't made his bed for four mornings in a row. I'd let him get away with it now and then, but four mornings was just too much. He was halfway down the block with a couple of his little buddies when I noticed his unmade bed and went running after him. When I caught up I said, "Brad, I really hate to do this, but this is the fourth morning in a row you haven't made your bed. So I'm going to have to ask you to please go back in and make it." He replied, "Mom, you wouldn't!" I said, "Well, I'm really sorry, but I'm going to have to do it." He responded, "But I'm going to be late for school!" I came back with, "I know you're going to be late for school, but we'll worry about that later." So he came home and made his bed. Then he said, "You know I'm going to need a note for my teacher." I replied, "Fine, I'll be happy to write you a note." I wrote him a note saying he was late because this was the fourth morning in a row he hadn't made his bed, and that the teacher could do whatever she wanted with him. You know what? I never had any trouble with Brad making his bed after that.

I'm not in a popularity contest to be the number one mom, but I *am* striving to be the mom God wants me to be. It was hard for me to do that to Brad. It was as hard for me to call him back into the house as it was for him to actually do it. But over the years the discipline paid off because it only happened one time.

Another key is to let them learn to make their own beds. Don't go in and remake it. If you do, they'll say, "Why should I bother? Mom just remakes it anyway." Let them have crooked bedding. As time passes the bedding will become straighter and straighter.

Helping Them Come to Breakfast

After we women make our beds we go into the kitchen. (We can get the first load of wash in beforehand if we like.) We get breakfast cooked and call everyone to the table for breakfast...but they don't come. Isn't that irritating? I (Emilie) think that was one of the things that bothered me the most. How to correct this problem? I said to the children, "We're going to have a meeting." I continued, "You know, I've really got a problem. I call you children for breakfast, but you don't come. Now is there anything that could help solve this problem?" They said to me, "Golly, Mom, if you'd just let us know a couple of minutes before breakfast is ready, we'd come right to the table." So that's what we did...and it worked.

You can ring a chime, play the piano, sing a song, or blow a whistle—whatever you want to do. Give your family a warning to let them know breakfast or dinner is going to be ready within a few minutes—and they'll come!

Another thing—serve everyone at one time, and don't be a short-order cook. In the beginning I wanted to please everybody, so I was fixing French toast for Brad and omelets and pancakes for Jenny. Or I was fixing oatmeal and whatever else they wanted. But what happened to me? I got exhausted. I thought, *This can't go on.* So that's when I came up with the Weekly Menus Planner we'll discuss next. I rotated what I cooked so everyone got what they liked at least once a week.

As your children come into the kitchen first thing in the morning, take the first 3 to 5 minutes to reconnect with your family after the long night before. Give each child your undivided attention for a couple of minutes. Share morning hugs and kisses. Look them straight in the eyes and listen as they talk to you. Smile as you greet them and serve breakfast. Remember, 60 percent of our communication is nonverbal. Kids (and husbands too) read your facial expressions. You are already setting the mood in the home early in the morning.

The Weekly Menus Planner

As I (Emilie) mentioned, I quit being a short-order cook. I would have a different breakfast every day, but everyone would eat the same thing every morning. So when Brad came to the table and said, "Yuck, I hate oatmeal," I replied, "Okay, so you don't like oatmeal. Tomorrow morning, as you see on the Menu Planner, we're going to have French toast, and that's your very favorite." So at least one morning a week I pleased at least one of the children. This worked so beautifully that I extended the idea and made menus for the entire week. Sometimes I even went two weeks! Also, I tried a new recipe at least once a week. That added a little variety and introduced my family to new foods.

The Shopping List

I made out my menus and then used my Shopping List (see chart on page 66). I checked off on the Shopping List everything I needed at the market to prepare the meals on the menu for that week. What happens when you do this? You don't go to the market and buy things you don't need. You save money, and you feel organized because you have your meals planned. You shop for them and have everything in the house that is going to be in those meals for the week. If you plan your meals, and buy only the items on your shopping list, you will save $35 to $50

If you have appointments or errands at different locations, schedule them so you go from one place to the next with a minimum of wasted time and travel. Eliminate additional trips by making back-to-back medical appointments for the whole family (or at least for all the kids).

Weekly Menus

Date: April 17

	Breakfast	Lunch	Dinner
Monday	7 grain cereal	Sack Lunch	Mexican mountains, salsa, dip
Tuesday	Pancakes w/ turkey patties		Baked chicken, baked potatoes
Wednesday	Scrambled eggs w/ wheat toast		Halibut w/ vegetables
Thursday	Belgian waffles w/ strawberries		Stir fry w/ noodles
Friday	Oatmeal w/ rye toast		Italian pasta salad
Saturday	Eat out at Cocos	Turkey w/ cheese sandwiches	Bar-B-Q chicken, beans, biscuits
Sunday	Bran muffins, melons	Meat loaf, potatoes, gravy	Soup, salad, crackers

Shopping List

Date: May 5

Qty.	Staples
___	Cereal
___	Flour
___	Jell-O
___	Mixes
___	Nuts
___	Stuffing
___	Sugar

Spices

Qty.	
___	Bacon Bits
___	Baking Powder
___	Chocolate
___	Coconut
✓	Salt/Pepper
___	Soda

Pasta

___	Inst. Potato
___	Mixes
✓	Pasta
✓	Rice
✓	Spaghetti

Drinks

✓	Apple Cider
___	Coffee
✓	Juice
✓	Sparkling
___	Tea

Canned Goods

___	Canned Fruit
1	Strawberry
___	
___	
___	
___	Canned Meals
___	Canned Meat
___	Canned Vegetables
___	
___	
___	Soups
1	chicken
3	Tuna

Qty.	Condiments
1	Ketchup
___	Honey
1	Jelly/Jam
___	Mayonnaise
___	Molasses
___	Mustard
___	Oil
1	Peanut Butter
___	Pickles
___	Relish
1	Salad Dressing
___	Shortening
___	Syrup
___	Tomato Paste
___	Tomato Sauce
___	Vinegar

Miscellaneous

___	Foil
___	Napkins
___	Paper Towels
1	Plastic Wrap
___	Tissues
___	Toilet Paper
___	Toothpicks
___	Trash Bags
___	Waxed Paper
___	Zip Bags
___	Small
1	Large

Household

___	Bleach
___	Laundry Soap
___	Dish Soap
___	Dishwasher Soap
1	Fabric Softener
___	Furniture Polish
___	Light Bulbs
___	Pet Food
___	Vacuum Bags
___	
___	
___	
___	

Qty.	Fresh Produce
___	Fruit
6	oranges
4	bananas
___	Vegetables
1	celery
1	lettuce

Personal Items

___	Body Soap
1	Deodorant
___	Fem. Protection
___	Hair Care
___	Makeup

Frozen Food

___	Ice Cream
___	
___	Juice
✓	orange
✓	pineapple
___	TV Dinners
___	Vegetables
___	

Pastry

2	Bread(s)
___	Buns
___	Chips
___	Cookies
1	Crackers
___	Croutons

Meat

___	Beef
3	Chicken
___	

Dairy

1	Butter
1#	Cheese
1	Cottage Cheese
12	Eggs
1 qt	Milk
___	Sour Cream

a week without ever clipping a coupon. "How?" you ask. Because many times you pick up items you may use sometimes but have no plans to use in the next week or two. Pretty soon your basket will be filled with items you don't need for the week ahead. That is money wasted and added to your grocery bill.

Also, if at all possible, don't shop with your children or husband. Many husbands and kids add extra items to the cart because they look good and like to snack. And don't shop when you're hungry because everything looks good then. You'll add several dollars to your grocery bill by purchasing items because you were "starving."

Now, let's say Wednesday night comes and your husband calls you and says, "Honey, I've had a terrible day. I don't even know if I can face anybody, but I want to be with you. Let's go somewhere, just you and me, for dinner." So you look at your Weekly Menu Planner and notice you had meat loaf listed for that night. What do you do? You move meat loaf over to the next week. Now you have everything in the house for one meal planned for next week! You give your kids waffles or hot dogs that night, and you go out with your husband and enjoy your time together.

You can be very flexible with your menu planning, especially if you work outside your home. It causes so much less stress when you plan ahead. If at four o'clock you start thinking about dinner, you can relax because you know it's already cooking in the Crock-Pot or ready for you to fix as soon as you get home. You almost get excited about going home from work to prepare dinner!

Do you realize that we make an average of 750 meals a year? That's a big area to be organized in. I did my food shopping on Thursday, so I always allowed plenty of time on my Weekly Calendar. When I got home from the market I organized my food for the rest of the week. If you've got several children, and particularly if they're hyperactive, let them help! As you come in from the market, start delegating. One person unloads the bags, one folds the bags, one puts away the frozen foods, one puts away the canned goods, and another puts away the dairy products and refrigerator foods. If you have a child who is a little older, have him or her do the job of cleaning all the vegetables right away.

The Salad Solution

We're big salad and vegetable eaters in our house, so I would buy head lettuce, romaine lettuce, red leaf lettuce, and spinach. I would dump them into the kitchen sink, fill it full of water, clean the lettuce carefully, and then set it aside to drain. But you know how it is—all the water never really gets out of the lettuce, so even if you put it in Tupperware or a baggie, the lettuce rusts. It won't last as long as you need it to.

Here's how to solve this problem. This is an "Emilie original" and one of the best ideas I've ever come up with. In the variety section of the supermarket, a big drugstore, or a department store, buy a lingerie bag. (It's a nylon mesh bag with a lot of holes in it.) Place all your lettuce greens in a sink of cold water with 2 to 3 tablespoons of white vinegar. Then rinse the lettuce leaves with cold water. Now take your lettuce and put it into the lingerie bag. Put the bag into the washing machine and turn on the machine at the spin cycle for approximately two minutes. Take it out and back into the kitchen. Tear the lettuce up and place it in your Tupperware bowl or plastic ziplock bag. Put it in the refrigerator—and it will last two to three weeks. I have used this method for more than 40 years, and Sheri has used it for 20 years. What have you just done? You've taken a few minutes to make a big tossed green salad. You don't have to worry the rest of the week about making a salad.

Now take all your other vegetables and clean them and cut them up (broccoli, zucchini, cauliflower, etc.). Put them in Tupperware or plastic ziplock bags and store them in the refrigerator. Now everything is ready for steamed vegetables, if you have that on your menu for the week. All you have to do is take the vegetables out of the refrigerator and put them in your steamer and you're done. You can even add some veggies and cut-up cooked chicken to your salad greens and have a complete salad meal for lunch or dinner. All you might add are rolls, and you're ready to eat. You'll save yourself hours throughout the week by investing a little bit of time in preparation.

I have another possible solution for you. If you feel funny about putting lettuce in the washing machine, buy a tea towel and fold it in half. Sew it up on two sides, making a bag. Attach a little bit of ribbon at the side. Now you have a lettuce bag. Put your lettuce in it, and the bag will absorb much of the water. Put the lettuce and bag into your Tupperware or the lettuce compartment in your refrigerator. After 24 hours remove the bag because it will be soaking wet. This method doesn't work as well as spinning the water out, but it still does a pretty good job. You can buy a plastic lettuce spinner at your local department store, but why spend more money when you already have a spinner in your laundry area? If you have a lettuce spinner, you can still get great use out of it. Place your serving of salad in the spinner, add one tablespoon of your favorite dressing and spin it. It will spread the dressing over the greens evenly and you won't use as much dressing. It cuts down on calories and fat.

Due to our busy schedules, the woman of today needs all the help she can get when it comes to creative meal planning. You want to feed your family healthful meals. There is a wealth of information available on the Internet. Go to your favorite search engine and type in exactly what you're looking for and get ready for lots of ideas!

Back to Breakfast

At breakfast time ask each family member, "Do you need me today? What for and where and when?" Check your Weekly Calendar as you go over the day's plans with them. Write down any commitments.

Then have everyone take their dishes to the sink. I (Emilie) had a rule in our family that no one ever went to the kitchen empty-handed. Each person always had to pick something up and take it to the sink. I filled the sink with hot, sudsy water when I'd get into the kitchen in the morning, and then each person would scrape their dishes and put the dishes into the sudsy water, where they would stay until I was ready to get to them. Now if you do this with your family, what happens? It's eliminating work for you. It's saving you steps so you have energy to do other things that are more important. I (Sheri) share with women that in order to raise responsible adult children, they must be given responsibility when they're young. Delegate as much responsibility as children can handle for their ages. It will help reduce your load and your family will benefit.

After breakfast quickly check each child's room with him or her. Also check the bathrooms, and have the children wipe the toothpaste off the counter and mirror. Once or twice a week you might want to go in and do a really good job, but get them used to cleaning up after themselves so they won't think you're the maid or that messes magically get cleaned up.

As they're leaving the house for school, check to see if they have their lunches, their lunch money, their books, their homework, their gym clothes, their reports, and whatever else they need. This way you won't get a phone call asking you to bring something to the school.

Proverbs 31:26 says, "When she speaks, her words are wise, and kindness is the rule for everything she says." So fit in a special moment with your husband. Ask him, "Honey, is there anything I can do for you today? Is there anything you need me to pick up for you?" He might fall over in a dead faint the first morning you ask, but he'll probably come up with a nice list of errands for the next time you ask.

Say Something Good

When your kids have done something well, be sure to compliment them. For years I (Emilie) taught a Friday morning Bible study in my home, and one day I threw out this suggestion to the women: "Write down six items you like about yourself." You wouldn't

believe how hard this was for
them! They hemmed and hawed
around. They couldn't figure out
anything to write down. You see,
what happens over the years is
that we've had parents, brothers,
sisters, teachers, even strangers
put us down. So as we've grown
up we've developed a bad self-
image.

> *Surely we have been given the
> gifts of creativity and sensitivity
> partly so we can grow more
> attuned to beauty, to the way
> things were meant to be.*
>
> EMILIE BARNES

Let's not do this in our families! So compliment your children
when they do something well. "Timmy, you did such a neat job
setting the table this morning. I loved the way you used your teddy
bear for the centerpiece." And do you know what's going to happen
tomorrow morning? He won't be able to wait to show what else he's
done for you, and he'll be eager to do chores. "Gina, I'm so pleased
with you today! You got your shoes on the right feet and your socks
match. I am so proud of you!" As you compliment them and build
their self-image, you're also sending them off with a loving hug and
a positive attitude. Plus you help them remember you as a smiling
mom!

Okay, everyone is gone, and you're alone. So what's next? We
gals can't fall back into bed! Besides, now the bed is made, so it's not
quite as tempting to get back into it. We need to keep going, to get
the second load of wash in and the dishes clean. Check the Menu
Planner to see what you're going to have for dinner tonight. Make
sure you've taken what you need out of the freezer or put something
into the Crock-Pot. Remember, everything you need is already in
the pantry or refrigerator/freezer! Wipe down the counters and
water your houseplants.

You can now rejoice because your basic housework is done by
nine o'clock in the morning! For you who work outside your home,
it might be seven when this is completed, and for you moms of pre-
schoolers it might be one in the afternoon.

The Right Priorities

Proverbs 31:27-29 says, "She watches carefully all that goes on throughout her household and is never lazy. Her children stand and bless her; so does her husband. He praises her with these words: 'There are many fine women in the world, but you are the best of them all!'" How can we receive this kind of praise from our children and our husbands? What will cause our families to give us that genuine support? Having our priorities as Christian women in order will certainly help.

Do you know what our priorities are? God tells us in Matthew 6:33 (NIV), "Seek first [God's] kingdom and his righteousness, and all these things will be given to you as well." Our number one priority is God and a personal relationship with Him strengthened through prayer and Bible study. There have been times in my life when I (Emilie) got my priorities out of order. But I quickly got back on track. Sometimes when I needed to have a special time with my Lord the only time available was at five in the morning, when the house was still. And that was hard because I might have been up three times during the night with the children. But I got up and spent that little bit of time with God. I committed my works to the Lord, and my plans were established (Proverbs 16:3). On some days I checked my calendar and said, "There's no way I'm going to get everything done that I have to do today." But then I would get up early in the morning, read a little in God's Word, put my hands on the calendar, and say, "Lord, You know what I have to do today. Will You help me and guide me through every moment? Show me what You want me to do." And do you know what happened on the days I did that? I got everything done and had time for a nap in the afternoon.

> *Isn't it splendid to think of all the things there are to find out about? It just makes me feel glad to be alive—it's such an interesting world.*
>
> LUCY MONTGOMERY, IN ANNE OF GREEN GABLES

Other Priorities

If you're married, your second priority is your husband. The third priority is your children. The fourth priority is your home. And number five on your list of priorities is everything else, such as helping a philanthropic group, being a Scout leader, leading a Bible study, having lunch with friends, shopping, and so on.

I'll never forget the day my husband came to me and said, "Emilie, you love those children more than you do me." My first thought was, *Well, I have to take care of the children.* I said, "They need me. I have to do all these things for them." But in my heart I knew Bob was right. I knew he was being neglected because he was telling me he didn't feel that he had priority in my life over the children.

I (Sheri) faced a similar dilemma when Tim and I had only been married a short time. I was working as a church secretary and taught Sunday school for the junior high and high school kids. I spent a lot of time at church (doing "good" things) and going on many outings with the youth. One night when I got home late, I didn't bother fixing dinner, and there were still dishes in the sink from lunch. Tim asked me if he was important to me at all. Of course he was, but I wasn't showing it by how I treated him and how he fit into my priorities. I began that day to make sure he was in the priority position where he belonged.

It's easy to get our priorities mixed up. Sometimes the number one priority, which is God, becomes number six or seven on the list. Husband can be number eight or nine. Children can be number one, and all the other things we do number two. But God tells us that our children will stand and bless us, and so will our husbands, as long as we have our priorities in order. So remember that God is with you. He's given those children to you and your husband as gifts. He's going to take care of them for you. Work on keeping them in the right priority order. Remember that if you're married, you were a wife to your husband before you were a mother to your children.

Someday, and it won't be long, your children are going to be out of the nest. They're going to be off to college, moving out, working, and starting families of their own. And then you and your husband will be alone for the first time in many years. If you haven't worked on developing a relationship by spending time together and making each other priorities, at that point you'll simply be two strangers. Great marriages don't just happen; they are grown through much tender care.

If you're working outside the home and have your priorities out of order, stop working until you get back to where they should be. You say, "But I have to work." I (Emilie) had a woman come to me after a class and say,

> I attended one of your other classes a while ago. And boy, I didn't like what you said. I was working and I loved my job. [Her husband was an unbeliever, and she was having trouble in her marriage.] That job was so important to me, but my house was all out of order. That's why I came to the organization class. But I rejected everything you said. After two weeks, things got even worse in my home.
>
> God began to work in my heart. He said, "You better get your home in order." So I decided I was going to quit my job and work on my priorities and get my home organized and in order. So I went to my husband and said to him, "Honey, I'm going to quit my job." He replied, "Who's going to pay the car payment?" I said, "Sell the car." He responded, "Well, okay." So I quit my job.
>
> I got my home in order. I got all the things done that I needed to do. Then my relationship with my husband was getting better. He'd never set a foot in my church, but I thought I would invite him one more time. I said, "We're having a Valentine's Day dinner at church, would you like to go with me?" He replied, "Yes, I would." If I'd planned that evening myself, it couldn't have been better. Later my husband said, "Let me know anytime you have something at church that's special. I'd like to go with you."

So you see, when you get your priorities in order, God will take care of the rest. Today that husband is a growing Christian.

If you're working and yearn to be at home but don't see how that would be possible, make it a matter of prayer and watch what God can do.

Evening Time

Five o'clock in the afternoon can be a terrible time. The children are tired of you, and you are certainly tired of them by then. So you may need to prepare yourself a bit. Freshen up your makeup. (Remember, it was six o'clock in the morning when you first put your makeup on.) Put on a little perfume. It is never an old-fashioned idea to look nice for your husband.

Start thinking toward a quiet and gentle spirit. But you say that right now it's four o'clock and a zoo around the house? There's spilled milk all over the kitchen floor, and something's boiling over on the stove. The dog and cat are hungry and nipping at your heels. You've got kids all around you. The phone rings. Your husband is due home at five. And you're supposed to have a quiet and gentle spirit? It's tough, isn't it? Do you know what I (Emilie) did? I would go into the bathroom and stick my head in the sink and pray several times, "Lord, You don't know what it's like out there. It's a war zone." I'd cry. Sometimes I'd have to make three or four trips in and out of the bathroom until I could finally pull myself together enough to settle the children down and organize as best I could.

Hopefully I would be ready for my husband's arrival. When I heard his car coming up the driveway or him walking up the side-walk, I would drop everything and go to greet him. Now I know you may be diapering that baby, but throw a diaper over him and go and greet your husband. What does it tell him when you run to the door to meet him as he comes in from work? You're telling him that he's important to you. You don't know how long he's been on the freeway. You don't know what happened at work today—whether he had to fire his best friend or whether the construction job fell through. You don't know what went on in his day.

That husband of yours could have gone a hundred different places tonight. There are tons of women out there who would like to have him. It doesn't matter what he looks like or what kind of shape he's in. They'd like to have him. But he has chosen to come home to you. He's coming through that door to you, so take those few minutes to go to the door, greet him, and throw your arms around him. Tell him you're happy he's home, you're thankful he's worked hard all day and provided for this home, for you, for your children. Then let him have 15 minutes to unwind with the newspaper, mail, or children. If possible, don't share the negative parts of your day until after dinner. You'll reap incredible rewards by making your husband feel special and respected.

> *Kindness is a language in which the deaf man can hear and the blind man read.*
>
> MARK TWAIN

It's evening time. You can get a fire lit and some candles burning. You might want to prepare a small plate with a few snacks, especially if dinner is still a few minutes from being ready. Remember, you've got everything already prepared. All the vegetables are cut, cleaned, and in the refrigerator. You can make a dip with a little sour cream, cottage cheese, garlic salt, and lemon juice. If the kids are bouncing off the walls, throw a sheet on the floor, give them some veggies and a little dip, and let them have a snack too.

Enjoy your family. God has given that family to you as a gift. Ill-mannered children are no fun to be around, even if they are your own. So lovingly discipline them. Teach them obedience and responsibility. Children are a very precious legacy. They will grow up to be beautiful if you take the time to teach, train, and discipline them with love.

Family Household Expenditures Chart

Ecclesiastes 3:1 (NIV) says, "There is a time for everything, and a season for every activity under heaven"—and that includes organization. Each month list your expenses for your house payment or rent, food, utilities, babysitting, insurance, telephone, clothing, hair dresser, taxes, and donations on the Family Household Expenditures Chart. (The charts are at the end of this chapter.) Then at the end of the year you'll have the totals for all the expenses you've had during the year, and this will be very easy to take to your tax person.

Family History Chart

On the Family History Chart (see end of chapter), list your children's names, their birth dates, their blood types, dates of their yearly physical, their dental exams, their eye exams, when they had their inoculations, and so forth. Everything is nicely organized so you can refer back to it when necessary.

Shopping Guide Chart

The Shopping Guide is a practical way of tracking family statistics. This will enable you to quickly give grandparents and other family members your children's clothing sizes and also can be used for medical growth questions and patterns. It will also be interesting to refer to in future years.

Credit Cards Sheet

The next chart is for credit cards. List the name of the company, the account number, the address, the telephone number, and when the card expires. If a card is lost or stolen, you can quickly go to your notebook and report it immediately. If you do some purchasing over the telephone, you have the number handy. This is *not* information you want to store in your computer. If someone gains access to your computer, your information could be stolen. Keep credit card info in a very safe place.

Important Numbers Sheet

On the Important Numbers Sheet list phone numbers for the police, the fire department, the ambulance service, the poison control service, the neighbors, and so forth.

One woman shared, "I was filling out my notebook pages when I came to the Important Numbers Sheet. I started listing all the telephone numbers. Then I noticed the Poison Control heading. Well, I hadn't even known there was such a thing! So I looked through the phone book, but I couldn't find the number. I called the information operator, but she didn't know much about it either. It took me several minutes to finally get the number of poison control. That listing on the chart could have saved a child's life. If my child had taken something and I had to try to find the number, it would have been four or five minutes before I found it."

Dates and Occasions

Make a list of dates and occasions you want to remember. Write down everyone's birthday, anniversaries, and all the other important dates for the year. As each month comes up, check to see whose birthday is listed. Mark on the chart if you send a card or what kind of gift you give. This will come in handy next year!

Home Instructions Sheet

The Home Instructions Sheet is especially important if you travel frequently or have small children that require a babysitter from time to time. If you have someone house sit while you go on vacation or someone comes into your home to take care of your children, they can see what needs to be done, what time Sunday school starts, where the church is located, any appointments you may have during the week, and when the trash is picked up. Maybe your mother-in-law sees this man walking around in your backyard one day, and she doesn't know who he is. She can check the Home Instructions Sheet and know it's probably the pool man or gardener.

The Entertainment Sheet

An Entertainment Sheet is handy. If you're going to host a party, a dinner buffet, or a tea party, list the guests, the time and date, what type of party, if you're going to have a theme, your menu, your table decorations, and so forth. You can also write down any notes you want to make for next time.

Deductible Items

Purchase a dozen large envelopes (at least 5 x 10). These are for all your receipts and check stubs, one for each month of the year. Insert your receipts and check stubs into the proper envelopes. Then take these envelopes, plus your Deductible Items Sheet, to your tax preparer, and everything is ready for your tax return.

Items Loaned and Borrowed

How many times have we borrowed from someone or loaned a dish to a friend and forgotten about it? The very basic and simple form at the end of this chapter will help you keep track of these items.

You can order these charts—plus the Weekly Calendar, Menu Planner, Shopping List, and Work Planner charts—from More Hours in My Day. They come professionally bound in an 8½ x 11 three-ring notebook or on a CD with a master set of charts for you to print and make your own notebook. Call (951) 682-4714 or visit www.EmilieBarnes.com.

Family Household Expenditures

Month of: _January_

House payment/ Rent	Food	Utilities	Furniture/ Repairs	Car/Gas	Insurance	Phone	Clothing	Cleaning: House, Clothing	Haircuts	School Expenses
929.00	72.13	102.40	car 76.02	21.00	427.00 car	72.00	15.00	14.00	25.00	5.00
	50.76			17.50	170.00 med.	23.00	41.00	45.00	7.00	4.00
	39.00			18.00			16.00		4.50	3.75
	83.40			20.00			30.00		5.00	6.04
	24.24									
	62.43									
T 929.00	331.96	102.40	76.02	76.50	597.00	95.00	102.00	59.00	41.50	18.79

Family History

Family Member Name	Birth Date	Blood Type	Date of Last:			Inoculation/ Date	Other
			Yearly Physical	Dental Exam	Eye Exam		
Christine	7/9/83	B	12/83	7/84	—	at 18 mo.	
			12/84	1/85	—	DPT	
			12/85	6/85	—	Rubella	
				12/85	12/85	Measles	
Chad	11/20/84	B	12/15/85	—	—	6 mo.- DPT	
						Polio 5/85	

Shopping Guide

Family Member Name	Sizes					Favorite Activities	Other Clubs, Interests, Etc.
	Dress/Suit	Shoes	Pants	Socks	Underwear		
Dad	46R	10½ D.	38x30	10–13	XL	Gardening	Reading
Mom	6	8	6	B	6	Cooking	Walking
Brad	42R	10 D	32x30	11–13	M	Biking	Running
Jennifer	7/8	7½	7	7–9½	M	Aerobics	Decorating
Christine	8	3	8	10–12	S	Dancing	Singing
Chad	7	2	6		S	Baseball	Swimming
Bevan	7	12	6	6/7	S	Legos	Baseball

Credit Cards

If lost or stolen, notify company at once

Company	Card Number	Company Address	Company Phone Number	Card Expires (Date)
Bank of America		7264 Archibald St., San Francisco, CA 94100	555-8421	
Shell Oil		1123 Sage Brush, Phoenix, AZ 85012	555-3321	
American Express		62431 Hilltop Ln, Boston, MA 02106	555-4306	
Diner's Club		2731 Hale Ave., Los Angeles, CA 90001	555-6626	

Important Numbers

Service Person	Phone Number	Service Person	Phone Number
Ambulance	555-4203	Neighbor – Sally	555-0011
Appliance Repair	555-4219	Newspaper	555-4738
Dentist – Merrihew	555-4703	Orthodontist	555-1104
Doctor – Turnbull	555-4909	Pastor	555-0767
Electrician – Rusty	555-1001	Poison Control	555-0013
Fire	555-9996	Police	555-5001
Gardener – Mike	555-4618	Pool Service	555-4379
Gas Co. Emergency	555-5551	Plumber	555-0114
Glass Repair		School(s) – Elem.	555-9013
Heating/Air Conditioning Repair	555-0013	School(s) – Jr. High	555-1111
Husband's Work	555-0321	Veterinarian	555-2409
Insurance (Car)	555-0112	Cat's Name	Tiger
Insurance (Home)	555-0112	Dog's Name	Mickie
		Animal Control	555-0014
		Security System	555-1163
		Trash	555-0731
		Newspaper carrier	555-4100

Dates and Occasions

Month	Date/Occasion	Name of Person(s)	Gift(s) Given
January	Jan. 10	Don Foor graduation	Dress shirt
February	Feb. 13	Bill Beck promotion	Necktie
March	Mar. 22	Yoli Brogger graduation	Sport dress
April	April 30	Bill's birthday	Sport shirt
May	May 22	Brad's birthday	Jogging shoes
June	June 8	Bob's birthday	3 days in San Diego
	June 9	Ken's birthday	Swim trunks Walk shorts

Dates and Occasions (continued)

Month	Date/Occasion	Name of Person(s)	Gift(s) Given
July	July 9	Christine's birthday	$50.00 Bond
August	Aug. 8	Great Grandma Gertie's 80th birthday	a cruise to Alaska
September	Sept. 30	Bob & Emilie's 46th anniversary	a cruise to Mexico
October			
November	Nov. 18 Nov. 20	Jenny's birthday Chad's birthday	Gift certificate $50.00 Bond
December	Dec. 13 Dec. 10	Bevan's birthday Bradley Joe's birthday	Winter coat

Home Instructions

	Routine Chores/Errands	Special Appointments
Sunday	Christine & Chad's Sunday school begins 9:45	Grandparents to take home after church
Monday	Water front plants Feed birds Bring in paper each morning	Chad's Dentist appointment 2:30
Tuesday	Set out trash	
Wednesday	Water front lawn Feed birds	mail off letters, bills
Thursday	Gardener comes today	
Friday	Set out trash Feed birds	
Saturday	Water indoor plants	

Entertainment

Date: January

Guests	Time/Date	Dinner/Party Type	Menu	Decorations/Centerpiece/Tablecloth
Delorenzos	1/8 6:30 P.M.	Beans & Cornbread	Beans, cornbread, salad	Farm animals
Merrihews	1/15 7:00 P.M.	Pasta & Salad	Pasta, salad, garlic bread	Dripping candles in old wine bottles
Planchons	1/22 6:00 P.M.	Mexican	Tacos, (chicken), fajitas, enchiladas	Sombrero gourds
Hendricksons	1/29 6:30 P.M.	French	Veal, sauces, potatoes	Candlelight w/ dinner music

Entertainment (continued)

Games/Entertainment	Dress	Help: Hired/Voluntary	Notes
Cards	Casual	—	A great time
Monopoly	Casual	—	We want them back
Charades	Mexican	—	Fun, Fun, Fun
No Structure	Casual	—	We will be with them in March

Deductible Items

Credit Card Charges	Investments	Medical/Dental	Medicines	Babysitting	Taxes	Donations	Savings	Other Misc. Expenses
47.00 B/A	60.00 *mutual fund*	25.00	18.00	—	225.00	175.00	100.00	60.00 *United Way*
								10.00 *Booster club*
								10.00 *Boy Scouts*
T 47.00	60.00	25.00	18.00		225.00	175.00	100.00	80.00

Items Loaned and Borrowed

Month/Year			
Date	Item	Who	Returned
1/20	Serving tray	Janice Gormley	1/25
2/14	Folding chairs	Carol Pewther	2/17

7

Effective Time Management

The Lord is not slow in keeping his promise, as
some understand slowness. He is patient with you,
not wanting anyone to perish, but everyone
to come to repentance.

2 PETER 3:9 NIV

On Bob and my (Emilie) first Volkswagen van we had a colorful rainbow with "More Hours in My Day" lettered on the side. We had a lot of people, from service station attendants to the nurseryman, comment, "How do you get more hours in your day?" Everyone is looking for that simple and easy secret that will give them that magic commodity called *time.* Unfortunately there isn't one simple trick that makes everything flow together; however, if you can eliminate long searches for whatever you're looking for it will help save time.

Group Your Shopping Trips Together

In your organizational/planning notebook keep a list of items you need to buy: books, videos, Christmas gifts, clothes, cosmetics, household items, birthday and anniversary gifts. When you see a sale or go to an outlet store, you can acquire what's on your list. This will save time and a lot of money because you can shop sales.

Purchase More Than One Like Item

If you have frequent demands for items such as toiletries, pens, rulers, tape, and scissors, store several of each in strategic spots around the house. Don't waste time running all over the house to obtain a basic item. This is especially true if you have a two-story home. An extra vacuum cleaner and cleaning items are great to keep upstairs.

Do More Than One Thing at a Time

Most women can multitask very easily with a little training. A cordless phone in the kitchen is a must. You can do any number of things while talking to a friend or relative. Also develop a "to read" folder to take with you when you know you're going to have to wait someplace. You can get caught up with all the junk mail, catalogs, magazines, letters, and correspondence. And carry along a few blank thank-you notes so you can write friends. If you exercise and have an indoor exercise machine, this is also a great time to read a magazine or your favorite book as you work out.

Cut Unwanted Calls Short

When salespeople, survey people, or people who just want to chat call and you're busy, cut the calls short by learning how to handle these people graciously. These types of calls can really eat up valuable time. One of the greatest inventions of our time is the answering machine. Turn it on and use it when you need to keep working on a project. Be sure you get back with your friends when you have time.

Determine What's Important

This is where a to-do list really comes in handy. Each evening before going to bed or before leaving the office, I (Emilie) make a list of what I need to do tomorrow, and then I go one step further. I rank items according to priority: one, two, three. The next morning I start working with number one, then go to number two. It's not long before I've made a real impact on that list. As has been mentioned, it's best to do the worst job first. By completing and deleting that item off your list, you are less stressed and can feel a sense of accomplishment. You'll be eager to tackle the next item on your list.

Use Your Body Clock

Each of us operates most efficiently at a certain time of day. Schedule taxing chores for the hours when your mind is sharpest. Do these chores when you have the most energy. Find out when your children are most alert and active. Schedule their chores during that time. It will help alleviate whining and complaining.

Prevent Interruptions

In a recent article I read that most people are interrupted at least once every five minutes. If this is true for you, analyze what's causing those interruptions. You are unique and will have unique situations. My family always wanted to know what we were having for breakfast or dinner so I posted the menu on the refrigerator door. No more interruptions.

Store Your Keys and Glasses in One Area

My Bob used to always waste time looking for the car keys and his glasses. One day I (Emilie) put up a decorative key hook by the phone in the kitchen and told him to put his car keys on the hook and to place his glasses on the counter underneath the keys. Done deal—problem solved!

Plastic Clothes Bins for School Homework

Reduce the early morning stress of looking for the children's homework and school-related materials. If you are into color-coding your children's belongings, purchase colored plastic clothes bins and put them by the front or back door. When the children leave each day for school, all they have to do is reach down and grab their school supplies.

Have It Picked Up and Delivered

We're returning back to the good old days. More and more companies are offering pick-up and delivery services. These are valuable time savers, and in many situations they are cost efficient.

Use a Daily Planner or Electronic Planner

Keep your keys, checkbook, list of appointments, address book, and so forth in a planner. There are many stylish organizers you can use that become a purse and will house your planner. This two-in-one organizer really helps consolidate these two areas of your life. Just remember to buy only what you will use. It makes no sense to invest money in an expensive leather planner or electronic PDA (personal digital assistant) if you will never use them.

Divide Big Jobs into Instant Tasks

Break the whole job into smaller tasks or "instant tasks." You will have to work at this concept if you are a "practicing perfectionist." Turning a big project into small tasks is a great help! A job may be overwhelming, but when it is broken down it's not so daunting. For example, cleaning the refrigerator. Clean one shelf on Monday, one shelf on Tuesday, and so on. By the end of the week, the entire refrigerator will be clean, and it only took 10 to 15 minutes a day!

Use a Timer

One of the best investments you will make is a digital timer, preferably a triple timer. If you tend to get distracted or you have a hard time getting started, a timer keeps you on task. And knowing you only have to do something for 15 minutes helps you tackle a job. Set a timer for your children and make a game out of picking up toys, cleaning rooms, and other chores. Reward them for jobs well done.

Become a List Maker

In my daily planner I (Emilie) have a list for almost everything I do—all the way from planning a tea for a group of friends to getting ready for a Christmas party. I save these notes so next time I can go back and review my comments. It's a great way to start planning since you already have a good beginning. You may want to get a journal or blank book for your project list making. Date them and then you have a point of reference for your next event or project.

Plan Your Errands

Do your errands at one time. You'll be amazed at how much you can accomplish! Create your list and then organize by the order of your stops. Arrange your errands in a big circle, moving from one place to the next, starting with the closest. Within a short time you'll be back. With gas prices out of sight, this will save you money too.

Stop Procrastinating

Your to-do list will help you get started. Rev your engine and get in gear. Even if "traffic" isn't flowing well, get moving. A car has to be moving in order for it to go somewhere. *Start now!*

It Doesn't Have to Be Perfect

This goes hand-in-hand with procrastination—not wanting to do something if it's not perfect. It's nice to want things done right, but not if you're crippled into inactivity. Besides, even if you know the difference, your friends and guests might not know or care. Some jobs don't need perfection. No one is going to show up with white gloves.

Become a person who takes control of your time. With a little study you can turn "time-interrupters" into positive "time-savers."

The busy person's greatest need is for "effective," not "efficient," planning. Being effective means choosing the right task from all the alternatives. Being efficient means doing any job that happens to be around. Planning is important because it saves you time in the end. Know what you have to do and have your priorities established.

8

Wardrobe Organization

Fix your thoughts on what is true and good and
right...and dwell on the fine, good things in others.

PHILIPPIANS 4:8

Now let's move to our closets! We can weed out some of those things we don't need and get our clothes in order.

The Right Equipment

As we get into our wardrobe, we'll need some equipment. First get some storage boxes with lids (preferably ones with the lids attached). Then we'll need some plastic shoe boxes. These can be purchased at most stores. Watch for sales and purchase several at a time. If you have the time, you can cover shoe boxes with pretty contact paper or wallpaper. Shoes that you don't wear often can go in the plastic shoe boxes labeled with a felt-tip pen. Stack them out of the way. This way you'll have a neat and organized closet instead of having shoes thrown here and there. And the shoes you wear most often will be handy and easy to get to.

Consider getting some small, clear plastic boxes. You can put your scarves, belts, and small clutch bags in them.

Use the storage boxes (cardboard or plastic) for the clothes and items you want to keep but aren't using right now. This is a great way to store seasonal clothing. Make sure you label each box. List on the box each item inside. Or you can create a "card catalog" with the information listed on 3 x 5 cards and numbering the boxes 1 through 10. For example:

Box 1— Jenny's summer shorts, T-shirts, skirts, sandals

Box 2—Costume clothing: 1950s outfit, black-and-white saddle shoes, purple angora sweater with holes, high school cheerleader's outfit

Box 3—Ski clothes, socks, underwear, sweaters, pants

Box 4—Scarves, belts, jewelry

Notes About Hangers

Wire hangers are messy and crease clothing. Replace them with plastic or cloth-covered hangers. Buy some plastic hangers in different colors. You may want to color-coordinate your wardrobe by using a different color hanger for each type of clothing.

Hang skirts on skirt hangers with clothespin-type clips. Pants can be hung on skirt hangers, pants hangers, or folded over plastic hangers. To save space get a slacks rack. You can hang five pairs of slacks and use the space of only one pair! (These are also wonderful to hang tablecloths on.)

Getting Started

How do you get started? Get three trash bags and label them "Put Away," "Give Away/Recycle," and "Throw Away." As you walk to each closet take everything out.

As you pull things out of your closet, keep in mind that if you haven't worn it or used it for the past year it goes in one of those three bags. If you haven't worn or used an item for two or three years, definitely give it away or throw it away.

Taking Inventory

Now let's start taking inventory. (You can use the Wardrobe Inventory sheet printed at the end of this chapter.) As you take your inventory, you'll quickly see what you have and need. For example, you may have way too many pairs of navy-blue pants. You only need one or two pair of quality navy-blue pants and maybe a couple pairs of nice jeans. You'll also see how you can better coordinate your wardrobe.

Everything in Its Place

Hang your clothes and accessories up when you change clothes. Each item should have a definite place. For example, all the extra hangers can go at the left end of your closet. Arrange all your blouses according to color, then your pants, then your skirts, and so forth. If you have a jacket that matches your pants, still separate them. Hang the jacket with the jackets and the pants with the pants. This way you can mix and match your things and not always wear the same jacket and pants together.

Put your shoes on shoe racks. Many neat shoe racks are now available. Remember to store shoes you don't wear often in cardboard or plastic shoe boxes.

It all comes down to a place for everything and everything in its place—just as soon as it comes into the house. Otherwise, you'll put it somewhere "for now," but it will really be forever.

EMILIE BARNES

Your smaller handbags can also go in clear plastic boxes. The larger ones can go on the shelf above your wardrobe. A hanging plastic shoe bag is great because you can also put purses and scarves in it. Storing smaller purses inside larger ones saves space. Belts and ties go on hooks. Ribbons can be hung on these hooks too, or you can hammer a big nail or decorative hook into the wall. You'll be surprised at how many belts you can get on a long nail!

Wardrobe Organization Equipment Needed

- ❏ 3 to 10 large storage boxes, preferably with lids
- ❏ 3 large black trash bags
- ❏ Plastic and cardboard shoe boxes
- ❏ Clear plastic boxes for scarves and clutch handbags
- ❏ Plastic hangers, all one color if you like
- ❏ 2 to 4 hooks
- ❏ Belt or tie holder

How to Get Started

A. Label trash bags:
1. Put Away
2. Throw Away
3. Give Away/Recycle

B. Plan a one- to two-hour time (or several days of shorter blocks of time).
1. Take everything out.
2. Get vicious and make decisions.
3. Put items in proper boxes. If you haven't worn it for one year, it must be put away or given away; if for two years, it doesn't belong in the closet; if for three years or longer, give it away or throw it away. (There might be very few exceptions.)
4. Return items to your closet and list them on your Wardrobe Inventory sheet.
   a. Suggested order for your clothes (left to right):

1) Extra hangers
2) Blouses
3) Pants
4) Skirts
5) Blazers and jackets
6) Sweaters (folded and put on a shelf or in a drawer)
7) Dresses
8) Gowns

b. For each item, put all similar colors together (example: light to dark).

c. Coats and heavy jackets can be kept in a hall closet or in an extra wardrobe closet.

d. Shoes go either in a shoe rack (floor type or hanging) or placed in covered shoe boxes on a shelf or neatly stacked on the floor.

e. Handbags:
   1) Smaller ones in clear plastic boxes.
   2) Larger ones on shelf above wardrobe (store smaller bags inside larger ones).
   3) A hanging plastic shoe bag is also great for handbags.

f. Belts and ties:
   1) Belt rack applied to wall with screws.
   2) Hooks or nails are great.

Give Away/Recycle

Be sure you give away the clothes and items you're not using. Maybe someone in your family or a friend can use them. Many people today have limited finances and would love to have what you're not using. Missions and thrift stores welcome slightly worn items. What can't be used as is may be remanufactured—so recycle!

Throw Away

Put these items in a black trash bag and put it in the garbage can. Don't forget to recycle if possible.

Helpful Hints

❏ When one leg in your panty hose gets a bad run, but the other is still okay, cut off the bad leg just below the panty part. Use it with another pair that has the same problem and you have saved a pair of panty hose. You can also use nylons with a run underneath dress slacks.

❏ When you buy something new for your wardrobe, make it a habit to throw something out or give something away.

❏ After wearing leather shoes, let them air out overnight before placing them in a shoe box and storing. To maximize the use of your shoes, rotate between two or three pairs.

❏ There are stores and websites on the Internet that are dedicated to home organization. The items they sell tend to be expensive, but sometimes they have just exactly what you need. Or they may spark some new ideas in you.

❏ Purchase plastic storage containers made specifically for use under the bed. Use bed risers to give you additional storage space. This is a great place to store out-of-season clothing that won't be needed from several months to a year. Bed risers can be purchased at home-improvement stores.

Wardrobe Inventory

Blouses	Pants	Skirts

Jackets	Sweaters	Dresses

Gowns	Lingerie	Shoes

Jewelry	

Things I Never Wear	Things I Need

Get in the habit of returning everything to its proper place and remind others to do so. If you do this daily, it takes less time than waiting until the situation is out of control. An even bigger bonus is that you needn't spend time looking for out-of-place objects.

9

What to Do with All that Paper

*You are no longer a slave, but a son; and since you
are a son, God has made you also an heir.*

GALATIANS 4:7 NIV

If you can't get on top of paperwork, it will absolutely bury you
and make you overwhelmed. This is the number one area of
disorganization for most women (and men too!). Have you noticed
that if you leave a stack of paper on the kitchen counter for more
than 15 minutes it gives birth to several more stacks that end up
all over your house? Paper can take over in a short amount of time.
The solution is to deal with it immediately when it comes into your
home.

Control Junk Mail

When you go through the mail each day (I stress *each day*—work
through today's mail before tomorrow's mail arrives), have a shredder, recycle bin, and trash can nearby. Get in the habit of quickly
deciding what goes in the recycle bin or trash. Don't procrastinate.
Remember that any mail with your name and address can become
a source of identity theft. Shred everything with personal information on it. If you receive an overwhelming amount of mail (most of

it junk) put the "toss" pile in a basket on top of your shredder. Then once a week have a teenager shred it all. This saves your time and gives a teen a chance to earn a few dollars (if it's not a "regular" chore).

Place Mail to Review in a Folder

When sorting mail, place the mail you want to read in a folder. Bob and I (Emilie) keep this folder behind our bed pillows and read the mail at night. (This won't work for all families, but for ours it does.) Have a trash can or recycle bin near the bed so you can toss the rejects into the container. Magazines can go on the living room coffee table, and last month's magazines can go into storage for future reference or recycle.

I (Sheri) have a basket on the kitchen counter that all the mail goes into for distribution. I have a reading file folder where I place magazines, catalogs, newsletters, and other reading material. I take that folder with me when I go somewhere and know I'll have some down time, such as waiting at the doctor's or dentist's office, the post office, and picking up kids from school. There is no such thing as "magazine police," so when you find something you want to save, tear it out that minute. If you wait, you probably won't remember the reason you saved the magazine. Toss the rest of the magazine in your recycle can and file the pages you saved in your file cabinet once you get home. Keep a supply of file folders and felt markers so you can create any necessary folders for the papers you are saving: "Recipes," "Home Remodeling," "Decorating Ideas." Then file the folders in your file cabinet. If you don't have a filing cabinet, use file storage boxes. Stack three in a corner and place a tablecloth over it and top with a vase of flowers or a lamp.

> *Next to the dog,*
> *the wastebasket*
> *is man's best friend.*
>
> AUTHOR UNKNOWN

Personal Mail Goes to the Person

When the children are home, place all personal mail into the folder of each individual member of the family, which is then placed at the person's work station. (This might be a desk, a kitchen table, or his or her bed.) This way everyone can find their daily mail. Make sure everyone returns the empty folders to a central place.

I (Sheri) have a mail sorter on my kitchen counter, out of the way, where all my family file folders are kept. I have color-coded my family so that everyone knows that when they see their color file folder, anything inside belongs to them. Green file folders at home belong to Tim, my folders are blue, and the kids have yellow and orange. Although my children now live in New York, they still receive mail at my home occasionally. I place it in their respective folders and once a month I place all their mail in a big manila envelope and send it with a love note from mom!

I have several other folders that stay in the mail sorter on the counter. One is labeled "Household bills." I place all the monthly bill statements in that folder. At the end of the month, Tim and I sit down at the kitchen table and pay the bills. This works well whether you pay by check or online. We place the leftover statement stubs back in the folder and file the entire folder in the file cabinet. It is the most effective way to file bills. Any time you need to refer to an old paid bill, it will always be under the date. You have only to open the file cabinet and pull out the folder for that particular month and presto! you'll be able to find what you need in a timely manner. It makes filing so much easier as well. Instead of stacks of paper sitting and waiting for time to file in separate folders, you just file the entire folder behind the last month. Remember: Don't pile it, file it.

File Important Papers

Somewhere in your office area (wherever that might be), set up a simple or elaborate file system to keep important tax records, health insurance, life insurance, and auto insurance papers. This area could include storage of papers detailing information about that favorite someday vacation, car records, childhood mementos, doctor references, pet information, and so forth.

One of the stresses of paper is that we put it down and soon have piles all over the house. Create a designated area for all papers.

Use Accordion Files

Accordion files are wonderful because they have many versatile uses—all the way from storing bills for future payment to storing important papers, from keeping photos sorted to greeting and thank-you cards. You can set the files up with labels for each heading, along with "Pay," "Read," "Answer," "Pending," and "Hold." Another great use for accordion files is the storage of computer software and user manuals and appliance and equipment manuals. Many appliances today come with an accompanying instructional CD or disk. You can place the disk and the corresponding instruction user manual in one pocket. Use one pocket for each computer program or appliance. If you need to reinstall a program or work on an appliance, you have everything you need handy. Another excellent storage idea for user manuals and computer software is a notebook with sheet protectors. Again, place the user manual/instruction book and warranty information, along with any computer CDs or disks, into the sheet protector. You can have a separate notebook for each computer or a notebook for all appliances. Most people keep instruction books, user manuals, and warranties for appliances and equipment they no longer have. Toss old stuff. Keeping everything together will make it easier to retrieve when you need it and easier to throw away when you can.

Plastic Business Card Holder

We all get business cards from people—our mechanic, painter, electrician, and life-insurance representative. Don't toss the cards in a drawer or drop them into your purse. Go to a stationery store and purchase a plastic business card holder that fits into your daily planner. The next time you get a business card, file it if you think you'll use the person's services.

Use a Master Family Calendar

Each family needs a "control center" where all members of the family can discover what's happening in the family. A bulletin board or a large monthly calendar can be posted on or near the refrigerator. This is the place for all announcements and where people jot down important notices—including birthdays and anniversaries. Once again, color-coding the calendar will make it easy to track who's doing what and where. Use the same color for each family member that you used for their file folders.

You can also use Post-it Notes to remind you to RSVP or call for an appointment. Place the note on the day the call needs to be made by. Once the call has been made, throw the note away.

Don't stress out in your battle against paper. Continue to be alert to weapons that will help you be better organized. There are so many handy gadgets and containers that can assist you. Check them out the next time you go shopping.

Get a notebook planner, either looseleaf or spiral-bound, that is small enough to carry around with you. This planner will become your "master list"—a continuous list that replaces all the slips of paper you've been using. Keep track of errands to run, things to buy, and notes to yourself about anything that requires action.

10

Stress Relievers

*Let no unwholesome word proceed from your
mouth, but only such a word as is good for
edification according to the need of the moment,
so that it will give grace to those who hear.*

EPHESIANS 4:29 NASB

Are you late for appointments on a regular basis? Do you pay the gas bill twice, fail to send in tax payments on time (and have to pay interest along with a large penalty), forget luncheon engagements with dear friends, or even miss a flight because you didn't get to the airport on time? Organized families know how to avoid these stresses. And that means happier family relationships. Let's look at a few stress busters, so we too can have calmer, healthier lives.

At Home

❏ Have a box or basket where clothes that need to be mended can be deposited. Mend only once a week or once a month. Or take clothes to the dry cleaners or laundry service and have them do the mending. Your time may be more valuable spent on something else. As your children get older, teach them how to do basic mending such as sewing on buttons and hemming garments.

❏ Use mats on both sides of entry doors. These will really cut down on dirt accumulation in the home, which means less mopping, less vacuuming, and less cleaning each week.

❑ Members of the family need to help keep their areas clean. Don't do it for them.

❑ When you're making repairs around the home and you aren't sure you'll remember how the parts go back together, draw a simple diagram. If you have a digital camera, take a picture. Another help is to lay the parts out in a line in the order you remove them. This makes it easier to reverse the process.

❑ After putting up your holiday decorations, take a photo so next year you'll know where everything goes. This will save a lot of time.

❑ Write chores on small slips of paper and put them into a small dish. Let the various members of the family draw out a slip and that becomes their chore for the next week. Go one step further and write the name of the family member on a master list next to the chore he or she has drawn.

To protect valuable mementos and records from fire or flood— and to keep them all in one place as well—store them in a fireproof and waterproof safe.

❑ Make sure that each bedroom has a clothes hamper or laundry container so that clothing will be tossed into it rather than on the floor. On the way to breakfast, have each person put the dirty clothes in a larger hamper in the wash area. If you have the space, put several large plastic containers in the laundry area and teach the children to sort.

❑ Keep a turntable under every bathroom sink in the house. The shampoos and hair sprays can go on them. The cleaning products can go in a little basket or bucket. This way everything is right there in one container that you can pick up and take with you when you're cleaning.

Speed-Ups for Procrastinators

❏ Set your household clock 5 to 10 minutes ahead of the correct time. Don't tell anyone.

❏ Call the office of your next appointment to make sure they're running on schedule.

❏ Rather than nag your children 5 minutes before they leave for school, church, or an activity, set a timer for five minutes before they need to leave. When the timer goes off, everyone knows to head out the door.

❏ If you have a friend who is always late, call the person a few hours before your appointment and confirm the time and place.

❏ Make your to-do list before going to bed or before leaving the office. Now you know where to begin tomorrow.

Make Shopping a Piece of Cake

❏ Shop early in the morning or late at night (avoid peak hours).

❏ Shop from a grocery list. Get in and out of the market as fast as possible. This will save a lot of money by avoiding impulse buys.

❏ Write your shopping list on the back of an envelope and place inside the envelope only those coupons that deal with items you're going to buy.

❏ Avoid shopping for food when you're hungry or with your children (or husband!).

❏ Take a calculator with you to compare unit costs and keep a running total of your costs.

❏ Shop via the Internet. This can be a real time- and money-saver.

❏ When shopping for clothes, wear garments that are easy to remove, ones with a minimum of buttons and zippers.

❑ Don't shop with negative people. They won't let you purchase anything because nothing is "just right."

❑ Tie a ribbon to your auto antenna when you aren't familiar with a parking lot so your car will stand out. If you don't have an antenna that stays up, make a mental note of where you parked. Pick a landmark. That will help you when it comes time to leave. If there are posted aisle numbers, jot down where you parked on your shopping list.

❑ Have extra household goods in the closet or pantry. If you run out, you have backups. This will save unnecessary trips at usually inconvenient times.

Promoting Peace

❑ Attach a list of most-used addresses to the back of your stationery box. Better yet, keep a small organizer close by so you have addresses readily available.

❑ Limit travel to non-busy times of the year. Stay away from holiday travel, if at all possible.

❑ When you make an appointment, write it on your calendar, along with the person's telephone number.

❑ Teach your children to select their clothes ahead of time for the next day's activities.

❑ Insist that all members of the family talk decently to each other. Encourage only positive remarks.

❑ Limit intimate friends to a number you can give appropriate attention to. More than that adds stress in your life.

TVs and Telephones

❑ Limit the amount of time you spend on the telephone with each caller. Set a timer if you need to.

❑ Make the best use of your cell phone. When you find yourself waiting to pick up children or at an office for an appointment, make phone calls to set up appointments or catch up with a friend.

❑ Turn your TV off at mealtimes (soft background music is very satisfying).

❑ Ignore the phone when it rings at mealtime. Let the answering machine pick up messages. Turn the ringer off during these times.

❑ TV and homework don't mix, no matter what the kids say.

❑ Schedule at least two "no TV" nights each week. These are times to read, communicate, get to know good music, play games, put puzzles together.

❑ Don't accept any telephone solicitations. Tell callers to send a letter stating their company's request and background. (You probably will never receive it.) To avoid telemarketers, register with the national do not call list at 1-888-382-1222 or go to www.donotcall.gov.

❑ When you're limited on time, call the people you need to give information to when they won't be home and leave your short message on their answering machines.

Stress Reducers

❑ Color-code that special key on your key chain so you don't have to continually search for it.

❑ Color-code your extension cords when you have several at one outlet. This way you don't have to plug and unplug to see which cord goes where.

❑ Keep an inventory of clothes you need for next winter or summer. In the in-between months, look for the items when they go on sale.

❑ Keep an extra pair of panty hose in your desk at the office or in the trunk of your car.

❏ Sew extra buttons for your clothing on the inside bottom of the garment. This way you know where to look if it needs mending. Do this with the extra buttons that come with new garments too so you won't have to search when you need one.

❏ Have a fully equipped emergency kit in the back of your car, including an old sweater, comfortable walking shoes, a flashlight, a blanket, some emergency food, and water.

❏ Tape the extra screws that come with furniture to the underside of chairs, sofas, and tables. They are there when you need them.

❏ Have a key hook in the kitchen or a special designated place where family members place keys when they come into the house. This saves a lot of time looking for keys. Don't keep it by the door in case a burglar comes in and wants to take your car.

Save Time

❏ If you have to remember something in the morning, tape a message to the front door or to your bathroom mirror.

❏ Write down addresses and telephone numbers in pencil. You can erase and rewrite them very easily.

❏ Put your daily pills in a plastic box marked for each day of the week. A quick glance tells you if you took your pills that day.

❏ Buy a couple pairs of reading glasses if you lose glasses often.

❏ Write down phone numbers, directions, and messages in a notebook you take with you.

❏ Don't wait until your car's gasoline tank is almost empty to refill. Get in the habit of filling it when it reaches half a tank. It's just as easy to fill the top half as the bottom half.

❏ Clean out your purse at least once a month.

11

Travel Safe, Travel Smart

*Don't be afraid, for I am with you. Don't be
discouraged, for I am your God.*

ISAIAH 41:10 NLT

As we open newspapers or turn on television we're bombarded with terrible news from all over the world, including citizens being attacked. What can we do to protect ourselves and our families?

Our first priority is to be secure, and our verse for today gives us a glimpse of where that security comes from—the Lord Jesus Christ. He is our protector and defender. However, we must do our part in keeping safe. The following ideas will help you.

Foil Car Thieves

❏ *Car thieves look for easy jobs.* Their most attractive quarry is a car with the keys left in it. Car thieves also like dark, secluded parking places, and cars with keys hidden in those little magnetic boxes. Thieves are especially fond of unlocked doors and windows, and they get access to 80 percent of their loot that way. *Always* lock your car and take the keys with you.

❏ *Protect your car keys.* Most car keys have an identification number printed on them. Have your car dealer or locksmith punch out those numbers, but keep a record of the numbers in a safe place in case you need a duplicate.

❏ *Park in attended lots.* If you park in an unattended parking lot, your car is five times more likely to be stolen than if you park on the street or in an attended lot.

❏ *Remove your house keys from your key ring* when you park your car in a lot with valet service. Or give the valet a key chain holding only your car keys. Ideally you shouldn't leave anything of value in the car. However, if you can't take items with you, hide your valuables in the trunk. Most newer models of cars have special valet keys or a system of locking your trunk so that it can't be opened by the valet service.

❏ *Keep a copy of your vehicle identification number* in a safe place. Trucks and RVs don't always have a number, so mark these vehicles with your own code number.

❏ *Don't leave your driver's license or other identification in the car.* Keep your registration and insurance papers out of sight. In high-crime areas, consider taking these papers out of your car—but keep them in your purse since you're required to have them when driving.

❏ *Park with your wheels turned sharply to the curb* to make towing difficult.

❏ *Conceal valuable equipment—iPods, laptop computers, cell phones, and radar detectors.* Keep valuable items in the trunk. Don't leave packages, your purse, or anything that might make a thief want to break into your car.

❏ *Get your bearings before you drive in new towns.* When you're in a strange town, ask the hotel concierge, tourist information office, or police department if there are unsafe areas you should avoid. If you must drive through them, keep your windows up and doors locked.

❏ *Get a car alarm system* to frighten off thieves with sirens, horns, lights—or all three. Always activate your alarm.

❏ *Consider public transportation.* Many areas are so congested with vehicles and people that driving a car isn't very practical. Besides, public transportation gives you a better opportunity to sightsee and cuts down on pollution. Traveling independently may be more fun than traveling in groups; however, there is safety in numbers.

Personal Safety

Whether you're going on a tour or traveling independently, don't let the pleasure and relaxation of travel make you careless about your own safety.

❑ When you set out, leave your valuables behind. You'll be less attractive to thieves, and you won't risk losing your belongings.

❑ Weed out your wallet. Don't take credit cards and other items you won't need.

❑ Wrap a rubber band around your wallet and keep it in your inside pocket. Some travel stores have special clamps to secure your wallet in your pocket. Another option is to carry your money in a money belt, leaving just enough money in your wallet for the day's activities.

It's best to not carry a purse. Even if you hide your purse under a jacket and hold on tight, it can be snatched. If you must take a purse, make it a fanny pack.

❑ Wear clothing with secure pockets, and don't take any more than you can carry in them.

❑ Note your traveler's check numbers, and photocopy your passport identification pages, driver's license, and all credit cards you're taking with you. Give copies to a friend, and tuck other copies in your wallet.

Use Precautions at the Airport

❑ Be very vigilant as you enter an airport. Pickpockets thrive on the crowds and confusion in entrance areas, so get past security checks and into the waiting area as soon as possible.

❑ Get your boarding pass in advance, if you can.

❑ Limit carry-on luggage so you don't have to fight through the baggage-claim area. If you do check luggage, make sure it's easy to identify.

❑ Don't check valuables if at all possible. Remember, you can no longer lock check-in luggage.

❑ Before checking luggage, wind colorful ribbon or yarn around the handles so you can quickly spot your bags and no one will claim them by mistake.

❑ If you use your home address on luggage tags, get tags that have a flap to conceal the information from casual observers. It's better to use an office address.

❑ Have your address and contact information inside your suit-case.

❑ Find out in advance about ground transportation from the air-port to help you ward off unscrupulous drivers and guides.

Beef Up Your Hotel Safety

❑ Book a room between the second and seventh floors. You'll have more protection from burglars than if you were on the ground floor, and you'll still be low enough for fire equipment to reach you in an emergency.

❑ Read the emergency directions in your room. Locate the nearest fire exit (stairs).

❑ Keep tickets, expensive jewelry, unneeded traveler's checks, and other valuables in a hotel safe-deposit box. Many hotels offer a small safe in the room for your convenience.

❑ Meet new acquaintances in the lobby, and don't give them your room number.

❑ If you're traveling alone, have a bellman escort you to your room. Wait in the hall until he or she has checked the room and unloaded your luggage. If the hotel has no bellman, when you enter your room, prop the door open with one of your suitcases and check the bathroom and closet areas before shutting the door.

International Travel

❑ Make a note of emergency numbers, including police, fire, your hotel, and the U.S. embassy and consulate. Learn how to use the pay phones, and have change handy.

❑ Check with your cell phone provider to see if you can add international calling for the duration of your trip. Many times it is far less expensive than you may think.

❑ Learn enough of your host country's language to be able to communicate your need for assistance. There are now electronic devices for language translation.

Take the Worry Out of Sightseeing

❑ Before you set out, ask your concierge, tour leader, or local police department which neighborhoods you should avoid, and what (if any) special precautions you should take.

❑ In high-crime locations dress casually and look confident.

❑ Be on guard for muggers that work in pairs.

❑ Walk in the middle of the sidewalk, away from doorways and streets. If someone does accost you, give the person what he wants. Nothing is as valuable as your *life* and your *safety*.

❑ There are valuable travel resources online and at your local library. Take advantage of what is available. Talk to friends who have traveled where you intend to go.

Many areas of the United States and foreign countries are quite safe and welcome visitors. One of the joys of travel is meeting new people, and you can usually trust your instincts on when and where you can open up to new friends and experiences. If you fortify yourself against the possible dangers, you'll be able to relax more.

12

Air Travel: The Perils of Packing

*If I go and prepare a place for you, I will come
again and receive you to Myself,
that where I am, there you may be also.*

JOHN 14:3 NASB

If you haven't flown in recent years, you are in for a shock the next time you fly. Since September 11, 2001, traveling has changed radically.

What you can pack is defined quite specifically now. You are allowed the following as carry-on luggage:

❑ Toiletries. (Liquids must be 3 oz. or less and placed in a quart-sized ziplock bag. You can only take what will fit in one bag. The only exceptions are baby formula, breast milk, prescription medications, and over-the-counter medications (liquids, gels, or aerosols). These can be in containers larger than three ounces and don't have to be inside a quart-sized plastic bag. But you do have to declare them at the security checkpoint.

❑ Solid cosmetics and personal hygiene items such as lipstick in a tube, solid deodorant, and lip balm can be carried on. These items must be *solid* and not liquid, gel, or aerosol. If you have questions or doubts about an item, place that item in your checked baggage.

❑ Medical equipment and medicines.

Other restrictions may apply, depending on the airline. To avoid having possessions confiscated or boarding delays, check the regulations for the airline you're using. You can use the Internet to find out if any new restrictions have been added since the last time you flew. Here are some very basic tips for flying.

❑ Pack smart and keep valuables such as jewelry and electronic equipment in your carry-on luggage. Remember, checked luggage can't be locked.

❑ Put baggage tags inside *and* outside the bags.

❑ Leave for the airport early. Allow for car trouble and over-crowded traffic near the airport.

❑ Check the routing of your baggage. Make sure the agent attaches the correct tags for your destination city.

❑ Abide by the amount and size of carry-on luggage you are allowed (check with the airline).

As a general rule, airlines limit the number of carry-on bags to one plus a purse, briefcase, or laptop. Carry-on luggage must meet certain size requirements. Many international governments are very specific. Usually there are guidelines that say something like, "No more carry-on luggage can be brought on board than can be safely stowed." All this really means is that what you can carry on depends on the individual airline as well as the particular type of aircraft that will be used on your flight.

Always check with your individual airline *before* you head for the airport regarding specific baggage rules. If going overseas, don't forget to check carriers you'll be using there too.

Here are some ideas on what to check in, what to carry on, and what to leave at home.

For Your Carry-on Bag

❏ Prescription medicines, along with photocopies of the prescriptions.

❏ A photocopy of your airline tickets, your itinerary, and (if traveling overseas) your passport.

❏ A small supply of replacement batteries for any electronic items you'll be using on the flight.

❏ An inflatable neck pillow.

❏ Reading material.

❏ A casual pair of warm-ups (in case your check-in luggage is late).

❏ Stationery—in-flight time is great for getting caught up on thank-you notes and overdue letters.

❏ Your iPod, laptop computer, or portable DVD player. You can listen to music, watch a movie, or answer emails that can be sent once you've landed.

For Check-in Bags

❏ A basic first aid kit.

❏ A small umbrella.

❏ A voltage converter plug and adapter kit for hair dryers and shavers (overseas flights only).

❏ Plastic bags for dirty items and shoes.

❏ Girth belts for luggage. You don't want to depend solely on the often-flimsy locks and zippers on luggage (particularly if you tend to overstuff your suitcases).

❏ An extra plastic or canvas bag for the souvenirs you can't fit into your checked-in bags on your return flight.

❏ A small battery-operated alarm clock. You need a backup in case the front desk attendant forgets to wake you up. Alarms are built into many cell phones.

❏ A small flashlight for emergencies.

❏ If you wear glasses, a repair kit is a must. Make sure it has a small screwdriver and small screws.

❏ Additional film or memory cards for your camera.

When you are away on vacation or away from your home for a period of time:

1. Instruct the post office to hold your mail until you return.

2. Stop deliveries of paper, milk, and so forth.

3. Buy a timer and hook it up so that a light goes on at dusk and off at midnight.

4. Inform a trusted neighbor that you will be away, and have him or her look after your home.

5. Invite a friend or college student to stay at your house while you're away.

PART TWO

More Hours...and Home Organization

13

The Organization Test

*There is an appointed time for everything. And
there is a time for every event under heaven.*

ECCLESIASTES 3:1 NASB

How organized are you? What would your spouse, your children, or your friends say about you? Have you ever felt this way?

I am completely overwhelmed with paperwork! It is closing in on me. I am getting less done and taking more time to do it. I can't find anything, and the paper monster is taking over my home.

It's never too late to get organized. By allotting just 15 to 30 minutes a day to organize your home, you will be amazed at how quickly things begin to take shape. In order to be completely successful, you must have a game plan. This isn't difficult; it's simply a matter of choosing a plan and sticking to it. But let's start at the beginning.

Just what is organization? Take this simple test to help you determine your current level of organization and how much work you have ahead of you.

1. At this moment do you know where your car keys are?
2. Could you find your most recent tax returns in five minutes or less?

3. Do you know where your children's birth certificates and shot records are?

4. Could you find a receipt for office supplies purchased two months ago?

5. Is the sink free of dirty dishes?

6. Are three or more piles of paper a rarity in your home/office?

7. Could you, at a quick glance, give me a subtotal of revenue receipts or expenses for the previous month for your home?

8. Do you have a current list of service names and phone numbers, and could you retrieve it in under three minutes?

9. Have your bills for the month all been paid on time?

10. Do you open and sort your mail the day it arrives?

Eight or more "yes" answers: You are very organized.

Six to eight "yes" answers: You could use a tune-up.

Four to six "yes" answers: It's a jungle in there.

Less than four "yes" answers: You need a complete overhaul.

One woman who had a very exciting and successful home-based business had to cope with a great deal of paperwork. She was being swallowed up by clutter. She barely had any walking room left in her entire house. A small path led from the front door to her office, another path led to the dining room, and yet another path led to the back bedrooms. She became so overwhelmed by the mess that she began to lose business and eventually closed down altogether. She was stressed to the point of exhaustion. Her problems could have been easily prevented if she had learned these very basic organizational principles:

❏ Do it now.

❏ Don't put it down, put it away.

❑ A place for everything, and everything in its place.

❑ To fail to plan is to plan to fail.

❑ Don't pile it, file it.

❑ Do the worst job first.

Webster's definition of organization is simple: "To arrange in an orderly way; to set oneself into an orderly state of mind." We need to arrange our homes and offices in an orderly fashion to make our work productive. We will accomplish much more if we are organized. But remember—organization means different things to different people. For some it means no clutter anywhere—no piles, no excess paper. For another person it may mean having *neat* piles. Some people's closets and drawers are organized and labeled. They don't keep any clutter on countertops, and they generally are not collectors of knickknacks. For others, organization means that drawers are neat, items are easy to locate, counter-tops are clean but neatly display decorative items, and their knickknack collection is dusted. Depending on your personality type, organization may mean something different for you. How boring it would be if we all were exactly the same! Our differences make life fun and exciting, and we can be organized to fit our lifestyles.

> He who every morning plans the transaction of the day and follows out that plan carries a thread that will guide him through the labyrinth of the most busy life…But where no plan is laid…chaos will soon reign.
>
> VICTOR HUGO

Most self-organizers fit into two distinct categories. We find they are either "conventional organizers" or "unconventional organizers." The conventional organizers design strict schedules and adhere to them consistently. The unconventional organizers have the appearance of being unorganized at times, but upon closer examination are found to be extremely organized. Their organizational systems are very complex—sometimes even more complex than the conventionally organized individuals. For example, conventional organizers might use complex planners and tickler files. Unconventional organizers may use simple to-do lists and unique filing systems using binders rather than traditional file folders.

Whether their systems are conventional or unconventional, self-organizers share these characteristics:

1. *They know they can be in charge of how they do things.* Self-organizers have discovered that even if it doesn't seem so, they're free to choose how they're going to do things. Also, they are willing to live with the consequences of their choices.

2. *They keep their priorities in mind and orchestrate their work around these goals.* Knowing what's really important to them pervades everything they do, from the hours they spend working to their choice of tasks.

3. *They take responsibility for what happens.* Since they realize they can usually structure their work the way they want, self-organizers have also learned they're responsible for what results they get. If they aren't getting what they want, they check to see if their approach needs to be modified. They take responsibility for problems as well as solutions.

4. *Although self-organizers often don't realize it, they have made a habit of following the basic principles of good systems organization.* They have learned the principles of good systems organization by osmosis. They picked it up from their parents, a teacher, or on the job. The most common way people learn organizing habits is from the way they were taught to clean up their rooms as young children.[1]

If you weren't blessed during childhood with learning the basic skills for creating and using organizational systems, don't despair. There's no need to struggle through the hazards of learning by trial and error. You can use the principles in this book to design an organizational plan that will work for your home.

Wouldn't it be wonderful if you could wake up in the morning and know exactly where you are going, why you are going, and how to get there? Do you wish you had the secret to having more time to spend with your husband and children? We're here to tell you that you *can* go to bed at night with the satisfaction of knowing you accomplished all you set out to do that morning in your family life and in your extended responsibilities. So keep reading for some exciting challenges as we work together to become all God designed us to become!

14

Prayer Organization

*Admit your faults to one another and pray for each
other so that you may be healed.*

JAMES 5:16

Some of you may not have a prayer life. Others of you may have a very vital prayer life. Some of you desire to have a vibrant, effective prayer life but are fumbling with it because you're not sure how to incorporate it into your life or how to organize it. Many people have been in that position. But we can help! That's what we're going to do now—offer steps to take to set up a prayer notebook and organize a prayer life.

One Set of Footprints

M.R. Powers

One night a man had a dream. In his dream he was walking along the beach with the Lord, when across the sky flashed all the events of his life. However, for each scene he noticed two sets of footprints in the sand, one belonging to him and the other to the Lord. When the last scene had flashed before him, he looked back at the footprints and noticed that many times along the path there was only one set of footprints in the sand. He also noticed that this happened during the lowest and saddest times of his life.

This really bothered him, so he said to the Lord, "You promised that once I decided to follow You, You would walk with me all the way, but I noticed that during the roughest times of my life there was only one set of footprints. I don't understand why You deserted me when I needed You the most."

The Lord replied, "My precious child, I love you and I would never leave you. During those times of trial and suffering when you saw only one set of footprints, it was then that I carried you."

God is always with us. When the times are the lowest, that's when He picks us up and carries us. Isn't that wonderful? Some of us have experienced that. Some of us right now are in a position where we're being carried through a rough situation or a difficult problem. It's comforting to know that we have our Lord to carry us when times get hard.

But so often we don't take advantage of spending time with our Lord in prayer and communication. But do you know what? He loves us anyway. He loves us unconditionally. But why not pull together some type of system in our lives so we do spend valuable time with Him. Sometimes we get turned off because we believe we must set aside an hour or more, but it doesn't have to be a lengthy prayer time.

How to Get Started—The Prayer Basket

As with everything else, the proper tools and materials make life easier. Start by making a prayer basket. Get a medium-sized basket with a handle. You might have one already. Tie a nice bow on the handle. You may want to stick a small bunch of silk flowers through the bow to make it very pretty. Here are the items you will want in your prayer basket:

❏ *A small notebook* or a $5\frac{1}{2}$ x $8\frac{1}{2}$ three-ring binder. Get colored tab dividers, paper, and a pen. Divide the paper into three categories with the tab dividers: Prayer Requests, Sermon Notes, and Notes.

❏ *A Bible.* You may want to have a couple of translations so you can read verses in different versions to augment your understanding. Keeping your Bible handy is great because you may want to do a little Bible study with yourself. For example, when you're praying God may reveal something to you in His Word. If you're praying for specific people, you may feel impressed by God to drop them a note and tell them you're praying for them and supporting them. At times like this you can include a Bible verse for encouragement. Colossians 4:2 (NASB) says "devote yourselves to prayer, keeping alert in it with an attitude of thanksgiving." Christ is waiting for you. His attitude toward you is love. And hopefully your attitude in return is one of thanksgiving.

❏ *Some tissues.* As you pray for specific situations or concerns or certain family members, you may get weepy. These tears never go unnoticed by our heavenly Father.

❏ *Note cards.* These are for those words of love and encouragement you may want to send to someone you're praying for.

Feel free to add other things to your basket, such as a devotional book, a journal, a small blanket. Personalize it so that it fits you and your lifestyle.

Why Should We Pray?

> *[Jesus] knelt down and began to pray.*
> Luke 22:41 NASB

Why do we pray? Because we want to communicate with God. Jesus said that people ought to pray always, without giving up (Luke 18:1). Prayer also gives us an opportunity to confess to God those things we feel guilty about. First John 1:9 says, "If we confess our sins to him, he can be depended on to forgive us and to cleanse us from every wrong." We can open our hearts to God and confess the very worst things in our lives and the very smallest things. God hears us! Nobody else has to know those things.

Prayer teaches us discipline. When we pray, we know we are in the hands of God and that God is here to touch us, to feed us, and to give us what He wants us to have. This draws us closer to the Lord. As we pray even brief prayers, we draw on the fellowship we have with Christ.

Prayer keeps us from being selfish. It keeps us from looking at ourselves and the things *we* want. When we pray for someone else, we focus on what the other person needs, is going through, and our love for him or her.

Prayer also keeps us from temptation. As we pray we draw closer to God, and as we draw closer to Him, we find that we want to do what He wants for us. We want to be the women He created us to be.

How to Pray

Luke 22:41 says that Jesus knelt and began to pray. This doesn't mean that every time we pray we have to get on our knees, though there are times when we will want to do this. Be flexible. We also have a tendency to think we have to keep asking God for something over and over. But Matthew 6:7 says, "Don't recite the same prayer over and over." We can give our needs to God without constantly reminding Him of them because He already knows all about them and He hears us the first time! So if we don't pray for that thing every day, God still knows. That doesn't mean we can't consistently pray for something; it just doesn't need to be every day.

A woman prayed for her husband for 35 years. She probably didn't get down on her knees every day and pray fervently for her husband for 15 minutes for 35 years. But she was in an attitude of prayer for 35 years, and then one day when her husband was in his seventies he received Christ and stepped into the kingdom of God. God hears our prayers!

The Best Approach

As we approach God in prayer, let's first praise Him, adore Him, and thank Him for all the things He's given us and for who He is. This opens our hearts to Him.

We can thank God for everything, even when life is difficult. He never leaves us! If we're depressed, thank God for even the smallest things. As we begin to list what we're thankful for, our selfishness will dissipate.

Next we can confess our sins and shortcomings to God, talking freely to Him, knowing He loves us no matter what. When we ask for His forgiveness—He grants it!

Now we submit ourselves to God. He wants to hear our needs and our supplications. Matthew 7:7-8 (NASB) says, "Ask, and it will be given to you; seek, and you will find; knock, and it will be opened to you. For everyone who asks receives, and he who seeks finds, and to him who knocks it will be opened." God *wants* to answer our prayers and to give us the desires of our hearts.

Make a List

When you organize your prayer notebook, make a list of the things you want to pray for. You could have a section for your family. Then you might have personal prayer requests. These could include financial needs or a situation between you and your husband or boyfriend.

Have a section in your notebook for your church, including your pastor and his or her spouse and children. All of us should pray for the rulers of our country, our state, and our city. If you have children in school, pray for the principal and all the teachers, plus the friends your children have.

And pray for yourself. Pray that you will incorporate some of the organization skills we've talked about. Pray for your personal needs. You may be struggling with anger toward someone or selfishness. Pray for wisdom and understanding.

If married, pray for your husband. That's vital. He's working, struggling in the world, trying to make a living. Situations and circumstances come into his life that will provide opportunities for you to uphold him and support him. Thank God for your husband and your family.

We also need to pray for missionaries as they spread God's Word to people throughout the world in areas we can't or don't reach.

Keeping Track

In your notebook label the tabs with each day of the week. So you have Monday, Tuesday, Wednesday, Thursday, Friday, Saturday, and Sunday tabs. Now spread out your prayer requests. For example, behind the Monday tab you might put your family prayer requests, listing those people in your family that you will pray for. When Monday morning comes and you have your quiet time with the Lord, pray for those needs. (You can pray for them at other times as well.)

Tuesday might be your prayer day for your country, your church, your pastor, and maybe your Bible-study members. (During your Bible-study you can note the prayer requests given and put them in your notebook. This way you can look on the page and see that, for example, Peter doesn't have a job. So you pray for Peter. Then when Peter gets a job you can say, "Thank You, Lord, for giving Peter a job.") Write down God's answers to your prayers next to the original request. (Always date your prayer requests and answers.)

Make appointments with friends. It's all too easy to let time slip by...Try setting up regular meeting times.

EDITH FLOWERS KILGO

Saturday is usually a difficult day because of family activities, so praying for miscellaneous requests works well. Sometimes on Saturday you may not even get a formal chance to pray. Your children are home, your schedule is off, and you're going on picnics and so forth. Keep Saturday fairly open.

On Sunday, instead of having a list of people to pray for, outline the pastor's sermons. If you do this you'll discover you're listening better and getting more from the message. When people come to you with prayer requests at church on Sunday, write them in your prayer notebook. That way you'll remember to pray for them on Monday, Tuesday, Wednesday, or Thursday as you're going through your times of prayer during the week.

God Hears Children Too

Give your children an opportunity to share in prayer with you also. Ask for their prayer requests. One great way to do this is to ask when you gather at the breakfast or dinner table. For example, "What kind of exam are you going to have today?" When you get together again, you have a point of reference and can ask, "How did your exam go?" And your kids can ask what your needs are and how your day went. They might say, "How did your speaking go?" Or they might ask, "How was your job today? Did you get the project done you were working on?" This way prayer requests become part of your family life.

When to Pray

When should we pray? Morning is an important time to pray. Maybe we can pray in a private place in our homes. Or maybe it can be somewhere else. I (Emilie) spend a lot of time in my car, and I find this a valuable time to spend in prayer. People may look at me on the streets or freeways and wonder why nobody else is in the car and my mouth is moving, but I'm talking to my Lord. Be sure not to close your eyes when you're driving and praying!

We also need to pray with other people. Matthew 18:20 (NASB) says, "Where two or three have gathered together in My name, I am there in their midst." As we pray together, we don't need to make our prayers long by praying for everything in the world and everything in our notebook. God doesn't care so much about our words; He cares primarily about our hearts and our attitudes.

We can pray short prayers in our Bible-study group, in our prayer group, or over the telephone. When people call with a problem, say, "Let's pray about it. I don't know all the details of your situation, and you don't have to spell them all out to me, but God knows all about them, so let's pray about it right now." And then do it.

The Desires of Our Hearts

God is interested in the desires of our hearts, even when we think, *I'd love to have it, but I'm afraid to ask because it seems selfish or even a little silly.* It's the *attitude* toward those things He's really concerned about. So make sure your list aligns with God's priorities. Pray, "Lord, if it's okay with You, I'd like to have this." Your list might include a lot of things: maybe a new sofa or finances for the women's overnight retreat you can't afford to attend. One lady prayed about a curling iron. Hers died and she didn't have enough money to buy a new one. She went into a beauty supply store and told the man she didn't have any money but needed a curling iron. He replied, "Don't worry about it—we have one that was brought back because the lady didn't want that size. She didn't have it in the right box, so you can have it." My friend couldn't believe that God was even interested in her curling iron!

Remember to thank God for all things because He is interested in everything that has to do with you. Ephesians 5:20 says, "Always give thanks for everything...in the name of our Lord Jesus Christ." God is interested in the desires of our hearts.

Prayer Organization Summary

Devote yourselves to prayer, keeping alert in it
with an attitude of thanksgiving.
Colossians 4:2 NASB

Materials Needed

- ❑ Small three-ring binder with front pocket
- ❑ Paper
- ❑ Seven dividers with tabs
- ❑ Pen
- ❑ Bible

Why Pray?

A. We pray because our Lord prayed:

He walked away, perhaps a stone's throw, and knelt down and prayed this prayer: "Father, if you are willing, please take away this cup of horror from me. But I want your will, not mine." Then an angel from heaven appeared and strengthened him, for he was in such agony of spirit that he broke into a sweat of blood, with great drops falling to the ground as he prayed more and more earnestly. At last he stood up again and returned to the disciples—only to find them asleep, exhausted from grief (Luke 22:41-45).

B. Prayer gives us the opportunity for confession.

C. Prayer brings discipline to our lives.

D. Prayer draws us closer to our Lord.

E. Praying for others keeps us from selfishness.

F. Prayer helps us love those we have difficulty loving.

G. Prayer keeps us from disobedience to God and temptation. God...will provide the way of escape (1 Corinthians 10:13 NASB).

How to Pray

He knelt down and began to pray (Luke 22:41 NASB).

A. "Don't recite the same prayer over and over as the heathen
do, who think prayers are answered only by repeating them
again and again. Remember, your Father knows exactly
what you need even before you ask him!" (Matthew 6:7-8).

B. A helpful reminder:

1. A—Adore God.

2. C—Confess to God.

3. T—Thank God for everything.

4. S—Supplication and submission unto God.

C. "Ask, and it will be given to you; seek, and you will find;
knock, and it will be opened to you. For everyone who asks
receives, and he who seeks finds, and to him who knocks it
will be opened" (Matthew 7:7-8 NASB).

What to Pray For

A. Make a list of all needs:

1. Family (children, in-laws, relatives)

2. Personal (finances, problems)

3. Friends

4. Church (pastor and family, church leaders)

5. Country (city, state, president)

6. School (teachers, principal, students)

7. Husband (work, personal)

8. Self (home, anger, organizing)

9. Missionaries

B. Delegate requests into days of the week: Monday through Saturday (use tabs).

C. Sunday's tab will be for sermon outlines and prayer requests.

1. Prayer requests will be added to all categories.

2. Date prayer requests and date God's answers. Answers may be "wait" ("not now"), "no," or "yes." Always give thanks.

D. Let the children give prayer requests. "All things you ask in prayer, believing, you will receive" (Matthew 21:22 NASB).

When to Pray

❏ Morning

❏ Noon

❏ Evening

❏ Meals

❏ Bedtime

Where to Pray

When you pray, go into your inner room, close your door and pray to your Father who is in secret, and your Father who sees what is done in secret will reward you (Matthew 6:6 NASB).

A. Home—in the closet, while doing dishes, vacuuming, cleaning

B. In the car, while jogging, exercising, walking

C. With others. "Where two or three have gathered together in My name, I am there in their midst" (Matthew 18:20 NASB).

1. Bible-study groups

2. Women's prayer groups

3. With a girlfriend

    4. On the phone with a friend

Wish Prayers

A. God already knows the desires of our hearts, but He wants us to ask Him for them. It's the *attitude* about those things that He is concerned about.

B. Check yourself by saying, "Lord, if it wouldn't be good for me to have this, then I really don't want it. But if it would be okay with You, I'll be very grateful and use it for Your glory."

C. Be prepared—God always answers. It may be an immediate "yes," a "wait a while," an absolute "no," or "the timing is not right at present." Record these answers in your notebook by item. Allow God to work in your life. He loves giving you what's best for you. Remember to thank Him in all things (Ephesians 5:20).

Seven days without prayer makes one weak!

AUTHOR UNKNOWN

15

Total Mess to Total Rest

If you wait for perfect conditions,
you will never get anything done.

ECCLESIASTES 11:4

Suppose I (Emilie) were to say to you, "Today I'm going to come home with you. I want you to take me into your house so I can see your closets, look under your bed, open your drawers, check your pantry, and go anyplace in your house."

Some of you would reply, "Well, that's okay. I've got my house in order, and things are really good here, so you can come over." Others of you would say, "Okay, but don't go into the third bedroom because I've been shoving things in that back room for a long time. That's my little hideaway. You can't go back there, but you can look everywhere else." Still others of you might say, "There is no way anybody is going to come into my house because the whole place is a total mess."

Controlling Your Home

Sheri and I are going to show you how you can change any mess—large or small—into a home that you'll be able to maintain and rest in. *You* will control your home instead of your home controlling you.

Emilie's program was the turning point in my (Sheri) life. When

I attended my first seminar in 1981, I was so afraid Emilie was going to make me get rid of my "stuff." And I didn't want to do that because I was very attached to it. However, I really wasn't sure what all my stuff included or exactly where my stuff was located. By learning and implementing the principles of "Total Mess to Total Rest," I was able to keep the things I wanted to keep and store my things and retrieve them in a timely fashion when I needed to. Emilie really was an answer to my prayer of frustration over the disorganization in my home.

Here's some of the equipment you'll need to work this program.

❏ 3 to 10 file boxes 16" deep x 12" wide by 10" high with lids (we call these "Perfect Boxes" because the lid is attached).

❏ a 3"x 5" card-file box and some 3"x 5" cards. Get 10 cards in each color—blue, yellow, pink, white, green, orange, cherry.

❏ 3 x 5 dividers for your card box

❏ a pen

❏ a black marker pen

❏ colored file folders

❏ regular manila file folders

❏ a filing cabinet or file boxes

❏ large black trash bags

❏ white or masking tape

Sheri and I (Emilie) have been teaching More Hours in My Day seminars for years now, and we've discovered something about women. Our intentions are good and we want to get started, but somehow we can't seem to get organized enough to get ourselves organized. So we get frustrated and throw the whole program out the window. So pray about this program. Ask God to help you be willing to get the materials and use them in your home.

Commit

You'll need to commit to five weeks in taking your entire house from total mess to total rest. Don't become overwhelmed thinking about it. You're going to tackle a small portion at a time—only one room a week for the next five weeks. You'll do it nice and slow so you'll gradually get your home under control. For those of you who tend to be perfectionists, this concept will take some getting used to. Normally you desire to clean and organize everything all at once and perfectly. But because we don't live in a perfect world, that's impossible. So instead of getting something done, you tend to do nothing at all.

Your entire home can be transformed in 15-minute time slots. On Monday, you're going into room one to clean like mad for 15 minutes, and then forget it until Tuesday. On Tuesday, you'll do the same as you did Monday, spending 15 minutes cleaning and organizing. You will continue this process throughout the week. Presto! By the end of the week you will have spent one hour and 30 minutes in the first room. You'll still have Sunday off and a nice, clean, well-organized room. You will continue this process until every room in the house is complete. You'll also set your timer so you stay on task and not overdo. Are you ready? Okay!

First, you'll get out three large black trash bags. I like black trash bags because they're lightweight, you can drag them through the house, and you can't see inside them—and your husband and children cannot see inside either. This means no rooting through and removing items. Take your three trash bags and, using the tape and marker pen, label one of them "Put Away," one "Throw Away," and one "Give Away/Recycle."

Now visualize yourself standing at the front door with these three big trash bags. Ring the doorbell, and then walk through the front door. The first room you come to will be the first room you're going to clean, with the exception of the kitchen. (If that's the room you walk into first, move on. You'll save the kitchen until the end because you'll need all the experience you can get before tackling it.) To make it easy, let's say we step into the living room, and on our right is the hall closet.

The Hall Closet

We open the hall closet. We're now going to take everything out of that hall closet. We've decided to get serious in making choices about what to do with all the stuff in that hall closet.

Let's put back into the hall closet only those things that actually belong in a hall closet. This includes sweaters, coats, umbrellas, boots, football blanket, binoculars, tennis rackets, and so forth.

But now we have all those other things that don't belong in there, such as old magazines we've collected for six or seven years. (We were going to look through them some rainy day and cut out the pictures and recipes, but we never did.) So we have to get rid of these things. We also had papers and receipts, and all sorts of other things in that hall closet. We may even have coats we haven't worn for five years! We'll put these extra items in the Put Away bag, the Throw Away bag, or the Give Away/Recycle bag.

Ask a friend to help you (and you help with her house). A friend isn't attached to your stuff so she can objectively tell you to throw it out or give it away. Don't invite a sentimental pack rat to help you!

As we go through our home every week for the next five weeks, we begin to fill up these bags. At the end of the fifth week we may have 3, 10, or 15 bags full of various items. Put a twist tie on the trash bags marked Throw Away and set them out for the trash collector. Now they're gone! You've got all those things out of the way.

Now you have two types of bags left: Give Away/Recycle bags and Put Away bags. The Give Away/Recycle bags will hold things you may want to hand down to other family members, clothing you want to give to a thrift shop, sell at a rummage sale, and donate to your church, and recyclable items. Separate out the recycle items and then recycle!

Maybe you'll decide to have a garage sale and make a little extra money. If you do, buy something for yourself or for the house or give the profits to your church or missionary group. Now you've cleaned these things out of your house and put them to good use in somebody else's hands!

The only items left are the "put away" ones. Return them to where they belong or, if you choose to store them, we'll handle that in the next section.

Keeping It Neat

Okay, we have our house totally clean. How are we going to keep it that way? We certainly never want to go through this total mess again! The cleanup lasted for five weeks, and we don't have to do it again. The way we maintain our organized house is to take our file box, the 3" x 5" cards, and the dividers. Label each of the divider tabs. The first tab will be "Daily." On these cards we list all those things we will do daily to maintain our house, such as washing the dishes and making the bed.

The second divider is labeled "Weekly" and consists of those things we do weekly. For example, on Monday we wash clothes; on Tuesday we iron and water the houseplants; on Wednesday we mop the floors; on Thursday we vacuum and do our marketing; and so on.

Now Thursday comes along, and Lisa, your best friend, calls you and says, "Let's go to lunch and go shopping. The department store has a big sale today." So you check your cards and say, "I've done all my daily things, but it's Thursday, so I have to vacuum and go to the market. I can do my marketing this afternoon when we get back from lunch, but I don't know about the vacuuming."

So you go with Lisa and get your bargains, but the vacuuming isn't done. You consider moving the vacuuming to Friday. But when you look on Friday's card and see all those other things to do, you take Friday's chores and move them to Saturday. But on Saturday you're going to the park with the kids. So you decide to move those things to Sunday. But on Sunday you can't do them either because you're going to church, and you've also got company coming afterward. So you're going in circles. You've moved jobs from day to day, and you're completely stymied.

What's the solution? Don't move the job. Instead, on Thursday when you go to lunch with Lisa and don't have time to vacuum, you move your vacuuming card to the back of the weekly section. This means you don't vacuum your house again until next Thursday, when the vacuuming card comes up in your file again. In other words, you rotate your cards daily whether you do the allotted jobs or not.

Yes, this means you're crunching along on dirty carpet for a week or two. You say, "I can't possibly do that." But now you're disciplining yourself to keep your priorities in order. So next week when Lisa calls and says, "Let's go to lunch," you tell her, "I'll go to lunch if I get my vacuuming done. If I don't get it done today it means another whole week before I can do it." Remember, *you* want to be in control of your home, and not the other way around.

Label the next divider tab "Monthly." This may include cleaning your appliances. Let's say you put down "clean the fridge." During Week 1 you clean the refrigerator (you have a whole week to do it, or you can delegate the job to a child). On Monday of that week, clean only one shelf, Tuesday, clean another shelf and so on. By the end of the week you've cleaned the refrigerator, and it only took 15 to 20 minutes each day. During Week 2 you do the oven, and so forth. This way every week you're doing a little bit to maintain your home. It's only going to take you a little time every day, and you'll never have to go through the Total Mess program again.

The next divider is labeled "Quarterly." List the items that must be done every three months to keep your home in good shape. Break it down over the three months. You might need to straighten the linen closet, move the furniture and vacuum, and clean the china cabinet.

Label the next divider "Semiannual." These tasks might include washing the curtains, cleaning the screens, washing the windows. And, finally, the next divider is labeled "Annual." Those jobs might include cleaning the basement, attic, and garage.

Your last tab, at the very back of your file, is labeled Storage. Take your 3 x 5 cards and number them #1, #2, #3, and so forth in the upper left corner. Then you take your "Put Away" large trash bags and divide your things into the "Perfect Boxes" with lids and number each box: #1, #2, #3. On your #1 card list all the items in box #1. On the top right corner of the index card, write where the box will be stored: "Garage," "Attic," "Basement," "Master Bedroom Closet." Write this on the box too. Place the cards behind the "Storage" tab in the file box and the boxes where you've decided. The next time you need to retrieve something, you simply go to your card file box and search for the card listing what you're looking for, see where the box is located, and find the item you want. It's as simple as that! No more searching for hours or days to find something you know you have but can't put your finger on.

Maintaining Memories

A number of years ago my (Emilie) son, Brad, came home from college and said to Bob, "Remember when you used to referee those football and basketball games, and you wore that black-and-white striped shirt? Well, I'd like to wear it because we're going to have a black-and-white party at school. You can't get into this party unless you wear black and white."

Bob looked at me and thought out loud, *I don't know where the shirt is. I haven't seen the shirt for 15 years.* But I knew where the shirt was! I went right to my card file, checked it out, and said, "Oh, yes, it's in Box #5." So I said to Brad and Bob, "Go out into the garage, look up on the shelf, find Box 5, pull it down, and inside that box you will find your black-and-white referee shirt." Sure enough, there it was. Brad took the shirt and wore it to the party. I noted on the card with a Post-it Note that Brad borrowed the shirt. When he returned it, we put it back in the box and tore up the note.

Moving on, now we take our file box, manila and colored file folders, and go to the piles of papers we found while cleaning our home. We found old newspaper clippings, warranties, instruction booklets, receipts from car and household repairs, and a lot of other things. Sort these papers into labeled file folders, list all those things on 3 x 5 cards, file the folders and file the cards in the main file box.

Don't forget to write where the folders are located for easy retrieval. You may have several file cabinets or file drawers. Once again, when you need a receipt, warranty booklet, or instruction manual, it will only take seconds to put your hands on the exact folder you need.

If you work outside your home, a simple file folder system on your kitchen counter will help keep you organized. You can have colored file folders in a box with these headings: Personal, Household Bills, Receipts, Paycheck Stubs, Credit Card Receipts, and Catalogs/Newsletters/Magazines. Add folders and headings as necessary.

Several years after Tim and I (Sheri) had our swimming pool built, we had some problems with the pool pump. Tim came into the house and asked me if I could locate the pump manual. I assured him I could. I went to my file box and saw that the file I was looking for was in the back office file cabinet. I went directly to the file drawer and pulled out the manual and gave it to him. It took less than two minutes! There was a time when it would have taken weeks for me to locate the manual. I was proud of the progress I'd made—and Tim was proud of me too!

Receipts Equal Money

I (Emilie) had a neat experience several years ago. The icemaker on our refrigerator broke for the second time. When I called the repairman he said, "Mrs. Barnes, that's the same thing I fixed about six months ago." I asked, "How much will it cost?" He replied, "Sixty-five dollars. However, it's under warranty if you can find the receipt."

Little did he know! I went right to my file, looked under Repair Receipts, and within 30 seconds had the receipt. I told him, "I have it right here." He replied, "Great! You just saved yourself 65 dollars."

The Children's File Box

When the children were about 12 or 13 years old, I (Emilie) set up a file box for each of them. (I wish I'd done it even earlier.) I gave them each 10 file folders. One day we went through the Total Mess program in their rooms. Then they began to file their report cards, their special reports, and their pictures and letters. Jenny was blessed to get some love letters, so she filed those in her file folders. She also pressed and filed the flowers from her special dates and proms. When she got her first car, the insurance papers went into the file box.

When the children went away to college, the first thing they took with them was their file box. It had all their important papers. When they came home for the summer, home came the file box. When Jenny married, she took her file box with her. All her treasures were in that box. Then she got another box and ten more file folders, and she set up a household file box. So now she has all those warranties, instruction booklets, and insurance papers in her household file.

What have we done? We've taken our *total mess*—and our children's total messes—and changed it into *total rest*. And we'll maintain that rest. What does that give us? More hours in our day and no guilt feelings about an unorganized house.

Total Mess to Total Rest Summary

Equipment

❏ 3 to 10 "Perfect Boxes" with flip-top lids attached

❏ 3 x 5 card file box

❏ 3 x 5 colored cards with dividers

❏ Twelve 8½ x 11 colored and manila file folders

How to Get Organized

A. Plan your five-week program: When will you do your 15 minutes a day work and in what order are you going to clean the rooms. Note the dates on your calendar.

B. Label three large trash bags:

1. Put Away

2. Throw Away

3. Give Away/Recycle

C. Start at your front door (usually the living room) and end with the kitchen.

1. Do closets, drawers, shelves.

2. Get ruthless!

Household Routine

A. Set up a 3 x 5 colored card file box with dividers and tabs.

B. Label dividers in this card file:

1. Daily

2. Weekly

3. Monthly

4. Quarterly

5. Semiannually

6. Annually

7. Storage

C. Make a list of jobs to be done:

1. Daily

    a. dishes

    b. make beds

    c. clean bathrooms

    d. pick up rooms

    e. pick up kitchen

2. Weekly

    a. Monday—wash, grocery shopping

    b. Tuesday—iron, water plants

    c. Wednesday—mop floors and dust electronic and computer equipment

    d. Thursday—vacuum, go shopping

    e. Friday—change bed linens

    f. Saturday—do yard work

    g. Sunday—free except to plan for next week

    Note: If you skip a job on an allotted day, *don't do it later.* Put the card at the back of the file section and skip the task until next week.

3. Monthly

    a. week 1—clean refrigerator

    b. week 2—clean oven

    c. week 3—mend clothing

    d. week 4—clean and dust baseboards

4. Quarterly

    a. clean drawers, windows

   b. clean closets, move furniture and vacuum

   c. clean china cabinets, cupboards, linen drawers

  5. Semiannually

   a. clean screens

   b. rearrange furniture

   c. change filter in the furnace

  6. Annually

   a. wash curtains

   b. touch up exterior paint

   c. clean drapes

   d. clean carpets

   e. make repairs around the home

   f. wash walls

   g. clean out garage

Storage

 A. Get "Perfect Boxes" with flip-top lids or plastic storage boxes and label them Box #1, Box #2, Box #3, etc.

 B. Assign each box a 3 x 5 card with a corresponding number. For example:

  Box 1—a. Bill's baby clothes

      b. Bill's baby book

  Box 2—Toys

  Box 3—Seasonal clothes

  Box 4—Fall decorations

  Box 5—Books: high school yearbooks and materials

  Box 6—Scrapbooks

Box 7—Old pictures

Box 8—Snow clothes

Box 9—Scrap fabrics

Note: I reserve boxes 15a, 15b, 15c, 15d for income tax materials to coordinate with April 15, the IRS filing deadline. I also reserve boxes 25a, 25b, 25c, 25d for all Christmas materials to go along with December 25.

C. Labeled file folders:

1. Report cards

2. Appliance instructions

3. Warranties

4. Decorating ideas

5. Insurance papers

6. Special notes, letters, cards

7. Car repair receipts

8. Receipts from purchases, such as furniture/antiques

Note: I put these file folders in my file cabinet or use a "Perfect Box."

In 15 minutes a day you can be on your way to having more hours in your day!

Helpful Hints

❏ Many household chores can be done during "in-between times"—in-between outings, appointments, or TV programs. Once you realize that it takes only 15 minutes to change bed sheets, you can fit this and similar tasks into the available time slots.

❏ The busy person's greatest need is for effective, not efficient, planning. Being effective means choosing the right task from all the alternatives. Being efficient means doing any job that happens to be around. Planning saves you time! Know what you have to do and have your priorities established.

❏ Get rid of extra paper. Almost 90 percent of the paper in your home or office is never referred to again. Recycle most of it as soon as possible.

❏ Break a project into a lot of small jobs and complete the little pieces, and you'll get the job done faster. Reward yourself with a treat for doing a good job.

❏ Studies show that the success rate for people who write down their goals is about 90 times greater than those who don't.

❏ Be positive in your approach to organization. Make a list. Eliminate what you don't need. Set a schedule; discourage interruptions. Remember: *You are in charge.*

❏ Total organization doesn't exist. Organization is a lifetime process. You are capable of handling your flow of appointments, clothes, money, and so forth.

❏ In budgeting your time on your daily calendar, leave a cushion of 15 minutes here and there on your schedule. This way you won't find yourself running from one appointment to another.

❏ Make a list of 10 goals you want to attain by the end of the year. Work toward fulfilling them.

16

Miracles in Minutes

*She watches carefully all that goes on throughout
her household and is never lazy.*

Proverbs 31:27

Do you ever find yourself standing in line at the bank, sitting at
the car wash, or waiting for a child to come out of school and
wishing you had something to do during those minutes of waiting?
We've all been there and there is a solution. The Miracles in Minutes File can be the answer. It helps you focus on the small tasks you
never seem to have time to do at home.

Recently I (Emilie) decided to estimate how many minutes the
average person wasted each day. I came up with 2½ hours. That's in
just one day! Now if we had 2½ hours free in a single block of time,
we could accomplish a great deal. But in small segments of time, not
much can get done. Or can it? Think of some little jobs that can be
accomplished in very limited amounts of time. You'll be surprised
by the short amount of time it takes to do many things.

I've always been in favor of utilizing any spare minutes. I advo-
cate taking along an article from a magazine or a book to read while
running errands. You never know when you'll have a few minutes
of waiting.

By now you realize that time is a premium commodity. I've
had women tell me over and over how much they appreciate even

an extra few minutes. Juggling a husband, children, a home, working outside the home, and a home business can test even the most organized.

Always take your planner with you whenever you go out on errands. You may be able to fit in something that you scheduled for later in the week.

Tasks that can be incorporated into the Miracles in Minutes File will free up time for other important jobs. So what is this miracle file? It's really quite simple.

What You Will Need

❑ Two sturdy, brightly colored file folders

❑ A lined pad of paper or a computer-generated form

❑ A timer, preferably one that allows you to set more than one time allotment at a time. (West Bend makes a great "triple timer," www.westbend.com.)

What You Do

❑ Label one of the file folders "To Be Read" or "Reading Material." Put inside the magazines, catalogs, newsletters, and other mail you want to read. You can grab the folder on your way out the door. (The file folders are brightly colored so you can spot them for quick retrieval.)

❑ Label one folder "Miracles in Minutes."

❑ Sit down with a cup of tea or coffee and make a list of chores and small tasks that can be completed in 5-, 10-, and 15-minute blocks of time. Organize them under time needed to complete. Go from room to room and jot down ideas if necessary. As you use your list, be open to improvements and adjustments depending on the actual amount of time it takes to complete each chore.

❑ Make a simple chart on your computer or your pad of paper. Include space to check off tasks that you've completed. Some of the items, such as cleaning the toilet or washing out the kitchen trash can, will be ongoing. However, one-time tasks can be eliminated after they're completed. Put inside Miracles in Minutes folder.

❑ Add and delete items on your list as needed. Keep the folder handy. I (Sheri) keep my folder in the kitchen where I have my other folders.

What jobs can be completed in small increments of time? I (Sheri) have tested these tasks using my timer. You'll need to work quickly and without distractions if possible. Set your timer and go!

5-Minute Tasks

❑ Clean the toilet in the guest bathroom.

❑ Shake a floor rug and sweep.

❑ Empty the trash cans. (Timesaving tip: Place a roll of trash can liners in the bottom of each can. You can remove the trash and put in a new liner immediately.)

❑ Spray and wipe down bathroom mirror(s).

❑ Wipe down outside glass shower door with window cleaner.

❑ Gather dirty bath towels and start a load of laundry.

❑ Fold a load of laundry from the dryer. (Save time by sorting into color-coded baskets for each family member. This makes it easier to put clothes in the proper rooms.)

❑ Refill business card holder.

10-Minute Tasks

❑ Sweep the front walkway.

❑ Pick some flowers from your garden and arrange them in a vase.

❑ Unload the dishwasher.

❑ Order items over the telephone or on the computer.

❑ Write a thank-you note.

❑ Go through the mail, filing letters in appropriate family members' color-coded folders. Place items to read later in your Reading File.

❑ Feed and water the animals.

❑ Wipe down computer, keyboard, and printer.

❑ Sharpen all your pencils.

❑ Refill paper in printer.

❑ Work on your to-do list for the next day.

❑ Telephone to confirm meetings for the next day.

15-Minute Tasks

❑ Clean out one drawer of your desk.

❑ Feather dust and vacuum master bedroom.

❑ Pull weeds.

❑ Straighten one or two shelves of your linen closet.

❑ Make a pitcher of iced tea.

❑ Clean out your silverware drawer.

❑ Check your email and send out several replies.

❑ Sit down and have a cup of tea or coffee and thank God for all His blessings!

When do you use the Miracles in Minutes File? Any time you have a few spare minutes! Waiting for a friend to pick you up? Do a 10-minute task. Waiting for an important phone call? Do a 5-minute task. You might have a few minutes before you leave to pick up a child from soccer practice. Do a 15-minute task.

Your children can utilize the Miracles in Minutes File too! Next time they're waiting for a ride, hand them the file and let them choose a task to complete in five minutes. They will be contributing to the family as a whole and utilizing their time responsibly. You may want to encourage older children to make folders of their own so they can learn how to better manage their time.

The main reason we don't get more accomplished is because we lack an organized way to determine what needs to be done. By writing down quick tasks and keeping them in a handy file, you will be organizing yourself and your family. And there is nothing more rewarding than getting jobs completed in a timely manner.

17

Speed Cleaning

All hard work brings profit,
but mere talk leads only to poverty.

Proverbs 14:23

One of the most frequent questions asked at our seminars is "What kind of a list is available for areas to be cleaned and maintained for each room of my home?" Now a few of you are thinking this is a silly question. Everyone knows what to clean and how to do it. But that's not true. Many young women who attend More Hours in My Day Seminars went to college, built a career, married, and now have husbands, homes, and children. They were not taught basic cleaning skills at home or given an example to follow. We've found this to be true all across the country.

The Speed Cleaning segment is one of the most popular parts of the More Hours in My Day organizational seminar. Women want clean homes, but they don't know how to get started.

If you become easily distracted when cleaning, the speed cleaning method is for you. Does this ever happen to you? I (Sheri) fill the sink with hot, sudsy water and start washing the dishes. I glance over to the counter and see a stack of books that don't belong there. So I stop doing the dishes, pick up the books, and take them to the back bedroom. While there I find dirty laundry on the floor, so I pick it up and take it to the laundry room. In the laundry room (the garage) I find Tim's tennis shoes on the floor, pick them up, and head back to the bedroom. I find more dirty towels, and go back to the garage. An hour passes and the dishes are still in the sink. Speed cleaning will help you! Let's get started.

It's amazing how our homes function much better when we maintain an organized and clean house. The idea of cleaning the entire place can be overwhelming, so how can we make it less intimidating? First, concentrate on how good it's going to look when you're finished cleaning the area. And then follow this plan.

Getting Started

1. *Decide as a family how clean your home needs to be.* Each family will differ in this area. Some people require more cleanliness than others. I (Emilie) saw a cross-stitch picture long ago in an antique store that said, "I need my home to be clean enough to be healthy and messy enough to make it warm." That's pretty good wisdom. Remember, a home is to be lived in.

2. *Decide what you're going to do beforehand.* The evening before your workday, jot down on your to-do list what needs to be done. This will help you get started the next day because you don't have to waste time deciding, "What do I do now?" To-do lists provide a starting point. When you're cleaning and get finished with each item, be sure to check it off. It will give you a great feeling of accomplishment to complete each task.

3. *Start early.* Don't procrastinate. Roll up your sleeves and be in the swing of cleaning by at least 9:00 AM.

4. *Stay focused.* Don't get distracted by the telephone or a neighbor dropping by to chat. Turn on the answering machine and get moving.

5. *Turn big tasks into smaller tasks.* This cannot be overstated! The whole refrigerator might be too big, but cleaning the bottom shelf on Monday, the middle shelf on Tuesday, the fruit and vegetable drawers on Wednesday, and the exterior on Thursday

is doable. We call these small parts "instant tasks." Don't look at the whole—it gets overwhelming. *Think small!*

The Nuts and Bolts

1. Get the proper tools. We both use plastic carry-all containers for permanent storage of cleaning equipment and supplies. In them we keep all-purpose cleaner, Comet cleanser, window spray, furniture polish, an ostrich feather duster (a must!), paint scraper or razor blades, 100-percent cotton dust cloths (diapers are perfect), a whisk broom, toothbrush, large paint brush, pumice stone (another must), and rubber gloves (optional). These items go in the carry-all and travel from room to room. No more running back and forth trying to locate all your cleaning products.

2. Clean one room at a time. Don't leave that room until it is completely done. If you find items that belong in another room, place them in a basket outside the door. Don't leave or you will become distracted by something else and the room you started in won't get done.

Go to your local janitorial supply houses and buy concentrates. Why pay for water when you have it at home? Use as many "natural" cleaning products as possible.

3. Work around the room once, and don't backtrack. Start at the door, going left to right or right to left, whichever feels good to you. Work from top to bottom—always. Vertical surfaces are never as dirty as horizontal surfaces, and upper shelves have less dirt than lower shelves.

4. The secret is to work fast and smart. Use your timer. Set the timer for 30 to 45 minutes and put on some fast, upbeat music. This helps you to speed up and keep your mind off the drudgery.

5. Next comes your list of what needs cleaning and when. Don't

clean it if it isn't dirty. Read the list you created last night. When you're working in a room, use your list. It will keep you on task. You can generate a computer list, one room per page, so you can print a new list each time you speed clean a room. Each list will be different because every home is different. Your list will reflect your lifestyle and will help you determine what needs cleaning. Once your list is complete, post it on the refrigerator to refer to or place it in a file folder to be retrieved when you're cleaning. Check items off as they are completed. After a while you may not need to refer to the list as often as you become proficient at cleaning.

6. If you are married and have a family, incorporate your family in the process and work as a team. Everyone over eight years old cleans and straightens his or her own room. Teach them the method of cleaning top to bottom and left to right. Kids can also help vacuum, dust, and so forth. Save the harder jobs for the older members of the family. You may want to organize and straighten storage and linen closets.

7. Praise all your workers. This garners good will for later jobs. And don't forget to plan a reward for afterward. It may be ordering pizza and watching a movie. Or you might want to go out for ice cream cones as a family. Just have some fun together.

8. If you're single, you may want to trade and share with another single. It's always more fun to work with someone.

Cleaning Insights

❏ Keep track of your time and how long each job or room takes. As you practice from week to week you'll get faster.

❏ If your time is limited, which it seems to be for most people, speed clean in small time slots. Fifteen minutes a day or 20 minutes in the morning and 20 minutes in the evening gets you started. A little headway every day will get you a long way.

❏ Use both hands. This may take some practice but you'll get done faster. Spray with one hand and dust with the other. Finish one step with one hand and start the next step with the other. Why should one hand do all the work? God gave us perfect equipment, so let's use them to work together!

❏ Used properly a feather duster can be a real time saver. Invest in a good ostrich duster. Real ostrich feathers work the best. They have little barbs that collect the dust instead of spreading it around in the air. The dust in a house needs to be controlled as much as possible. Your feather duster is used to maintain a basically clean house on a regular basis. Use slow motions, trying not to flip the duster from side to side. The dust will adhere to the feathers, and what doesn't will fall to the floor where you'll be vacuuming soon (remember, we're cleaning top to bottom). If you have heavy dust, you may need to vacuum the surface first and/or wipe the dust up with polish and/or a cloth. If you regularly (you must determine what regular is) feather dust your home, you will cut your dusting time in half.

❏ The ostrich feather duster is the perfect tool for dusting mini blinds. Lower your blinds full length. Turn slats to the closed position. Grasp the cord that runs through them and pull the blinds away from the window. Reach behind them with your feather duster using long downward strokes top to bottom again. Go slowly stopping your duster at the bottom. This will catch the dust in the duster, preventing the dust from flying around the room. Take the duster outside and shake well. Then turn your mini blind slats the opposite way and dust the front in the same long slow strokes stopping at the bottom. If your mini blinds are very dirty or greasy, you may need to remove them from the brackets and wash them in a bathtub with hot sudsy water. Put a tablespoon of automatic dishwasher powder in the water, and the blinds will dry as the water sheets off. You can also take them outside and hose them off using a soft brush or cloth and a bucket of water with the dishwasher powder. Once sparkling clean, maintain them with your feather duster twice a month. Use your feather duster on the TV, VCR, picture frames, windowsills, knickknacks. Don't forget: Slow strokes stopping at the end until finished, and then shake the duster outside to remove the dust.

❏ Use a natural pumice stone to get the ugly ring out of the toilet bowl caused by rust and mineral deposits. It's so amazing how fast it removes the stain. Just rub it on the ring gently and it's gone. *It will not scratch the porcelain in your toilet.* Pumice will also clean ovens, remove carbon build-up on grills and iron cookware, get paint off concrete and masonry walls, and eliminate calcium build-up on swimming pool tiles.

❏ Your old toothbrush will clean hard to get corners of shower floors and around faucets and sinks. The tough stuff can be gently scraped with a razor blade.

❏ White vinegar is excellent for kitchen floors and tile.

❏ A good trick to remember is to vacuum windowsills, window panes, and cross frames on the windows before cleaning your windows. You can also use a large, soft bristle paintbrush or your feather duster.

❏ Rubbing alcohol in a spray bottle is great for windows, glass tabletops, tile (to eliminate streaks), and mirrored wardrobe closets. Use with a soft, 100-percent cotton cloth. When cleaning the outside, go top to bottom and the inside left to right. Should you miss a spot you'll quickly know what side you missed.

❏ Your hair dryer works great for blowing off the dust from silk flowers. Preferably go outside to do this. If your flowers aren't too bad or just need to be maintained, use the feather duster.

❏ Change your heat and air conditioner filters at least once a year or, better yet, twice a year. This prevents the black soot from staining your walls and ceilings at the air vents. Keep your vents clean by feather dusting once a month.

❏ Anytime you clean a bookshelf or the shelves in your refrigerator, do the left to right method. No need to take everything out, merely move all items to the right and clean and then shift to the left and clean. Remember the method: top to bottom. Use a spray cleaner. It's easy to apply and wipe dry. If your fridge shelves are too full, remove only enough food so you can move the rest from side to side. Drawers and bins should be removed so they can be cleaned inside and out. Be sure to catch the area under the bottom drawers. Water and gunk accumulate there.

Additional Tips

1. *Take care of everything you have.* Much of what we throw out is wasted through neglect. Keep your belongings clean and repaired.
2. *Do it now.* Don't wait to clean up that spill, spot, or soil. Do it while it's fresh on your mind. The longer we wait to clean, the more irritated we become.
3. *Train the family to clean up after themselves.* By not doing this, they increase your job. If they take care of their own messes, they will learn some very valuable lessons regarding responsibility.

Some people complain because God puts thorns on roses, while others praise God for putting roses among the thorns.

AUTHOR UNKNOWN

18

Using the Right Cleanser

Create in me a clean heart, O God, and renew
a steadfast spirit within me.

PSALM 51:10 NASB

Having the right tool makes any job easier. This is also true of cleaning products. Many women share with both of us products to take out stains, spots, and soils on fabric. So we're passing that information, along with our own experiences, on to you. Remember, all household cleaning products come with specific directions on the label. Read and follow them. Use the product only for recommended surfaces. Note any warnings on the label.

When purchasing cleaning products, buying concentrates from a janitorial supply company will usually save you money.

Abrasive Cleansers

Powder: For baked-on food residue, cooking utensils, tough stains on sinks and tubs. Wet surface, apply cleanser, rub/scour as needed, and rinse.

Liquid: For ceramic bathtubs, sinks, toilet bowls. Apply to surface, rub gently, and rinse.

Air, Carpet, and Room Refreshers and Deodorizers

For counteracting odors in carpets, rooms, rugs, and upholstery.

Sprinkle powdered carpet freshener on, leave 10 to 15 minutes, and then vacuum. For other forms follow package directions. Baking soda works well for absorbing odors in carpet. It's also great to freshen up cloth upholstery in your car. Sprinkle liberally, wait a few hours, and then vacuum.

All-Purpose Cleaners

Powder and Liquid: For appliance surfaces, glass, ceramic, and porcelain enamel tops/cook tops, chrome countertops, painted walls, painted and stainless steel, small plastic appliances, resilient and masonry floors, tile, window blinds, washable shades, painted woodwork.

Mix with water or use liquid full strength according to package directions. Generally no rinsing is required, except for no wax floors,

Spray: For appliances (surface and trim); chrome fixtures; countertops; small washable areas; smudges on painted walls, woodwork, doors, and around switch plates.

Spray on surface. Sponge or wipe clean; dry with towel or cloth.

Ammonia

For mirrors, glass, chrome fixtures, manually cleaned ovens, painted walls, stainless steel, windows, painted woodwork.

Note: Do not use to clean plastic windows or aluminum storm-door windows. Clouding and pitting can occur.

You can control the cleaning strength by increasing the ammonia from one half cup to one cup per gallon of water (depending upon the difficulty of the job).

For spray-bottle use: Mix 1 part ammonia to 16 parts water. For windows, mirrors, and glass, use one tablespoon ammonia per one quart of water.

Note: Use in a well-ventilated area.

Warning: Do not mix ammonia with vinegar, chlorine bleach, or toilet bowl cleaner. Fumes can be toxic and cause illness.

Baking Soda

For removing odor from utensils, chopping boards, coffeepots, baked-on food, freezers, and refrigerators. Also use on bathtubs, sinks, shower, chrome fixtures, fiberglass, shower stalls, plastic laminates, and stains on plastic utensils, dishes, and vacuum bottles.

Dry: Sprinkle straight from the box. Rub with a damp sponge or cloth; rinse and dry.

Solution: Mix four tablespoons baking soda per one quart water.

Paste: Mix three parts baking soda to one part water.

Carpet Cleaners (liquid, foam, powder)

For rugs and carpets (spots and general cleaning). Follow package directions. Some can be applied by hand; others require equipment.

Chlorine Bleach

For disinfecting cutting boards; mildew on grout, ceramic tile, patio bricks; stains on hard surfaces and toilet bowls.

Mix three-fourths cup bleach to one gallon water. Increase strength as needed.

Warning: Do not mix with ammonia, vinegar, or toilet bowl cleaner. Toxic fumes may cause illness.

Drain Cleaners (liquid and granular)

For dissolving grease, hair, soap-scum build-up, sluggish drains in kitchen and bathroom. Follow package directions precisely.

Dusting Products (aerosol and pump, liquid, and paste)

For furniture: Apply product to cloth, wipe over surface, buff to shine.

Glass Cleaners (liquid and spray)

For chrome, mirrors, windows, doors, and glass tabletops. Spray directly on windows or on cloth or sponge for mirror or picture glass. Wipe dry.

Note: Do not use on acrylic plastic doors, windows, or clock face protectors.

Metal Cleaner/Polish

For brass, copper, silver, and so forth. Some contain an anti-oxidant to protect cleaned surface from rapid retarnishing. Follow package directions.

Mildew Removers

For ceramic tile grout in showers, bathrooms. Follow package directions.

Note: Use in well-ventilated areas. Avoid contact with fabrics.

Oven Cleaners (liquid, sponge, spray)

For removing burned fats and food deposits from ovens and barbecue grills. Follow package directions.

Note: Use gloves while working with these products.

Pumice Stones

For toilet bowls, urinals, sinks and showers, concrete, masonry, and iron. Use plenty of water with back-and-forth motion.

Note: Do not use on highly polished metals, glass, fiberglass, and unbaked enamel surfaces.

Scouring Pads (soap-impregnated)

For baked-on food, barbecue grills, broilers, cooking utensils, ovens. Wet and use.

Toilet Bowl Cleaners (crystal, liquid, in-tank)

For cleaning; some also disinfect. Follow package directions. Keep bathroom well ventilated.

Warning: Do not mix with chlorine bleach, vinegar, or ammonia. Fumes can be toxic and may cause illness.

Tub, Tile, and Sink Cleaners (liquid and spray)

For ceramic walls; tiles; shower stalls; sinks; toilet bowl exteriors; fiberglass, plastic, and porcelain bathtubs. Apply to surface, rub gently, rinse thoroughly, and wipe dry with cloth.

Upholstery Cleaners (liquid, aerosol sprays, powder)

For upholstery fabric. Follow package directions. Test a hidden spot on the fabric first to make sure it won't stain.

Vinegar (white)

This natural product works well for hard-water deposits on bathtubs, shower stalls/curtains, appliance exteriors, chrome, glass windows and doors, and mirrors. Use full strength or diluted, depending on use. Other uses for white vinegar:

1. To clean coffeemaker, fill water holder with vinegar and water and run through a brew cycle. Follow with a cycle of clear water to rinse.

2. To remove pet urine smells, saturate the stain with white vinegar. Do not dilute. Pat the area dry and repeat several times. It neutralizes the

Assign convenient, permanent locations for small items that would otherwise end up on a tabletop or being mislaid: a hook hidden near the door for keys, a small dish on the bureau to collect loose change or earrings, a mug on the desk to hold pens and pencils, a specific cupboard for cleaners.

odor. Make sure to test a hidden area before treating with vinegar.

3. Add ½ to 1 cup of white vinegar to the rinse cycle of your laundry for sweet-smelling clothes. It works especially well on towels. Vinegar strips all soap residue from cloth.

   Add vinegar the first time you wash clothing to hold colors fast and avoid fading.

4. Add a cup of vinegar to the dishwasher as it is filling up. It will get rid of calcium build-up in the washer.

5. Soak shower head in a cup of straight white vinegar to get rid of calcium build-up.

6. Straight white vinegar kills hand and foot fungus. Soak for several minutes over several days, then wait for the damaged nail to grow out. As a precaution, if you have regular manicures/pedicures, soak your hands or feet for a few minutes after returning home. It will kill any fungus that might be present.

7. Clean all vegetables and greens with vinegar after returning home from grocery shopping. Fill the sink with cold water. Add 2 to 3 tablespoons of white vinegar. Soak for a few minutes and then rinse with cold water. It strips off dirt and pesticides.

These are just a few of the ways to use white vinegar. You'll wonder what you ever did without it!

Warning: Do not mix vinegar with chlorine bleach, ammonia, or toilet bowl cleaner. Toxic fumes may cause illness.

19

Setting Up a Desk and Work Area

Commit your work to the Lord, then it will succeed.

PROVERBS 16:3

As I (Sheri) began to get my home in order and eliminate the clutter, I soon realized I didn't have a special area to handle all the mail and paper that came into our home. Since a main cleaning motto is "Don't put it down, put it away," dealing with the paper was a problem. Much of our clutter consisted of little piles of materials that we temporarily set down and never got back to.

In the corners of our home we had piles of paper stacked in no organized fashion. In our new program we implemented "Don't pile it, file it." We now have folders in a mail sorter in the kitchen with headings such as:

❑ Household Bills, mo./yr.

❑ Receipts

❑ Taxes

❑ Family members' names

❑ To Be Read

Now when paper comes in it gets filed right away. No more piles! Remember to handle paper only once.

But during all these changes in our home, we still had no central desk or work area so we could function with maximum effectiveness. Effective paper handling depends upon a good physical setup in a practical location furnished with a comfortable working surface and a good inventory of supplies. Ideally, this office will become a permanent fixture where the business procedures of your home are done. The area should have easy access for supplies and files and be located where other household operations won't interfere. If your desk/work area can't be this ideal, don't let this stop you from getting started. Your work area might have to be portable for now, but that's okay. Work with what's available.

Resolve to make every day count. Treat each day as a treasure. Self-talk yourself into accomplishing something new. Live for today, not always anticipating tomorrow.

Since a desk or work area is so basic to a smoothly functioning lifestyle, we offer some practical steps in setting up this area.

Choosing the Location

The selection of your office location depends on how long you will spend in your office daily. If you have a business inside your home, you need to use different criteria in selecting that special site over the person who only needs a place to open mail, answer mail, pay bills, and file papers. Choose a location that agrees with your spirit. If, after a short while, you find you aren't using your new space, but instead find yourself working in the room with a big window, you might have initially selected the wrong location. Make sure your office is where you're comfortable. It's not always practical to be located in the "ideal" location. To help you choose that best setting, ask yourself these questions:

❑ Do I need to be in a place where it's quiet or is it better for me to be near people?

❏ Do big windows distract me or do I like being near them?

❏ Do I prefer a sunny room or a shaded one?

❏ Do I prefer to work in the morning or in the afternoon?

These last two questions are related because different rooms receive varying amounts of light at different times of the day.

The answers to these questions narrow your alternatives. Walk around your home to see which areas match your answers. After selecting at least two locations, you might ask yourself another set of questions:

❏ Is there enough space for my computer, printer, and/or fax machine?

❏ Are there enough electrical outlets and telephone jacks?

❏ Is there enough space for a desk?

❏ Is this location out of the way of other household functions? If not, can they be shifted so they won't interfere with my office hours?

❏ Is the area structurally sound?

Add the answers to these questions to your previously selected alternatives, and narrow your choices to an office area selection. Do you feel good about this choice? Live with it a few days before moving everything in. Walk to and through it several times to see that it feels good. Sit down in the area and read a magazine or book. If it still feels good, then you'll probably like your choice and use it.

Don't begin tearing out walls, adding electrical outlets, moving phone jacks, and building bookcases until you're sure you've found the right location.

Selection of Desk, Equipment, and Supplies

After you've selected the location for your office, take a sheet of paper and make a diagram of the floor plan with the dimensions listed. You will use this information when you want to make or select furniture for your new work area.

The Desk

In actuality, all you really need is a writing surface. In some cases a portable piece of plywood is adequate. Look around. Do you already have a suitable desk or table that will fit the dimensions of the work area? If you decide on a table, it should be sturdy, the right height to write comfortably, and large enough to hold various implements.

If you can't find a desk or table in your home, buy a desk. It's an investment you won't regret. Check on the Internet for used furniture or go to yard sales. Check local classified ads to find a bargain. Discount furniture stores usually have some real bargains if you take the time to thoroughly search them. Check for small scratches that might gain you an additional discount. Many times these stores will also deliver to your home free or with a minimal charge. You should have no trouble finding a desk that has the practical characteristics of office models but is still attractive in your home. Here are a few specifications to keep in mind.

To keep clutter under control, put a bowl or basket in a central location to temporarily house small objects that have no current home.

1. *Writing surface:* Your desk should be sturdy and comfortable to use, with a surface that doesn't wobble.

2. *Place for supplies:* Have at least one large drawer in which paper and envelopes can be kept in folders. If you find a desk with large drawers on each side, so much the better. A shallow drawer with compartments for paper clips, rubber bands, and other supplies is handy. At your local stationery store you can purchase small trays with dividers for organizing these

items. Some trays will fit above large drawers to give you a place for small items.

3. *Files and records:* A home office seldom has need for more than one file drawer, sometimes two. If your desk has at least one drawer big enough to contain letter-size file folders (legal-size is preferable), all your files will probably be comfortably accommodated. If you can't purchase a file cabinet at this time, buy a few cardboard file boxes ("Perfect Boxes") with the lids attached. These make excellent files until you are able to purchase a cabinet. Watch your newspaper for stationery sales.

4. *Typing platform:* If you have a computer and plan to use it in your work area, try to get a desk with a built-in platform for the computer and printer. You'll also want a pull-out shelf for your keyboard. If you have enough room in your office, you might want to designate a separate area in your office for computer work.

If you don't have enough space for a regular desk in your home, look into portable storage to house your supplies. Go to your local office supply store and have them recommend products that will fill this need. You'll still need a file cabinet or its short-term substitute (the "Perfect Box").

The Chair

Next to finding that perfect place for an office and locating a nice desk, the perfect chair is vitally important—especially if you will be spending long stretches of time sitting in front of a computer. You need a chair that is of very high quality. You don't want bargains here. You truly get what you pay for when it comes to desk chairs. It needs to be the right height so your feet are flat on the floor and your knees fit comfortably under the desk. The back of the chair needs to be high enough to give you good back support. Make sure it swivels so you can turn from one position to another easily. Wheels are also a great feature for shifting positions. And, of course, it needs to be comfortable. Try lots of different sizes, styles, and types to find the perfect chair for you.

Computers, Printers, and Other Large Equipment

So much has changed over the years since the personal computers were introduced to the public. When I (Sheri) started my home-based typing service in 1979, it was exactly that...a typing service. I had one of the first IBM electronic typewriters manufactured, and it was fabulous. I was in business for seven years before we purchased our first home computer.

You will have to do your homework to determine exactly what you need, but you certainly want to purchase the best computer for your money. The quality of the computer is very important. Research to determine exactly what your needs are and how much you can afford. For home you may want a desktop computer. If you travel extensively and need to have your information with you, a laptop may be the best way to go. There are great sales all the time at larger electronic chain stores. Take advantage of their special offers when purchasing large ticket items. Here are some basic questions to ask before making a computer purchase.

1. How much can I spend?
2. Do I need a desktop or laptop computer?
3. How much hard drive space comes with the computer? Is it enough?
4. How much RAM (Rapid Access Memory) does it have? Is it enough to do what I'll be working on?
5. Will I need to purchase additional software programs?
6. Do I need a printer? Ink Jet? Laser? Color?
7. Do I need a fax machine?
8. Do I need a copy machine?

9. Would a combination printer, copier, fax be a better option?

10. Should I purchase a warranty with my computer?

11. Will I need to take classes to operate my computer effectively?

12. If so, are they included in the price of the computer?

Storage Ideas

❏ Wall organizers are helpful for pads, pens, calendars, and other supplies.

❏ Paper, pencils, and supplies can be kept in stackable plastic or vinyl storage cubes under the desk.

Decorative objects, such as a ceramic mug, look attractive holding pencils and pens.

❏ Use an extra file cabinet placed next to your desk for your printer and/or copier.

❏ A bookshelf can hold a basket of supplies and/or extra paper for the printer.

❏ Use stackable, expandable plastic bins for bulky items. Use the small style for small items and supplies and a larger-sized bin for magazines and newspapers.

Supplies

For your shopping convenience we've put together a list of supplies to stock your office. Purchase these items on sale or at an office supply discount store. Watch your local paper for sales. Consider purchasing bulk items from Costco or Sam's Club. Many times bulk buying is where you'll get your best prices.

❏ Address book or Rolodex—I (Emilie) like both. The address book I take with me when traveling or on business, and I keep a Rolodex on my desk. The Rolodex has more room for adding other information I might want to use when addressing a particular person or business. It is also very easy to color code your rolodex—white for family, blue for friends, green for business clients.

❏ Appointment calendar—Ideally the calendar should be small enough to carry around with your notebook, as well as for use at your desk. If you search around, you can find a combination notebook and calendar that isn't too bulky to carry in your briefcase or handbag. The date squares should be large enough to list appointments comfortably.

❏ Bulletin board—This is a good place to collect notes and reminders to yourself. Attach notes with pushpins.

❏ Dry-erase board—This works great for reminders and phone messages while you're working. Keep it close to your desk if possible.

❏ Business cards—a must time-saver. You can order business cards for free (you pay only shipping) from www.vistaprint. com. You can design your own from their website. Start with something simple and, as your business grows, you can invest in a more expensive business card that reflects what you do in a very professional manner.

❏ Desk lamp—A three-way lamp gives you a choice of light intensity.

❏ Dictionary and/or electronic speller.

❏ File folders—colored and manila "third-cut" folders. The colors give a more attractive appearance to your file drawer and can help you organize.

❏ Letter opener.

❏ Marking pens—Have on hand a few marking pens in different colors. I do a lot of color-coding on my calendar. I also use a yellow "Hi-Liter" pen when I want some information to pop out at me for rereading.

❑ Paper clips—regular and large.

❑ Postcards—save money on your mailing.

❑ Pencil sharpener—If you use a lot of pencils, I recommend a desktop electric model.

❑ Pencils and pens.

❑ Postage scale—a small, inexpensive type.

❑ Rubber bands—mixed sizes.

❑ Rubber stamp and ink pad—There are all kinds of rubber stamps you can use in your office. These are much cheaper than printed stationery or labels. If you use a certain one over and over, consider having a self-inking stamp made. It's a great time-saver.

❑ Ruler.

❑ Scissors.

❑ Scratch paper—Use lined pads for this. 3-M Post-it Notes are also great.

❑ Scotch tape and dispenser.

❑ Stamps—In addition to regular stamps, keep appropriate postage on hand for additional weight and special handling if you do these types of mailings regularly. Postcards will save you money on certain types of correspondence.

❑ Stapler, staples, staple remover—If you do a lot of stapling, consider an electric model. It saves time and the palms of your hands.

❑ Stationery and envelopes—Usually the $8\frac{1}{2} \times 11$ plain white, 20# bond paper with matching business-size envelopes is all you need. If you use printed letterhead stationery, you'll need to get some matching colored second sheets. Large manila envelopes are good for mailing bulk documents, books, and magazines. Padded mailing envelopes are useful to ship items that need protection from rough handling in transit.

❑ Telephone—A cordless extension right at your desk works
   great. If you have a home-based business, you may want to
   consider adding an extra line specifically for the business.
   You can then purchase a two-line telephone for the office so
   you won't have to go to another room to answer the home
   telephone.

❑ Liquid Paper or other correction fluid or tape.

❑ Wastebasket.

❑ Shredder (spend a little extra money to get a really durable
   shredder). Make sure it can shred CDs, credit cards, and
   thick envelopes. I (Sheri) line my shredder with medium-
   sized trash can liners. When it is full, I tie it up and put it in
   my recycle trash can.

Congratulations! You now have an office space that meets your
needs. This addition to your lifestyle will make you more efficient
in other areas of your life. You'll also enjoy working there more.

20

Record Keeping Made Simple

*If you are untrustworthy about worldly wealth, who
will trust you with the true riches of heaven?*

Luke 16:11

This is the year to get records, bills, and receipts out of shoe boxes,
closets, drawers, and old envelopes. I (Emilie) found that I could
clean out my wardrobe closet fairly easily. An old skirt, stained
blouse, or misfit jacket posed little difficulty for me to toss; however,
where and when I should toss old financial records was very hard.

At income-tax time my neck always got stiff because I knew
Bob was going to ask for a canceled check or a paid invoice, and
I wasn't sure where it was. I finally made the decision to get my
record keeping in order so it would be a very easy process to keep
my records up-to-date.

I sat down and looked at the whole process of record keeping and
broke it down into logical steps. My first step was to decide what
to keep. Since I like things to be in order with minimal amount of
paper, I used to have a tendency to throw away records that should
have been saved. I found that throwing away Bob's salary stubs,
last year's tax return, and current receipts for medical or business
expenses brought problems further down the road.

Experts say that throwing away financial records is one of the
biggest mistakes people make. Throwing away records that later

turn out to be important causes people a lot of unnecessary work and worry. If you have an IRS audit and you can't prove your deductions by a canceled check or a paid invoice, you'll lose that deduction for that year plus be subject to a fine.

Any system of organization must be right for you. There is no best way to be organized. Whatever methods you select, make sure they fit your lifestyle and business needs.

Good financial records will also help you make decisions quickly. In just a few moments you can retrieve valuable information so that a decision can be made for budget planning, future purchases, and anticipated future income.

I developed a seven-step plan. I think you'll find it helpful too.

Step 1: Know what to keep. I discovered that records generally fall into two categories: *permanent records* (important to keep throughout your life) and *transitory records* (dealing with your current circumstances).

Permanent records include documents required for applying for credit, qualifying for a job, and proving entitlement to Social Security and other government programs. Birth and marriage certificates, Social Security cards, property records, college transcripts, diplomas, and licenses fall into this category.

Deciding how long to retain transitory records can be more difficult because often you don't know how long you'll need them. Generally, keep any records that would be necessary should you be audited for seven years. As a rule of thumb, I suggest you keep all employment records until you leave the job. Other transitory records you want to keep are receipts for any major purchases you have made (jewelry, autos, art), stock certificates, tax returns, receipts for at least three years, health insurance policies, credit union memberships, and company stock ownership plans. Canceled checks not relating directly to specifics such as home improvements should be kept for a minimum of three years in case of a tax audit; however, I usually keep five to six years just to make sure I'm not tossing any records I might need for an audit.

If you own your home, condo, or manufactured home, be sure to retain the receipts for any improvements you make until you sell the property. They become proof that you added to the property's value and may reduce any capital gains taxes you might owe. Don't discard the receipts or tax returns from the year in which you paid for the improvements. I usually make a copy of these types of receipts and keep a permanent copy in my folder labeled "Home." I've found that this saves a lot of valuable time when I need to justify each record. In my "Home" folder I also keep a running log with date, improvement made, cost, and receipt for each expenditure. At any given time we know how much money we've invested in our property. This information really helps to establish a selling price when it's time to move.

Your tax return, wage statements, and other papers supporting your income and deductions should be kept at least three years (that's the IRS statute of limitations for examining your return). I retain our records for six years because the IRS has the right to audit within six years if they believe you omitted an item accounting for more than 25 percent of your reported income...or indefinitely if they believe you've committed fraud.

Step 2: Know yourself when you set up your system. Keep your system as simple as you can. The more disorganized you are, the simpler the system should be. It doesn't make sense to set up an elaborate filing system if it's too complicated to follow. Consider these points when setting up your system:

❏ How much time can you devote to record keeping? The less time you have, the simpler your system should be.

❏ Do you like working with numbers? Are you good at math? If so, your system can be more complex.

❏ How familiar are you with tax deductions and financial planning? If you are a beginner, set up a simple system.

❏ Will anyone else be contributing records to the system?

This last point is a very important consideration if you're married. Our mates may have a different opinion on what type of system we should have. I've found among married couples that it's best to determine who is most gifted in this area and let that person take care of the records. Bob and I get along very well in this area. I write the checks for our home expenses and balance this checking account statement. Then I forward the statement to Bob for record keeping. In our family he's the most gifted in this area.

We've also found that the simplest way to organize receipts for tax purposes is to keep two file folders: one for deduction items and another for questionable items. At tax time all we have to do is total up each category and fill in the blanks. Be sure to double-check for overlooked possibilities.

If your return is more complex, set up a system with individual folders for the various deductions you claim: medical and dental expenses, business, travel, entertainment, property taxes, interest on loans, and child-care services. When you pay a bill, drop the receipt into the right folder. At the end of the year you'll be able to tally the receipts and be set to enter the totals on your tax forms.

Be sure to take your questionable deduction folder with you when you go to your CPA or accountant. Go over each item to see if it is eligible for a deduction. As you can tell by reading this chapter, I strongly endorse using a professional tax preparer. Our tax returns have become difficult and the tax laws so complex that good stewardship of our money requires a professional. You might save much more than you will spend for a professional's services.

Your checkbook can be your best record keeper if you check off entries that might count as tax deductions. There are also some excellent software programs available that will help you keep track of your records.

Step 3: Set aside a spot for your records. Generally your home, rather than the office, is the best place for personal documents. A fireproof and waterproof file cabinet or safe will do for transitory records. However, I use and have thousands of other ladies all across the United States using "Perfect Boxes" for storage of general records.

Permanent documents generally should be kept in a safe-deposit box. However, a will and important final instructions should be kept elsewhere because, in many states, safe-deposit boxes are sealed following the owner's death—even if someone else has a key.

Step 4: Tell someone where your records are. As I travel around the country conducting seminars, many of the ladies share with me that they don't know where their husbands have anything written down, such as whom to contact in case of their deaths. We don't like to think about death, but we must share our important information with someone who will need to know.

Each year Bob reviews with me his "data sheet" listing all the information regarding insurance policies, stock and investments, mortgage locations, banking account information, contents in safe-deposit boxes, and so forth. That information is very helpful and reassuring to me in case of any changes in our status.

Even if you're a whiz at keeping financial records, it's not much use if no one else knows where any of your records are located. Make a list noting where your records are located and give it to a family member or trusted friend.

Step 5: Get professional advice on handling records. As I've shared previously in this chapter, seek professional advice on how better records can translate into tax savings in the future. The expense is well worth the investment of time and money. You can also go to your local bookstore and purchase any number of good paperback books on this topic. Be a reader and a learner. They will serve you well.

Step 6: Change your record keeping system when you make a life change. Major life shifts—a job change or retirement, marriage, death, births, divorce, separation—signal a time to revamp your records. Starting a home-based business also means it's time to talk to a professional regarding new tax allowances. A life change necessitates a change in record keeping.

The costs of looking for a new job in the same field and a job-related move can mean you're eligible for a tax deduction, so be sure to keep and file all related receipts.

Step 7: Set aside time for your record keeping. Set a regular time each month to go over your financial records so you won't be a wreck come April when you have to file your tax return. The best system in the world won't work if you don't use it or keep it current.

Practice a 45/15 rule. After every 45-minute work cycle, take a 15-minute break and do something different. You can take a short walk, go outside for some fresh air, call someone, email someone, or get a drink of water. Doing this will keep you refreshed and motivated.

Many people prefer to update records when they pay bills. Others file receipts, update a ledger of expenses, and look over permanent records once a month when reconciling a checking account. Doing whatever works best for you is what's important. You should update at least once a month. If not, you'll experience a lot of stress when you play catch-up. Simple record keeping is supposed to reduce stress in our lives, not increase it.

Time is worth money. When I can save time, I can increase money because my energy is better spent on constructive efforts rather than dealing with emergencies.

21

Kitchen Organization

*Her sons brought the pots and pans to her, and
she filled one after another! Soon every container
was full to the brim!*

2 KINGS 4:5-6

Do you realize that one of the reasons you yearn for kitchen organization is because you spend an average of 1,092 hours a year in there? That's a lot of hours in an area that definitely needs to be organized.

What You'll Need

❑ Some jars. Start collecting jars of all sizes. Condiment jars work great. Tupperware and Rubbermaid are also wonderful storage containers.

❑ Lazy Susans are super in the kitchen and pantry areas.

❑ Small boxes. They can be plastic or cardboard. You may want to cover the cardboard boxes in paper that match your kitchen decor. Many times you can find plastic containers in bulk at Costco or Sam's Club. They come in a large box with a number of different sizes and shapes.

❑ Larger boxes with lids for storing seldom-used items in the garage or elsewhere.

❑ A timer

❏ Large black trash bags
❏ A felt-tip marker
❏ Labels

Scheduling Time

Proverbs 16:3 states that we are to commit our works to the Lord, and then they will succeed. If we want to stick with organizing our kitchen, we need to pray about it. God is interested in everything about us—even tiny things such as getting the cupboards clean. Dedicate your works to Him. Ask Him to give you the time and enthusiasm you need to organize.

Give yourself deadlines. Color-code the due dates on your calendar so you can visually see those dates each day. You might even color-code a few intermediate dates along the way to make sure you are on track.

The next crucial thing is to schedule a time. Here's what I recommend: Set the timer on your stove for 15 minutes, and then work as fast as you can until the timer goes off. Then move on to whatever else you have to do. If you're working toward a deadline, you will have a tendency to move a little faster. So schedule times in the days ahead when you're going to work on your kitchen.

Getting Started

OK, let's dig in! Open some of the cupboard doors. You don't want to open them all because you'll be knocking your head and passing out, but you need to start with, let's say, the upper cupboards. So you open all those and pull everything out, starting with the cupboards closest to the sink (because these are the ones used most often and are probably the biggest mess). When everything is out, wipe out all the shelves. This is the time to repaint and/or repaper the shelves with contact paper if you want.

Now, you know you have things in your kitchen you've been storing for a long time and not using, such as broken dishes, mugs, and vases. And you may have spices and other things that are partially used but you'll never use again. Put these items in your Throw Away bag, your Give Away/Recycle bag, or in a box you designate use as a temporary kitchen overflow container. (Mark some of your boxes "Kitchen Overflow.") You may also find you don't need as many gadgets as you thought, so don't hesitate to donate items to a thrift store or mission. Seldom-used items can be stored on garage shelves or elsewhere.

The Next Step

Put those things you use all the time back into the cupboards. Take a minute to think about how you want to organize them. Spices, dishes, pots and pans, and so forth, should be put back neatly. I use turntables for my spices. (I don't think you can have enough turntables.) Or you can use a spice rack. (A spice rack also comes in handy for vitamin bottles.)

The things you don't use very often should go into the cupboards on the highest shelves. This includes such things as the big platter for your Thanksgiving turkey, plate chargers, sterling silver serving dishes.

Work Together, Store Together

Things that work together should be stored together. What does that mean? If you're going to organize baking items—your mixing bowls, your hand mixer, your measuring cups—all can be stored in one small area together. I (Emilie) bake homemade bread often, so I have on one shelf all those things I use to bake bread. I have my pans, the oil, the honey, the flour, the yeast, and other ingredients handy so when I'm ready to bake I don't have to run from cupboard to cupboard to get things. After I bake the bread I put everything back on the shelf.

Once items in your kitchen have a place, they should go back to that place. When your family members get used to it, they will also put things back where they belong.

Kitchen Counters

Get your broken appliances repaired or toss them. They're sitting around waiting for somebody to pay attention to them. Those with repairs that will cost more than half the value of a new appliance should be thrown out or recycled.

For those who have high school students going into college, save your working appliances that are a little old-fashioned or extra. We found that when our children went off to college and moved into their own apartments, they wanted an iron, a toaster, etc. So save these things for them. Put them in a box, label the box, and number it. Then put this information in your card file box. (See "Keeping It Neat" in chapter 15.)

Kitchen Overflow

Now for your overflow. At one time my (Emilie) family lived in a condominium. We had moved from a big two-story house to a small three-bedroom condo. When I was organizing the kitchen I realized I didn't have a place for everything. That's when I discovered what I call "kitchen overflow," things such as a waffle iron, an extra set of dishes, or even extra canned goods. If you're lucky enough to have a shelf or cabinets in the garage, that's a good place to put the boxed up overflow items.

Many of you may be living in apartments, manufactured homes, or smaller quarters where you don't have a lot of cupboard space. This is a frequent complaint. Women ask, "What do I do with all this stuff? I don't have enough room for it." Well, when the overflow is in uniform boxes, you can stack them neatly in a closet or attic.

What should you do with gadgets and large utensils if you're short on space? Put them in a crock and tie a little bow around it.

The crock looks cute on the counter, and all your whips and wooden spoons and spatulas will probably fit in it. Set the crock close to the stove or at some other handy spot. Remember: Get rid of what you seldom or don't use.

Unavoidable Junk

Yes, there are junk drawers. There is no way to eliminate these, so don't be concerned that you have them. We all have them. The problem is, they are usually very messy. You can take that junk and clean it up. Use a silverware sectional container in your junk drawer. In mine I put a hammer, a screwdriver, and a couple of small artichoke jars that now hold cup hooks, nails, screws, and thumbtacks—all those little things. You may want to get two or three jars to put in your junk drawer so you'll have everything fairly organized. (Jars are nice because you can see what's inside them.)

It's not what you do that makes you tired; it's what you don't do. The mental pressure about all those things we need to do makes us worry, which makes us tired. Hang in there and get the job done.

When I (Sheri) was helping my nephew move into his first house, I discovered his junk drawer. He hadn't even unpacked yet and he already had one in the kitchen…and it was full!

Another handy organizer for the junk drawer is an empty egg carton. This is fabulous to use for little screws, nails, and hooks. You can cut apart the cartons so you have small sections.

Pantry Space

What a blessing if you have a pantry! If you don't have one, you may have a cupboard in your kitchen that you're using for storage. Not many of us are fortunate enough to have a walk-in pantry like Grandma used to have, where she could put all her bowls and flour and sugar. I've opened pantry doors in houses to get something out for someone and found toys, books, and such that should be in other parts of the house. If you have small children and need to keep some of their things in the pantry, get a plastic laundry basket to keep all their toys in.

Potatoes or onions can be kept in colored plastic stack trays. Onions will stay fresher longer if you place them in old, clean nylons and tie a knot between each onion. When you need one, just cut it off and chop.

Making the Pantry Attractive

The pantry can be organized in a really fun and cute way. Label the shelves with one of those tape labelers. (Maybe you already have one.) I have a friend who has everything labeled in her pantry— where the soups go, where the ketchup goes, etc. Why does she do that? Because she has older children who put groceries away when she comes in from the market. Also, she entertains a lot, and various people put things back into the pantry. I have another friend whose husband has taken wooden dowels and fastened them along the shelf of the pantry so that the canned goods slide in. That's real organization!

For packaged items, such as dried taco mixes, salad dressings, and gravies, get a small plastic box or cardboard shoe box (cover it with the wallpaper from your kitchen, extra wallpaper from another room, or contact paper) and place the packages in the box. They will look delightful in the pantry and be easy to locate when you need them. You can go as far as having your pantry custom organized with baskets, bins, and slide out shelves. This is an investment but well worth it if you're going to live in your home for a while.

Put everything you can in jars. My jars in the pantry hold rice, Bisquick, popcorn, beans, sugar, flour, graham crackers, cookies, raisins, coffee filters, dog biscuits—everything. Tupperware also carries clear storage containers in a variety of sizes and colors. Jars and others containers are critter proof too.

Knives

Get all your knives sharpened so you don't have to search for the "sharp" one. If you never use a particular knife, give it away or throw it out.

Pots

Pots and pans should be kept neatly near the stove. You can line the shelves for the pots with plain or light-colored paper—maybe brown paper. I bought some rubber pads to keep my frying pans and other heavy cookware from scratching and ruining my shelf lining. Determine the best possible position for your pans because you use them often and need to get them out quickly. If you want, draw a circle or square the size of the pan with a black felt pen and write the pan size inside the circle or square. For example, here is where the nine-inch frying pan goes and that's where the two-quart saucepan goes. If you have people other than yourself doing things in your kitchen, this is a wonderful way for them to know where things go.

The Refrigerator

What about the refrigerator? If you're working through your card file, you'll remember that a refrigerator only needs to be cleaned once a month. So the first week of every month you're going to do it. (Remember, you have a whole week to do it—see chapter 15.) Look at the refrigerator as just another closet because basically that's what it is—a cold-storage closet.

Your vegetables can be put in Tupperware, plastic containers, or plastic bags. The cheese and meats go on the coldest shelf. Put them in see-through containers also. You can even put some of these things in jars if you like. And remember to rotate your eggs.

Turntables are great space-savers in your refrigerator. I (Emilie) have two of them. One is on the top shelf and holds the milk and half-and-half. The other one holds sour cream, cottage cheese, etc.

You can also buy dispensers and bottle racks for your refrigerator. Can dispensers are good if you use a lot of soft drinks. Some dispensers you set right onto the shelf in your refrigerator. There are also special milk dispensers, juice dispensers, and so forth. Your children will love these. So if you buy a dispenser for the first time, put something really healthful in it, such as milk or orange juice, because they'll love to get a drink just to use the new gadget.

The Freezer

Now what about the freezer? When I go to the market and come home with hamburger meat, I prepare it for the freezer. I make patties, stick them on a cookie sheet, and put them right into the freezer. They'll freeze in an hour or two. Then, as soon as they're frozen, I take them out and put them in baggies or a plastic container so that when I'm ready a week later to get the hamburger out, the patties don't stick together. This way I can bring out two hamburger patties or ten. If I'm going to make meat loaf, I take out five or six hamburger patties.

An excellent investment is a vacuum-seal Food Saver. It allows you to store foods in a bag and then the machine takes the air out of the bag and seals it airtight so the food will last longer and stay fresher. I (Sheri) love my Food Saver and use it all the time. You can freeze fish for 18 months to two years and beef for up to four years! I'm not kidding. You can place cheese in a Food Saver bag and put it in the refrigerator, and it will last without molding for several months.

Also, keep ahead of your ice cubes, especially if it's summertime or you don't have an icemaker. Bag up some ice cubes and put them in the freezer so you'll have extras when you need them. If you place them in a brand-new brown paper lunch bag, they won't stick to one another.

All your frozen vegetables should be put in one section and your meats in another. Casseroles that you pre-make can also be put together. When I (Emilie) make a lasagna casserole or spaghetti sauce, I make enough for that night plus one for the freezer. I always label and date containers so I know how long they've been in the freezer. If you don't label dishes that go in the freezer, you'll find mystery packages when you clean it out. It's amazing how things change when they're frozen. They don't look the same.

I also try to keep emergency meals in the freezer in case company drops in or I've been too busy to prepare anything. You can buy plastic containers especially for making TV dinners. With these, if you have leftovers from a meal, you can put together one TV dinner with foil around the top, label it, and put it into the freezer. When you get four or five of these accumulated, you've got a nice meal that's just a little different for everyone.

Ice cream and frozen desserts need to go together in your freezer.

Did you know that you can freeze potato chips, corn chips, crackers, tortillas, muffins, and bread? If you use wheat flour, be sure to keep that in the freezer so it will keep nice and fresh.

This and That

Let's talk about some miscellaneous items. Kitchen towels and cloths can be kept in a drawer or on a shelf that's close at hand, and potholders near the point of use. Anytime you put something on a rack, it will be a space-saver for you. Plastic racks come in all sizes and are inexpensive. For example, your dishes can go on plate holders especially designed for that purpose.

Next look at the cleaning items you use daily. Place these on a turntable that is made specifically for using underneath your kitchen sink. You can put all your cleansers and so forth on this handy tray. It saves space and you can easily retrieve what you need.

Keep a coffee can full of baking soda near the stove in case of a grease fire, and label the can with a felt-tip pen. Be sure to teach your children what the baking soda is for and how to use it.

Don't cook over an open flame in billowy, long sleeves. Roll the sleeves up tightly or change clothes. We don't want you injured!

Always load sharp knives in the dishwasher with the blades down. Teach your children to do this also, so they don't cut themselves. All of us have cut ourselves at one time or another on a freshly sharpened knife, so we need to be careful with cutlery.

Joyful in the Process

First Thessalonians 5:16-18 says, "Always be joyful. Always keep on praying. No matter what happens, always be thankful, for this is God's will for you who belong to Christ Jesus." We sometimes become overwhelmed with our homes as we struggle from "total mess to total rest." Some of you haven't gotten the organization done, but that's okay as long as you're in the process. This is particularly true of your kitchen. You've got a lot of things to organize—and maybe not a lot of room in which to do it—so don't let it become overwhelming.

God says we are to be joyful in our homes and around our husbands. So we need to keep on praying no matter what happens. Sometimes we don't feel like having an attitude of prayer, and that's when we need to ask God to give us that joyful attribute no matter what happens. We need to continue with an attitude of prayer as we organize our kitchen.

Another wonderful thing to do is to turn on some good music. If you have Christian CDs or can get good Christian radio stations, turn the music on and allow God to speak to you as you straighten up your house.

You spend a lot of time in your home, so make it a happy place. Pray about your attitude toward your kitchen and your meals and the presentation of those meals to your family. Then let the music flow in your heart because of the love of our Lord Jesus Christ.

Kitchen Organization Summary

This is the day which the LORD *has made;*
let us rejoice and be glad in it.
Psalm 118:24 NASB

Equipment Needed

❏ Jars (assorted sizes)

❏ Tupperware (assorted sizes)

❏ Plastic turntables (Lazy Susans)

❏ Large "Perfect Boxes" labeled "Kitchen Overflow"

❏ Contact paper that matches the colors of your kitchen

❏ Trash bags marked "Throw Away" and "Give Away/Recycle"

❏ Felt-tip pen

❏ Labels

Schedule Time

Commit your work to the Lord, then it will succeed.
Proverbs 16:3

A. Open some cupboard doors.

   1. Begin with cupboard closest to sink.

   2. Take *everything* out.

   3. Wipe out shelves and repaint and/or repaper with Contact paper if needed.

   4. Eliminate, throw away, or set aside any item that is not used daily (example: odd mugs, glasses, plastic forks, utensils). Sharpen dull knives or throw them away.

B. The Next Step—Reshelving

   1. Spices used often

2. Glasses

3. Dishes

4. Pots and pans, etc.

C. Seldom-used equipment goes to the back of cupboards or on the highest shelves.

D. Put aside broken appliances to get repaired or get rid of them now. Schedule a repair time.

Things that Work Together Should Be Stored Together

A. Baking items, mixing bowls, hand mixer, measuring cups, etc.

B. Coffeepot, filters, coffee, and perhaps mugs.

Overflow

Box and store in garage vases, dishes, platters, pans, camping equipment (can be put into its own marked box), canned goods, seldom-used appliances (waffle iron, juicer, blender).

Gadgets and Utensils

Put wooden spoons, ladles, long-handled spoons and forks, and potato masher into a crock or ceramic pot. This saves space and looks decorative on the countertop.

Junk Drawers

Get plastic dividers (usually used for flatware). Use them to hold such things as a small hammer, thumbtacks, small plastic boxes or small jars with nails and cup hooks, a screwdriver, pliers, tweezers, glue, flashlight batteries, fuses, matches, scissors, and other miscellaneous items. Egg cartons also make great organizers.

Pantry

You're blessed if you have one. *It's for food only*—not papers, books, or toys.

A. Sort food items.

B. Label shelves: soups, fruits, vegetables, cereals, salad dressings. Baking section includes flour, sugar, baking soda, mixes.

C. Packaged items such as dry taco mix, salad dressing, gravy, etc., should be put into large jars or small plastic or cardboard shoe boxes covered with contact paper or wallpaper.

D. Put everything you can in jars—tea bags, plastic spoons and forks, nuts, flour, cereal, sugar, chips, croutons, beans, noodles, rice, oatmeal, popcorn, spaghetti, graham crackers, cookies, raisins, coffee filters, dog biscuits.

Pots and Pans

A. To keep these neat, line shelves with plain or light-colored paper.

B. Determine the best possible position for each item.

C. Draw an exaggerated outline of the item on the shelf paper with a felt-tip pen. You can also write the pan's description within the borders of the outline.

Refrigerator

A. Look at it as just another closet.

B. Fruits and vegetables should be put into plastic containers with lids, or in plastic bags, or in refrigerator drawers.

C. Cheese and meats go on the coldest shelf (use see-through containers with tight lids).

    D. Eggs—remember to rotate the oldest to the front or to the right depending on whether you have a drawer or shelf for eggs.

    E. Turntables will hold sour cream, cottage cheese, jellies, peanut butter, yogurt, and mustard. A turntable on the top shelf will hold milk, half-and-half, an orange juice jar, and a bottle of cold water.

    F. You can also buy can dispensers and bottle racks that attach to refrigerator shelves.

Freezer

    A. Freeze hamburger meat shaped into patties on a cookie sheet and then transfer the meat to plastic bags. The patties won't stick together that way. (They thaw quickly for meat loaf, burgers, tacos, casseroles, and spaghetti sauce.)

    B. Keep ahead of ice cubes. Periodically put a bunch in brown paper bags and store them.

    C. Keep frozen packaged vegetables together.

    D. Date and label all leftovers. Avoid mystery packages. Leftovers store great in ziplock bags or wrap them tightly with foil to avoid freezer burn.

    E. Ice cream and frozen desserts go together.

    F. Potato chips, corn chips, nuts, breads, muffins, wheat flour, tortillas, and corn freeze well.

    G. Make ahead: lasagna, noodle-and-cheese casseroles, soups, beans, spaghetti sauce, enchiladas. Be sure to date and label before freezing. Also, if you are freezing in jars, be sure to leave $1\frac{1}{2}$ inches at the top to allow for expansion.

Miscellaneous

    A. Kitchen towels and cloths

1. Put in a drawer or on a shelf close to the sink.

2. Keep potholders near point of use.

B. Racks

1. They double your dish space and cupboard space.

2. Plastic utensil drawers can be purchased at hardware stores at low expense. They come in various sizes and will fit together.

C. Cleaning products should be put in one area with dust cloths and a few rags. Include window cleaner, waxes, Comet-type cleansers.

Helpful Hints

❏ To avoid a smelly garbage disposal, run cold water with the disposal for a while after each use.

❏ Use pressure cookers, microwaves, electric pans, and small electric ovens when you can. They use less energy than your stove or regular oven.

❏ Do not store cookies, cereal, or other items kids like by the stove. Children can get burned climbing on the stove to reach an item overhead.

❏ Use glass or ceramic pans for baking; you can reduce your oven temperature by 25° F.

❏ An easy way to clean the cheese grater: Before using it, spray it with no-stick vegetable spray.

❏ Put a decorative hook by the sink. Hang your watch and rings on it while you work. (Diamond rings will score the inside of glasses while you wash, creating a breaking and cutting hazard.)

❏ Match the size of the pan to the heating element so more heat will get to the pan.

❏ If you have a gas stove, make sure the pilot light is burning efficiently with a blue flame. A yellowish flame needs adjustment.

❏ Cook with a clock or timer; don't open the oven door continually to check food.

❏ Glue a 12-inch square of cork to the inside of a cabinet door over your kitchen work area. On the corkboard tack the recipe card you're using and newspaper clippings of recipes you plan to try within a few days. This keeps them at eye level and spatter-free.

❏ Increase your efficiency! Cook, set the table, and clean out a drawer—all while talking on the phone.

❏ Meat slices easier if it's partially frozen.

❏ Want to mix frozen juice in a hurry without using the blender? Use your potato masher on the concentrate.

❏ Peel garlic cloves faster by mashing them lightly with the side of a heavy or broad knife.

❏ To keep bugs out of your flour canister, put in a stick of spearmint gum.

❏ Plan a cooking marathon with a friend or your family. Bake or cook a few entrees such as breads, cakes, casseroles, and soups. Freeze the items—some in family portions and some in individual servings. Date and label each item. On a day when you're sick or there's no time to cook, you can open your freezer and take your pick.

Ten Benefits of Meal Planning

1. *Saves you time.*
2. *Saves you money.*
3. *Prevents stress.*
4. *Prevents bad choices.*
5. *Gives you better nutrition.*
6. *Makes happy homes.*
7. *Makes happy meals.*
8. *Makes happy children.*
9. *Makes happy husbands.*
10. *Makes a very happy mom.*

22

Odds and Ends

*I can do everything God asks me to with the help
of Christ who gives me the strength and power.*

Now we can take care of the odds and ends throughout our homes. Once or twice a year I go to a card shop where they have all kinds of greeting cards—birthday cards, anniversary cards, sympathy cards, and more. Rather than running out to buy a card 15 or 20 times during the year, I spend 30 minutes to an hour once or twice a year. I take the sheet labeled "Dates and Occasions" from my organizational notebook to help me pick out the cards for everyone I'm going to send a card to throughout the year. Along with those I add some anniversary cards, get-well cards, and sympathy cards. I file all the cards in a file folder marked "Greeting Cards."

I (Sheri) have a large 5 x 8 card file box. I took colored permanent markers and decorated it with flowers and designs. I bought dividers and labeled them "Birthday," "Thank You," "Get Well," "Sympathy," "New Baby," and "Miscellaneous." Behind each divider I placed several cards that I purchased all at once. I have a section in the back for stamps and stickers. I have a couple of pens inside so I'm ready at a moment's notice to write a card or note. I just grab my box, my Rolodex, and I'm ready to go.

The Gift Shelf

Somewhere in your home it's nice to have a gift shelf. At any store that has a nice sale, pick up a few gift items—a little box of stationery, a small stuffed teddy bear, something useful. Keep them on your gift shelf. I (Emilie) have always had a gift shelf in my home. When my children had a birthday party to go to, I let them pick out from the shelf what they wanted to give. A gift shelf gives you access to presents all the time so you're not continually running out to a department store and spending a lot of time and money. You also save gas and stress. A gift shelf is a must for mothers!

The Gift Wrap Shelf

I also like to have a gift-wrap shelf (or box or drawer). Once a year I'll go to where they have gift wrap on sale. (We have several places in our area, and you may also.) Once a year I buy all my Christmas wrap plus some dried flowers, ribbon, and everything I need to wrap packages. One year I had red and white polka-dot paper for Christmas. I didn't stop using it once Christmas was over. I could put a red ribbon on that paper or a white or blue or yellow ribbon. I used that same wrap for all occasions throughout the year.

In that gift-wrap section you should have some colored ribbon, wired-edge ribbon, Scotch tape, and a few dried or silk flowers to put on a package. Another cute idea is to go out to the yard and pick some fresh flowers or greenery and stick it on your present. You should also have some padded mailing envelopes and small boxes, along with mailing labels and clear mailing tape.

The Home Office

Your desk should have scissors, paper clips, pens, pencils, Scotch tape, thank-you notes, marking pens, postcards, and stamps. I hate to stand in line at the post office. Every time I go, the line seems longer. So I go once or twice a year. I buy a nice, big, fat roll of stamps that costs a lot of money. I figure it's worth it because I don't have to go so often.

A glue stick, rubber stamp pad, and rubber stamp are handy. When our children were about 15 years old, I put a rubber stamp pad and a rubber stamp with their name, address, and telephone number in their Christmas stockings. They used these on their school papers and for a return address on the cards and thank-you notes they sent out. (Don't give this to a five-year-old because he or she will be stamping his or her name all over the wallpaper and everywhere else.) Kids love those little rubber stamps, and they make super gifts.

Even though most of us would like the pleasure and peace of mind that a clean, orderly home and office bring, remember that most working-at-home mothers never have their homes in perfect order.

Get some stationery, a letter opener, a memo pad, a paper-weight, some string, a dictionary, and a file box with your colored file folders.

Telephone Items

What do you keep next to your telephone? One of the things I dislike is a telephone address book because every so many years (or months) you have to redo it, which is a waste of time. I found a handy telephone address file that has separate cards that can be pulled out. One brand is Rolodex. With this system you fill out a separate card for each person, then if there's a change you can either erase the information or fill out a new card. This way you change the cards gradually as time goes on instead of rewriting a whole book once a year. On these cards you can list birthdays, anniversaries, clothing sizes, likes and dislikes, directions to homes, and other pertinent information.

By your telephone you should have some pens and pencils, scissors, a letter opener, a memo pad, and a calling card file. A calling card file is a little packet that has plastic pages inside for business cards. Remember that Put Away bag that now has those business cards from drawers and all over the place? Well, now you have a place to put them—in this nice little packet. This can go in a drawer by the telephone. (It makes a great gift for Father's Day or a stocking stuffer at Christmas.)

Also by your telephone you should have emergency telephone numbers.

Your Own Business Card

Consider having your own business card. I know you're saying, "But I'm just a mom; I don't need a business card or calling card." My sister-in-law gave me some calling cards when my children were little. The cards had my name, address, and telephone number on it. All over the card were the fun things I like to do. I couldn't believe how much I used those cards. I'd see mothers at school who would tell me their son or daughter was going to come home with my son or daughter to play, and I'd give them a card so they'd have my phone number and address. Instead of fumbling through my purse to find a pen and piece of paper, all I did was zip out my business card and hand it to them. They'd look at it and say, "That's neat. I didn't know you knew how to make homemade bread" or "I didn't know you taught a time-management class." You can go to www.vistaprint.com and get free business cards that you design. You pay only the shipping.

Your Car

Consider what you keep in the glove compartment and trunk of your automobile. You should have a flashlight, some maps, a can opener, change for emergency telephone calls, reading material, business cards, matches, stationery, pens and pencils, a blanket, a towel, and scissors. Some drinkable water and sealed snacks are great to have. You should also have a few fuses, a rope, a fire extinguisher, jumper cables, flares, and a first-aid kit. These things will help to keep you at ease.

23

Garage Organization

*We can make our plans, but the
final outcome is in God's hands.*

PROVERBS 16:1

Just the thought of tackling the garage sends most people into a tailspin. It's an overwhelming job that requires patience and several hours to complete. For many people the garage is where everything that doesn't have a place ends up. Cleaning the garage is not for the faint of heart. We are frustrated before we even begin. There is so much to do. Here are some necessary and practical ideas to help you get started.

What You'll Need

1. Trash bags.
2. Jars—mayonnaise, peanut butter, jelly, or plastic and glass jars from a discount store or small metal cabinets with plastic drawers. You can purchase these at a hardware store to take the place of jars.
3. Large hooks—the type to hang bicycles on.
4. Boxes—cardboard-type used for apples and oranges or use "Perfect Boxes."
5. Broom and rake hooks—hardware stores have these.

6. One to four plastic trash cans for uses *other* than trash.

7. Two to six empty coffee cans.

8. Several large black marking pens.

9. Three black trash bags marked "Put Away," "Throw Away," and "Give Away/Recycle." (You may have to add more bags depending on how much clutter you find.)

How to Begin

1. Call a family meeting and ask the family to help "poor mom" clean the garage. Set a date. Example: Saturday, 9 AM.

2. Make a list of all jobs.

3. On the cleaning day, delegate responsibilities to each member of the family. Responsibilities could be written on pieces of paper and put into a basket. Have each family member, friend, neighbor, cat, and dog draw three jobs from the basket.

An Example

1. Jenny: Sort the nails and screws into different jars or into the metal organizational cabinet with the plastic drawers (that you purchased last week).

2. Brad: Separate hammers, screwdrivers, wrenches, and small tools into piles, and then put them into the empty coffee cans (you prelabeled them with a black marking pen).

3. Husband: Sort possessions—papers, pipes, bolts, etc.—and put them into jars and cardboard boxes. Label with black marking pen.

4. Bill: Neatly roll up the hoses, extension cords, wires, ropes, and other roll-up type of materials. Put all gardening tools with long handles (rake, shovel, edger, broom, etc.) into one of the trash cans or hang on a wall in the garage with the special hooks purchased especially for them.

5. Chad: Empty the large bag of dried dog food into one of the plastic trash cans with a tight lid. It will keep fresh and prevent mice and other little animals from enjoying the food.

6. Bevan (a ten-year-old neighbor boy): Collect all the clean rags, old towels, sheets, etc., and put those into a trash can with a lid or into a cardboard box marked accordingly.

7. Mom: Number the cardboard boxes (1, 2, 3) and arrange them on shelves (hopefully you have some) in the garage according to priority. For example: You don't need the Christmas ornament boxes on the lower shelf because you will only get them down once a year. Put them on a top shelf.

More Suggestions

Bicycles can be hung on rafters with the large hooks you purchased at the hardware store. Most regular cars will easily drive under them. These are for bicycles not used every day. Maybe a family member could make a bike rack for the bikes used most often.

The partially used bags of cement, fertilizer, and other dry materials can also be stored in plastic trash cans with lids. This will prevent the materials from getting wet.

Gardening pots, bricks, flats, etc., can be neatly stored on a shelf in the garage or outside the garage in a convenient spot—or build a few shelves outside for them. Winter weather won't hurt them, and you have little need for them during those months.

We must not forget the trash bags marked "Put Away," "Throw Away," and "Give Away/Recycle." Be sure to fill them. You'll find newspapers, magazines, and old packaging materials. Put those in the Throw Away trash bag or recycle them. Have a separate bag for empty or dried up cans of paint. Recycle them when your trash pick-up includes a hazardous waste day.

You'll also find many items that are in perfectly good condition that you never or seldom use. Put these into the Give Away/Recycle bag and divide them up among neighbors, youth groups, needy families, thrift shops, churches, or have a garage sale and make a little extra money. Whenever we have a garage sale we let the children keep whatever money comes from their items. This encourages them to clean out and get rid of little-used items. Be careful, however, because children can get overexcited and sell their beds, desks, cats, or even baby brothers!

The Put Away trash bag will have items you'll need to store in cardboard boxes, such as athletic equipment (mitts, baseballs, baseball caps, Frisbees, cleats).

A good way to label the boxes is to mark the items on 3 x 5 white cards and tape or staple the cards to the front of the boxes (see chapter 15, "Total Mess to Total Rest").

When storing clothing, you may want to put the clothes in a small trash bag with a few whole cloves before placing them into cardboard storage. This prevents silverfish and other critters from having a picnic.

Spray-paint cans and smaller paint cans can be put into a storage box and labeled too. (Are you beginning to feel all boxed up? Great! That will free you from the guilt of garage disorganization, *and* you'll now know where everything is!)

Sweep and hose out the garage. Put hamburgers on the barbecue, kick back, and enjoy your family—being thankful that you worked together and got a big job done.

Safety Tips for Your Garage

❏ Throw away paint- or oil-stained rags or store in metal containers.

❏ Dispose of combustibles such as newspapers, magazines, empty boxes, and old furniture.

❏ Install extra lighting in work areas, especially where power tools are used.

❏ Make sure ladders are sturdy and have non-slip treads on rungs.

❏ Check that each electrical fuse is the proper size; never use any substitute for the proper fuse.

❏ Keep flammable and volatile liquids in tightly capped safety cans far from any heat source. Gas fumes travel. Never store gasoline in the home.

❏ Power tools should have double insulation and/or grounded plugs.

Garage Sale Checklist

Ask neighbors and friends if they want to join you. Sales advertised as "several families" or "neighborhood" attract more buyers.

1. Check with your city to learn if there are any garage sale restrictions, and if you need a permit.

2. Advertise in local newspapers, noting several of the best or most unusual items for sale.

3. Separate clothing by size and hang them for display.

4. Mark prices on each item so people don't have to ask. If you know you will have a sale when you're cleaning closets, stick prices on items you're going to sell so you'll have less to price the week before the sale.

5. Price items objectively and reasonably. If several families are participating in the sale, use colored stick-on tags with a different color for each family. As you sell an item, remove the tag and stick it in a notebook by the price received. Each family will know exactly how much they earned.

6. Place large, eye-catching items on the lawn or driveway to attract customers.

7. Have boxes, newspapers, and paper or plastic bags to package sold items.

8. Be ready for the "early birds" who show up an hour or two before the sale to get the best bargains.

9. Keep someone at the money box at all times, and arrange the tables so buyers have to pass the check-out as they leave.

10. Don't accept personal checks or large bills unless you know the buyer. (A new scam is to pass large counterfeit bills to unsuspecting families.) Have plenty of change ready at the beginning of the sale. You can keep coins in muffin tins.

11. Since the object of the sale is to get rid of stuff, be ready to bargain. You earn no money at all if you give or throw away the items, so why not give discounts?

12. Give leftover items to a charity.

PART THREE

More Hours…and Resource Savers

24

Dollar Mistakes to Avoid

*You may say to yourself, "My power and the
strength of my hands have produced this wealth
for me." But remember the Lord your God, for it is
he who gives you the ability to produce wealth.*

DEUTERONOMY 8:17-18 NIV

A re you someone who just can't pass up a good deal? A special
high-tech device, another camera gadget, one more power tool,
another set of golf clubs, an all-weather coat you can't do without?
We've all had that extra impulse that makes us go deeper into debt,
slowly sinking our money ship. Even though these may seem like
small expenditures, do we really need them? There are four cor-
nerstones for money management:

❏ *Recognize that God owns everything.* He owns your home, your car,
your marriage, your children, your jobs, your businesses, and
your talents. You may possess them, but you don't own them.
Possession is not ownership. In Haggai 2:8 (NIV) God states,
"The silver is mine and the gold is mine." Psalm 24:1 (NASB)
properly states, "The earth is the LORD's, and all it contains,
the world, and those who dwell in it."

❏ *The goal of financial responsibility is financial freedom.* In order to
be financially free you must meet these qualifications: Your
income exceeds your expenses; you are able to pay your debts

as they fall due; you have no unpaid bills; and, above all, you are content at your present income level.

❑ *Establish a spiritual purpose for your life.* If your spiritual purpose is to serve God (Matthew 6:33), all of your resources minister toward that end. The more money we give to God's work, the more our hearts will be fixed on Him. The opposite is also true: Don't give money to God's work, and your heart will not be fixed on Him.

❑ *Give money to the Lord on a regular basis.* God doesn't care how much we give as deeply as He cares *why* we give. When we lovingly and obediently fulfill our role as givers, no matter what the amount, God will use what we give to minister to others, and we will receive blessings in return. Scripture clearly shows us many directions for our giving:

  ▪ to God through our tithes, gifts, and offerings (Proverbs 3:9-10; 1 Corinthians 16:2).

  ▪ to the poor (Proverbs 19:17).

  ▪ to other believers in need (Romans 12:13; Galatians 6:9-10).

  ▪ to those who minister to us (Galatians 6:6; 1 Timothy 5:17-18).

  ▪ to widows (1 Timothy 5:3-16).

  ▪ to family members (1 Timothy 5:8).

With the above directions set for money management, let's look at some common financial mistakes that cost a lot of money.

1. *Attempting to get rich too fast.* There is no quick way to get rich. If it's too good to be true, it's probably not true. Stay away from quick ways to make a dollar. Too many folks have been taken in by smooth-talking salespeople. Build up sales resistance by saying "no" often.

2. *Believing the credit-card delusion.* Credit on credit cards does not give you a higher standard of living—it will be the ruin of your

finances. With rare exceptions, don't charge any more than you can pay off when the bill comes due.

3. *Not taking advantage of your benefit plans at work.* Most companies offer employee 401(k) or 403(b) saving plans, which permit you to avoid paying current taxes while saving money for retirement. Talk to your personnel office at work to see if your company has such a plan. If not, consider opening one yourself or open your own IRA plan.

4. *Overpaying your house payment (mortgage).* If you didn't refinance your home mortgage when interest rates were at an all-time low, you may be overpaying your monthly mortgage. You can reduce your house payment significantly by refinancing. Shop around to see what interest rates are available and what fees there are. Start with your present lender and go from there.

5. *Paying too much for insurance (auto, home, life, and health).* Review with each of your carriers to see if you can reduce your premiums. In some cases you may be buying more coverage than you need. This also provides an opportunity to reevaluate where you need more coverage.

6. *Investing for your children's college education the wrong way.* Since tax laws and education savings incentives vary from year to year, it's important to consult your tax advisor or bank representative to discuss your options and establish the best plan for you.

7. *Falling for a "hot tip."* Avoid these with a passion. Don't invest your hard-earned money in anything you don't understand. *Never* be swayed by a phone solicitor. Only deal with reputable parties—and make sure you understand the offering and the risk. Request a copy of the prospectus. Read it thoroughly and ask questions *before* you give money.

And now for some money-management practices to follow.

1. *Maintain excellent credit.* Protect this status as if it were gold. If your credit report contains incorrect information, take care of it

immediately. If you don't, it will delay or prevent you from getting a loan or refinancing your home mortgage. It's always a good idea to request a copy of your credit report once a year to check for accuracy and potential fraud. You can find the numbers for the credit bureaus on the Internet.

Due to reporting and processing variances, your credit report may not be identical at each of the credit bureaus.

2. *Keep your money invested in areas that provide good returns.* If most of your money is in no- or low-interest checking or money market accounts, think about shifting that money into five-year CDs or purchasing U.S. Treasury EE bonds. For a small risk, consider short-term bond funds or short-term U.S. Treasury notes. Call a good brokerage firm in your area for more information. Many banks also offer this service.

3. *Keep good financial records.* Your system doesn't have to be fancy, but your records need to be saved in a fashion where you can be sure to deduct the expenses on your tax return. Keep track of home improvements so you'll have proof of these expenses when you get ready to sell your home. Listing home improvement costs may decrease the tax on your capital gains. All it takes is a simple log recording the date of each improvement, what it was, how much it cost, and a running total in the last column—very easy and it takes just a few minutes. Be sure to keep receipts for these improvements.

4. *If married, make sure your mate is part of the money-management process.* If you lose your husband to disability or death you need to know about the family's finances. Make sure each of you are involved in the decisions and know what's happening.

5. *Be willing to take a few risks.* This is different than the too-good-to-be-true story. A well-balanced portfolio will have a diversified approach to stocks, bonds, CDs, real estate, and money-market accounts. You might want to consider keeping some of your savings in investments with growth potential. You can choose stocks

or mutual funds for some of your personal savings. Again, check with your bank representative or stockbroker.

6. *Be sure to leave a trust or a will.* Contact a local attorney who specializes in these and set up a date and time for your meeting. This is so important if you want to leave your estate to those you choose to benefit from your lifetime of work. Shop around for fees, however. The range will surprise you.

25

Investing Made Easy

*The man who received $5,000 began
immediately to buy and sell with it
and soon earned another $5,000.*

MATTHEW 25:16

Every day we hear of very successful people—athletes, actors, writers, speakers, doctors, and other professionals—who have high incomes but then go broke or lose large sums of money because they didn't pay attention to small details. Of all the activities that you cram into your daily schedule, managing your money is the one you can least afford to overlook. In the past, managing money fell completely on the husband. However, today with many more single parent homes, women in the workforce, women knowledge-able about finances, and singles waiting longer to get married, more women want to know how to save and invest money. Here are several quick, worry-free techniques that will help you as you work toward becoming a good steward of your money.

1. *Company saving plans.* If your employer offers this service, it's one of the sweetest ways to see your money grow. Under this type of plan you sign an authorization card requesting that your employer invest a certain percentage of your salary through automatic payroll deductions. The big plus is that your employer usually matches part or all of your contributions. Most of these types of plans have a 401(k)

feature, which means some of your contribution is tax-deferred and reduces your taxable income.

You will pay no tax on your company's matching contribution until you withdraw it at the time of retirement. If you resign from the company before you are fully vested (usually two to six years), you are not eligible to take out your employer's matching contribution. All funds in your account must stay in the retirement account or roll over into a new retirement account to avoid large penalties and taxes.

2. *Dollar cost averaging.* This is a great technique for the person who doesn't want to spend a great amount of time tracking individual stocks. Choose a stock or a mutual fund that meets your financial goals criteria for the next 5 to 10 years.

With the dollar-cost-averaging technique you invest a fixed amount (say 75 dollars) every month regardless of whether the price of shares is going down or going up. Over a long period of time—5 to 10 years—you'll find the cost per share will even out to the median price of the stock.

This type of purchase avoids two common errors: investing all your money when prices are up and selling at a loss when prices are low.

To simplify this technique, you can authorize payroll deductions or a checking-account transfer between your company or bank and a mutual fund or individual stock of your choice.

3. *Prepay your mortgage.* "You mean to say that an extra 25 dollars a month on my house payment will save me $18,221 on a $100,000 30-year loan at 7 percent interest?" Yes, it does! And if you are able to contribute more than that you will get a more remarkable savings of interest. This discipline really works. Sit down with your mortgage holder and review the figures to see what plan would be best for your financial position. Most mortgages no longer carry prepayment penalties. Check your mortgage agreement or call your lender to find out if any restrictions apply.

When you include an extra amount, write a note stating that you want the extra money to go toward the principal.

4. *Dividend reinvestment plans.* This is one of the great techniques of owning stock (available in many companies) without paying commission to a broker. These companies let you invest your quarterly dividends in purchasing additional shares without charging you any fees. Many of these companies will also give you a $5- to $10-dollar discount on the price of the stock.

> *In all realms of life it takes courage to stretch your limits, express your power, and fulfill your potential. It's no different in the financial realm.*
>
> SUZE ORMAN

On top of the quarterly reinvestment of dividends, you have the opportunity to contribute X number of dollars for added purchases. Each company will have its own monthly or yearly limitation amounts.

To participate in this type of program, you need to initially own 1 to 100 shares, depending on the company. Check with your financial advisor or bank representative to get more information on these types of plans.

5. *Asset-management accounts.* This is a great way to track all of your investment income and securities transactions for a year. The banks and brokerage firms that offer this service send very detailed listings of these transactions. At the end of the year you have a comprehensive summary for tax purposes. Many of these services will even list your deductible expenses and capital gains and losses.

This type of account will combine a brokerage margin account with a money-market account, a checking account, and a credit card. Most of these accounts offer unlimited free checking, plus a debit or credit card to make purchases or withdraw cash at banks and ATMs worldwide. Some plans let you deposit your paycheck and have your fixed monthly bills paid automatically.

Dividends, interest, deposits, and proceeds from the sale of your stocks are automatically invested in a taxable or tax-free money fund.

6. *Automatic payroll deduction plans.* Very little effort is involved in this type of plan. If your employer doesn't offer this type of savings program, check with your bank or credit union to see if they do. You simply fill out an authorization form, and your bank will deduct a certain amount from your checking account on the day you designate and transfer it to an IRA, money-market fund, savings account, or EE savings bonds.

7. *Company profit-sharing plans.* This investing strategy varies with the kind of company you work for. Company plans vary, but many offer an easy way to plan for retirement. Check with your personnel office for details.

Some companies distribute part of profits as a yearly bonus, but many will hold the profits in trust as a retirement plan for you. The tax advantage to this type of program is that you pay no taxes until you withdraw the shares from your account. Many of these profit-sharing plans allow voluntary contributions under a 401(k) option.

8. *Employee stock purchase plans.* If you work for a company that offers stocks, you are eligible to purchase shares on a regular basis. There usually aren't any administrative or commission charges for such transactions. One advantage to this type of investment is that you're not taxed on any gain or loss until you sell the stock. Most plans won't permit you to borrow against your account or take out cash until you retire or terminate your employment. Don't invest all your money in one company, no matter how well it seems to be doing.

9. *Deferred-pay 401(k) plans.* If your company offers this type of plan, jump on the bandwagon as quickly as possible. This type of program helps you reduce your taxable income by making a portion nonreportable on your W-2 form. Your earnings are compounded and tax-deferred too. Many companies will match all or part of your contributions.

The downside is that you may not withdraw funds until you reach a certain age without having to pay a 10-percent penalty—unless the funds are rolled over into an IRA account within 60 days. The only way to avoid a withholding fee by the IRS when you withdraw funds from this account is by depositing the full amount into an IRA within 60 days or telling your employer to transfer your money directly into an IRA.

These techniques will help you reduce the stress of having to invest large amounts of time in managing your finances.

26

Bulk Buying
Saving Time and Money

*Turn to Me and be saved, all the ends of the earth;
for I am God, and there is no other.*

Isaiah 45:22 NASB

When my Bob and I (Emilie) go to one of the large discount stores, he teases me because it costs 150 dollars to get out the door. He jokes that it is "free getting in, but costs our family inheritance to get out." One of Sheri's friends says they should just call it the $200 Store because that's what it costs every time someone shops there. Yes, it's true that you pay more up front buying in bulk, but if you're careful about what you purchase and avoid impulse buying, you'll save so much in money and time later on. Rushing off to the store every time you need an item wastes time, energy, and money.

By purchasing nonperishable items in bulk (and when they are on sale), you will spend less unscheduled time at the store, seldom run out of necessities, and save money. Buying by the case or in large quantities usually costs less than buying single items. But do your homework. Know what an item costs in a regular grocery or department store or you may find yourself caught up in the frenzy of buying in bulk and not realize any savings.

Take stress out of your life by keeping these items on hand.

- ❏ Paper products such as greeting cards, gift-wrapping paper, ribbon, boxes, mailing tape
- ❏ Extra school supplies
- ❏ Tape, glue, bulk office supplies
- ❏ Pet food
- ❏ Envelopes (legal and letter size)
- ❏ Paper plates, plastic silverware
- ❏ Special-occasion and party supplies, such as birthday candles
- ❏ Small gifts for friends, neighbors, and holiday drop-ins
- ❏ Postage stamps
- ❏ Shampoo and soap
- ❏ Toothpaste, toothbrushes, mouthwash
- ❏ Laundry and cleaning supplies
- ❏ Snacks for lunches
- ❏ Canned and bottled foods, condiments, soft drinks
- ❏ Basic dry foods
- ❏ Blank CDs/DVDs
- ❏ Bestselling books and movies
- ❏ Camera accessories
- ❏ Various sizes of light bulbs
- ❏ Candles
- ❏ Small and large appliances and electronics

27

Space Saving Ideas

Any kingdom divided against itself will be ruined,
and a house divided against itself will fall.

LUKE 11:17 NIV

One of the first comments women make about home management is, "But I don't have space. We live in a small home (or apartment or manufactured home)." Most of us do live in a smaller residence than we would like. That's when we really have to work smart. In the 1950s the average-size home was approximately 900 square feet. Today that figure is closer to 2,300 square feet—and we still complain about having no space. The truth is that we have too much stuff!

My (Sheri) children, Nick and Terra, recently moved from California to New York. Initially they shared a 450-square foot apartment. After sharing the apartment for a year and a half, my daughter moved into her own place in Brooklyn Heights. The term "apartment" applies loosely because the size of her new home is 200 square feet. Yes, I said 200. It isn't much larger than a bedroom. Along with the help of her dad, she has made great use of the small amount of space she does have. This chapter will help you stretch your small space. It will amaze you what a little pre-planning can do.

Living Areas

❏ Install a towel rack on the inside of the linen-closet door to hang tablecloths.

❏ Remodel an antique armoire to house your entertainment center (TV, CD player, VCR, DVD player).

❏ Use "Perfect Boxes" covered with wallpaper matching your room colors. These will accommodate a lot of storage items. Stack three of these boxes on top of each other, place a plywood round on top, cover with a colorful fabric from tabletop to floor, and you have a very attractive end or corner table.

❏ Hang your stereo speakers high on a wall to free up space on the floor or shelf.

❏ Use the tops of cabinets, hutches, and the refrigerator to store floral arrangements or other decorative items.

❏ Build a window seat under deep-set windows, and use the space underneath for storage.

❏ Use the area under stairs for added storage. Remember to install shelves.

❏ Put tall, slim bookcases in a room to create storage.

Bedrooms

❏ Move some of the children's sports equipment out of their bedrooms and into the garage, attic, or basement. Store these items in large, plastic trash bins or on wall hooks.

❏ Use egg-carton bottoms or ice-cube trays to organize small items in drawers.

❏ The early Shaker settlers used wooden pegs around their rooms to hang clothing. These work great.

❏ Seldom-used luggage is ideal for storing out-of-season clothing.

Store under the bed. You can raise the height of beds by placing bed risers under the wheels. This will give you several additional inches for storage.

❏ Follow a Barnes motto: "A new item of clothes purchased; an old item given away to someone in need."

❏ Convert an antique armoire into a cabinet to store sweaters, bulky shirts, or whatever else will fit.

❏ Use the space under beds to store boxes of overflow items or your gift wrap container.

❏ Build a plate shelf 9- to 12-inches wide and place high on the walls around your room. A lot of decorative items can be placed here.

❏ Select a headboard for your bed that has storage space.

❏ Go through your bedroom at least once a quarter and reorganize it. Toss out items not being used.

Clothes Closets

❏ Redo your single-clothes-rod closet to accommodate the new closet organizers. You can really improve closet efficiency.

❏ Keep clothes that need mending in a designated place (such as the laundry area). Keep on top of the mending—don't let it pile up.

❏ Store off-season clothes in another closet or in a trunk instead of the main closet. If your children are grown and no longer home, use their closets for this. If you store clothes in your attic or basement, be sure to guard against mildew.

❏ Put hooks on the wall inside the closet to hang nightgowns, robes, and shoulder bags.

❏ Hang a rotating tie rack from your husband's top rod. This can store a lot of ties.

❏ Install a mug rack on the closet wall for small hats, purses, and scarves.

❏ When redoing your closet into a space-saver unit, have some vertical shoe storage racks built in (make sure they are wide enough to accommodate your largest pair of shoes side by side).

❏ Take heavy boots out of the closet and store them in the garage on a shelf close to the door for seasonal use.

❏ Hang a mesh laundry bag with a drawstring for dirty hose and lingerie. Toss the full bag into the washer on the delicate cycle.

Children's Closets

❏ Use hangers and storage bins to color-coordinate your children's belongings. Get towels in each child's color. This saves a lot of identification time. They can easily see what is theirs.

❏ Keep small, everyday clothing items in colorful plastic bins on reachable shelves.

❏ Store a small step stool in the closet to help children reach high shelves.

❏ Install a commercially built closet organizer that has one rod to store long hanging clothes, separated by shelving for storage. On the other side, have two rods for shorter clothing and out-of-season clothing. Put often-worn clothing on the lower rod.

❏ Get color-coordinated child-size hangers. Children can handle them easier and are more likely to hang up their clothes.

❏ Use a lot of hooks inside the closets so the children can hang robes, nightclothes, and coats.

❏ Build a shelf that runs across the back or side of the closet to keep shoes organized.

❏ Compliment the children when they keep their clothes picked up.

❏ Let your children help you redecorate their rooms. They will take more pride in their areas if they've had a part in the selection of colors, wallpapers, and fabrics.

❏ Keep an empty basket by your children's bedroom doors. When you find toys and articles of clothing scattered around, place them in the respective baskets or delegate this job to one of your children. Have the children put these items away daily.

Storage Space

❏ Organize and store items in places convenient for their use. Store like things together. Arrange frequently used objects on waist-to-eye-level shelves, in drawers, or on hooks. Try not to bend or reach more than necessary. Before you buy something new, make sure you know where it will be stored.

❏ Identify nontraditional storage areas in your home: an old trunk, a sink cavity, a high plate rail around a room, under beds, under staircases, in attics, basements, and garages. Consider attaching racks to the back of closet and pantry doors.

❏ Study your storage situation and ask yourself these basic questions:

  ▪ Has the item been worn or used in the last year?

  ▪ Does the item have personal or monetary value?

  ▪ Will the item be worn or used again in the near future?

If your answer is no to any one of these questions, don't store the item in prime space. One of our mottos is: "Less is best."

❏ Before you add more *stuff* to your limited space, ask yourself:

  ▪ Do I really need this stuff?

  ▪ How often will I use it?

  ▪ How much space will be required to store it?

  ▪ Does it need to be cared for? How much care is needed?

If you don't need it or can't store it, don't buy it. When it comes to gift time in our family, we tell our children not to give us anything that needs storage, dusting, or attention (in other words, we only want consumable items). We have enough stuff.

28

Earth Saver Ideas

God saw all that He had made, and behold,
it was very good. And there was evening and
there was morning, the sixth day.

GENESIS 1:31 NASB

We live in a time where we are very conscious of our environment and the depletion of some of our most valuable resources. We have a responsibility to take care of the world that God created for us to live in. With everyone pitching in and doing their part, we will begin to see the benefits of being environmentally conservative. So why not make conservation a family project? The children will think it's neat because that's what they're studying in school.

You don't need to implement all these ideas at one time, but choose a new one each week and keep practicing the old ones. Let's make our world safer from "progress pollution."

- ❑ *Say no.* Don't purchase disposable products that aren't biodegradable.

- ❑ *Separate your recyclables.* Cooperate with your local waste-management programs.

- ❑ *Fix leaky faucets and toilets.* You don't think a little leak adds up to very much, but it does. In fact, a leaky faucet can waste 3000 gallons of water a year, and a leaky toilet can use an extra 20,000 gallons a year—enough to fill a good-sized swimming pool.

❑ *Use paper bags instead of plastic.* Paper is easier to recycle. Better yet, use canvas bags to do your grocery shopping. They're reusable and don't create any waste. Most stores now offer reusable bags for a very small price.

❑ *Flush the solid waste before tossing disposable diapers.*

❑ *Recycle bottles and cans.* Not only does recycling clean up the waste, but it can also be a great way to earn extra money.

❑ *Carpool to work.* More than 33 percent of all private vehicle mileage is due to work travel. Carpooling saves gas and cuts down on pollution, plus it greatly decreases automobile expenses.

❑ *Drive less.* Walk, cycle, or use mass transit more often.

❑ *Turn the lights out.* Get the whole family used to turning off lights when leaving a room.

❑ *Limit use of your garbage disposal.* It uses a lot of water, plus the garbage has to be removed at the sewage plant. Start a compost pile for your waste.

❑ *Scrutinize packaging.* If sending a package, don't use excess paper or Styrofoam. Encourage manufacturers not to package their products with excess packing.

❑ *Turn your water heater to the lowest setting.* Also turn it off when you go on long trips.

❑ *Dress appropriately.* Reduce your heating and air-conditioning needs by wearing the right clothing. It's healthier to keep your house on the cool side. Lap blankets are great when relaxing for the evening.

❑ *Try composting.* It's amazing how many pounds of compost a family can generate in a year. Your plants will love the nutrients you add to the soil. The compost also reduces the amount of water needed per plant.

❏ *Set your sprinklers properly.* Make sure the water hits the plants and not sidewalks, streets, and driveways.

❏ *Pick up litter.* Even if it is not your own. Not only does it make the area look clean, but removing litter can also prevent someone from tripping or having an accident.

❏ *Take a shower—not a bath.* Surprisingly, a shower uses only half the amount of water a bath does.

❏ *Shop big.* Buy products in larger sizes rather than in a lot of smaller cartons. There will be less waste.

❏ *Pull out weeds by hand.* This saves on toxic sprays that can get into the water supply.

❏ *Don't hose down the sidewalks or driveways.* Use a blower or broom to clean these areas without using water.

❏ *Don't overcool.* A lot of people keep their refrigerators too cold, thus using unnecessary energy. Refrigerators should be kept at 40° F and the freezer at 5° F. (Use ice cream to test your freezer compartment. If it's too soft, set the freezer slightly colder; if too hard, set the control slightly warmer.)

❏ *Take care with your wash.* Use biodegradable products. Phosphates contribute to the growth of algae.

❏ *Don't preheat the oven.* If your recipe will take more than one hour to cook, you can start with a cold oven. You can also turn your oven off before your meal is fully cooked. The oven will retain the heat to finish the job. However, when cooking cakes and pastries you should preheat.

❏ *Look for energy-efficient appliances.* As your old appliances wear out, look for those that have an energy-efficient rating. In many cities, purchasing energy-efficient appliances will get you a nice rebate. Check with your local utility company.

❏ *Reuse paper.* Turn it over and use the backside for printing documents from your computer that you won't be sending out. You can always use the back of papers for notes. Take these sheets that have writing on one side and cut them into fourths. Staple the sheets together, and you have a zero-cost notepad. I (Sheri) save my recycled paper for several weeks and then take it to one of our local print shops. They cut the paper into fourths, "pad" the tops and make notepads for me to use at home. I share them with family and friends.

❑ *Wash your car from a bucket.* Fill a gallon bucket of warm water with a few drops of auto wash detergent. Use a soft terrycloth rag to wash the car. Only use the hose for rinsing. This technique can save 100 to 150 gallons of water. Use a large (beach) towel to dry the car. Start at the top and work down.

❑ *Plant a tree.* Our countrysides and cities need more trees. Plant one for any occasion. Trees take in carbon dioxide and produce oxygen.

❑ *Recycle newspaper.* Many communities have newspaper recycling boxes. It only takes a minute to drop newspapers off, and it will save cutting down trees. Better still, if you have access to the Internet, read your local newspaper online and eliminate the print newspaper altogether.

❑ *Stop unwanted junk mail.* Thousands of tons of paper are used to mail out junk mail. If you want to stop the waste, visit this website: www.proquo.com. It will take a few minutes, but it will be well worth your time.

❑ *Recycle old items you aren't using.* When you do your "Total Mess to Total Rest" program, take those Give Away items that are not being used and recycle them by giving them to charity or by selling them at a garage sale.

❑ *Recharge those batteries.* With more and more toys and equipment using batteries as a power source, buy rechargeable ones rather than disposables.

❑ *Clean your dryer screens.* A clogged screen makes the dryer work harder, using as much as 20 percent more energy to dry one load of clothes. Clean it out before every load.

❑ *Conserve water while brushing your teeth.* Even though it's one of America's biggest habits, turn off the faucet when you brush your teeth.

❑ *Let solar heat work for you.* During the winter open your curtains, draperies, and blinds. This way the sun can help heat your home.

❑ *Keep curtains closed.* You can have a cooler home during the summertime if you close your blinds, drapes, and curtains during the day or while gone from your home for a long period of time.

❑ *Use attic fans to reduce cooling costs.* Our attics are pockets for catching extreme heat during those long, hot days of summer. Install one or more thermostat-controlled attic fans.

❑ *Weather-strip your windows and doors.* For a few dollars you can purchase weather-stripping from your local hardware store. This will drastically cut down your energy bills each month.

❑ *Close that unused damper in the fireplace.* Fires are beautiful and give some low-cost heating, but if the damper is left open when you aren't using the fireplace, you have an unseen shaft that lets valuable energy escape.

❑ *Install ceiling fans.* Ceiling fans are excellent for summer and winter use.

29

Water Saving Ideas

God called the dry ground "land," and the
gathered waters he called "seas." And God
saw that it was good.

GENESIS 1:10 NIV

We need to be aware of misusing water and, as informed consumers, be sensitive to the fact that water costs money. These simple water saving steps can cut hundreds of gallons out of your weekly usage. Whether you want to cut back 15, 25, or even 50 percent, the more steps you take, the more you'll save. It's easier than you think to save water.

In the Bathroom

❏ Replace your regular showerheads with low-flow showerheads (saves 230 gallons a week).

❏ Keep your showers down to five minutes or less (saves 75 gallons a week per person). If you need to, set a timer when you get into the shower.

❏ In the shower turn the water off while lathering. Turn the water back on to quickly rinse (saves 75 gallons a week per person).

❏ Take shallow baths—no more than three inches of water (saves 100 gallons a week per person).

❏ Replace your old toilets with new ultra-low-flush models (saves 350 gallons a week).

❏ Put a water displacement device inside the tank of every toilet. You can make one with a plastic bottle of water and pebbles (saves 50 gallons a week for each toilet).

❏ Check your toilets for leaks. Drop a dye tablet or a teaspoon of food coloring in the tank. If the color appears in the bowl after 15 minutes, replace the "flapper" valve (saves 100 gallons a week for each toilet repaired).

❏ Flush the toilet only when necessary. And never use the toilet as an ashtray or wastebasket (saves 150 gallons a week).

❏ Don't let the water run while brushing your teeth or shaving (saves 35 gallons a week per person).

In the Kitchen

❏ Hand wash dishes once a day using the least amount of detergent possible. This will cut down on rinsing. Use a sprayer or short blasts of water to rinse (saves 100 gallons a week).

❏ Run your dishwasher only when you have a full load (saves 30 gallons a week).

❏ Scrape food off dishes into the garbage can or rinse them off with very short blasts of hot water (saves 60 gallons a week).

❏ Run your garbage disposal only on alternate days (saves 25 gallons a week).

❏ Rinse vegetables and fruits in a sink or pan filled with water instead of under running water (saves 30 gallons a week).

Around the House

❏ Repair leaky faucets, fixtures, and pipes inside and outside your home (saves 150 gallons a week for each leak).

❏ Use the water level settings on your washing machine.

Outdoors

❏ Water your lawn and landscaping no more than once a week. Only water early in the morning or after the sun sets, when there's less evaporation (saves 250 gallons a week).

❏ Deactivate automatic sprinklers and operate them manually. Adjust your sprinklers so they don't spray on sidewalks, driveways, or streets (saves 250 gallons a week).

❏ Set lawn mower blades one notch higher since longer grass reduces evaporation. Use chunks of bark, peat moss, or gravel to cover bare ground in gardens and around trees (saves 200 gallons a week).

❏ Never hose off your driveway, patio, or sidewalk—use a broom instead (saves 100 gallons or more a week).

❏ If you have a pool, use a cover to cut down evaporation. This will also keep your pool cleaner and reduce the need to add chemicals (saves 250 gallons a week).

Without love our life is…a ship without a rudder…
like a body without a soul.

SHOLEM ALEICHEM

30

Technology
A Blessing and a Curse

*Do not conform any longer to the
pattern of this world, but be transformed
by the renewing of your mind.*

ROMANS 12:2 NIV

Technology, as defined by Webster, is "the branch of knowledge that deals with the creation and use of technical means and their interrelation with life, society, and the environment; the sum of the ways in which social groups provide themselves with the material objects of their civilization." In other words, it's a fact of life, it's here to stay, and it's changing by the nanosecond.

By the time we purchase our latest and greatest gadget and get it home, it has already become obsolete. So how do we stay connected to technology without spending a fortune and driving ourselves crazy trying to keep up and knowledgeable? That is the million dollar question. I (Sheri) have finally come to the realization that I was born 15 years too late to really embrace all technology has to offer. I know just enough to get myself into trouble sometimes. I've been around long enough to know there are many advantages of technology. I don't know how I would live without my computer, printer, and fax machine. And my heart palpitates if I leave the house without my cell phone.

Technology started the day we harnessed energy and has not looked back. What would we have done without the telephone, the television, the electric typewriter, and the calculator, just to name a few? Technology has improved our appliances and comforts of home so that we would not, or even could not, live without them today.

My all-time favorite television series is *Little House on the Prairie.* I love watching the Ingalls family and how they worked together and worked hard to carve out a simple life for themselves. But when I really sit back and observe what Caroline Ingalls had to do just to cook a meal, wash the laundry, and clean her small but efficient home, I am once again delighted to live in the twenty-first century with all my modern day "servants." How could I live without my microwave oven, food processor, dishwasher, washer and dryer, and vacuum cleaner?

Technology is a wonderful thing, but it moves at breakneck speed. We must be wise about what items we purchase and how much time it takes us away from the things that really matter. Finding the balance between utilizing technology and letting technology run our lives is hard. Moderation is the fundamental key to us being in control and not letting technology control us. Making use of technology in our families without running the risk of technology separating the family is a delicate dance.

How can you choose, maintain, and organize the different technological wonders that may enter your family dynamic and your home? These helpful suggestions are not all inclusive, but we wanted to give you some basic, practical guidance for handling the technology that can be such an important part of daily life.

We are raising children in a technological world that adults may struggle with but kids understand completely. Recently Tim and I were getting ready to visit some friends, and he wanted to take along his new iPod to show everyone. I told him he might be able to find one of the kids there who could help him figure out all the bells and whistles. He admitted, "Yeah, even a kid with a pacifier will know more than I do." There is a lot of truth in that statement. Children born after 1980 seem to be wired with "technology genes." They "get it" without a lot of instruction.

Marketing experts persuade us that we need the newest, latest, and greatest model or we somehow are missing out on something. We need to be careful, however, that we control technology. We don't want technology to take over our lives—especially with our children. Technology is wonderful, and what it allows us to access is almost unfathomable, and yet it comes with a warning to be very careful. Inappropriate use of technology has caused much pain and suffering to families and individuals. From misuse and overuse of the Internet, computers, computer and video games, email, MySpace, iPods, MP3s, and other technologies we've heard and may know firsthand how gadgets can become a primary focus. Without us realizing it, the damaging effects may hit our homes and those we love.

> *Technology...is a queer thing. It brings you great gifts with one hand, and it stabs you in the back with the other.*
>
> C.P. SNOW

Technology can separate us if we are not careful. Many modern homes today think nothing of having televisions and computers in every room of the house. Instead of drawing us together to enjoy the benefits, technology separates us from one another. Mom is in the kitchen answering email. Dad is in the den working on a project from the office. One son is in his room connected with earphones to the latest songs from his favorite band. Younger sister is on the computer in her room talking to her friends via chat rooms on the Internet, and the youngest child is playing video games in his room. All may be worthwhile endeavors, but the result is still a disconnected family. As parents and adults we understand the negative impact that some technology has had on the family. We must choose wisely what we will embrace and what is unnecessary. Each family is different and so decisions must be made based on your particular family and what you need.

Recently I was listening to Beth Moore on television and a statement she made was so profound that I haven't forgotten it. It really stuck with me. I share it often and believe it is a timely warning: "If Satan cannot tempt us to destruction, he will settle for distraction."

Doesn't that just about sum up our culture today? The fast-paced speed in which we are all traveling is verging on being out of control. Beth Moore's statement really spoke to me about how I spend my time and has caused me to make some necessary changes to be a better steward of my time. Am I always successful? No. But my heart's desire is to be efficient and effective, not just busy. Many times it is busyness doing really good things, but is it really the *best* use of my time right now? This is a question we all must ask ourselves.

Three things we need to consider as criteria for embracing technology are:

1. *Time*—How much time will it take to learn about a particular product? How much time will I need to invest on a daily basis to use it? How much time do I have to devote to this particular piece of equipment?

2. *Finances*—How much will it cost? Is it worth the investment? Can I purchase it used? How long will I need to save for it? How much can I set aside weekly or monthly to purchase it? Will I have to go into debt to buy it? Can I use it as a tax deduction?

3. *Fulfillment*—Is it necessary to better my life at home or at work? Will it save me time or cause me more frustration? Will the entire family benefit from it? Will we be better off with or without it?

Once you've decided what you really need, you can purchase exactly the right device, program, or gadget that will enhance your life and help you work smarter.

By embracing the use of technology in moderation, balance, and efficiency, you'll be amazed at what it can do to make your life easier, keep you informed, and help you stay connected. The key is balance and moderation.

Computers

When I started my home-based typing business in 1979, there were no personal computers readily available for purchase for the home. I did buy one of the very first IBM electronic typewriters, an IBM Electronic 75. At the time I thought it could do everything but make me a sandwich for lunch. It had built-in memory, font cartridges, and proportional spacing. The term "electronic" was relatively new, and I was on the cutting edge of technology.

> *I like my new telephone, my computer works just fine, my calculator is perfect, but Lord, I miss my mind.*
>
> AUTHOR UNKNOWN

In 1986 I bought my first personal computer and laser printer. Once again I was on the cutting edge of technology. My computer was one of the first computers to have a hard drive—20-megabytes (yes megabyte!). When the salesman sold me the computer he told me I would never fill up the hard drive. My first system cost $8,000! I pretty much stayed on the cutting edge of technology for another five years or so. Then I gradually realized I couldn't afford every new upgrade and program. Computer technology changes so quickly that by the time a new product reaches the retail market, it is already obsolete. So what are some guidelines for purchasing computers and software programs?

1. Do I need to buy new?
2. What features are necessary, and how much RAM and hard drive space will I need?
3. Do I need to purchase additional software?

4. Should I purchase a warranty?

5. Is my equipment upgradeable?

6. Am I getting a computer that will also be used for games? (If so, get as much video memory as possible.)

7. Desktop or laptop? Consider getting a desktop computer over a laptop unless you are going to take it with you when you travel. Laptops are more costly, have a higher risk of being broken or stolen, and generally don't perform as well.

8. Custom or factory setup? Consider using a local vender (OEM integrator) to build a custom computer system to avoid all the junk that comes preloaded on name-brand machines. You'll pay a little more, but I (Sheri) believe you get what you pay for.

9. Are there any sales going on? If you do get a prefab (name-brand) computer system, look for specials or blowouts.

10. How big should the monitor be? Don't be tempted to buy a gigantic monitor. If it's too big, you'll end up pushing it way back on your desk, eliminating the benefit.

After you've made your purchase, here are some tips for organizing your computer equipment.

1. *Desktop organization.* Keep only programs on your desktop that you utilize on a daily basis. This will keep your desktop neater and make it easier to locate programs. You can group several "like" programs into a folder on the desktop to keep it even more tidy. For example, all your word processing programs could go in a folder labeled "Word Processing Programs," all publishing programs in another folder, and so on.

2. For personal files and folders in a program, file each by last name, a date, or a topic. For example:

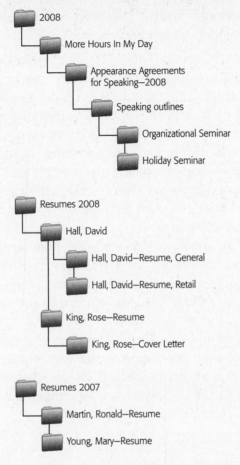

By keeping files organized either by date, name, or topic, you'll be able to find them faster later on.

3. Organize your photos by both date and name. You can also add an event name such as: 2007—December—Torelli—Christmas.

4. Keep emails organized the same way. If you receive email that you want to save, create a folder with a heading that is appropriate. When appropriate use the date and last name. For additional categories such as "Recipes" or "Travel Information" you can save using those category titles. Remember

to title a folder so you will remember what it's called and how you saved it so you can find it later.

5. Back up, back up, and back up! It is imperative that you back up your files regularly. This is so very easy to put off, and you'll realize too late when your computer "crashes" and you have no back up of important files and programs. If your computer is used for your job, and the work you create on the computer is not available any other place, backing up on a daily basis is essential. Otherwise get into the habit of backing up your computer on a weekly basis. Keep a separate back up file for programs and make two copies. Place one in a fireproof safe and another copy at a different location from where your computer is located. You only need to back up program files when you purchase a new program. Keep your document files on a separate disk (different from the back up of your programs). Again, store one copy in a fireproof safe and one at an offsite location. It is especially important to back up your picture files and make several copies. Double-check the copies to make sure they copied correctly. Don't assume they are on the CD/DVD unless you double check. Remember DVDs hold more information than CDs. They may be a better value for your money.

Entertainment

Technology in the entertainment arena is over the top. High Definition televisions, digital cameras, digital video cameras, iPods, MP3 players, portable DVD players, cell phones, and equipment that combines all of the above have changed the face of personal entertainment. Now you can have one device that serves as your cell phone, an MP3 player, a personal DVD player, your to-do list…and provides access to the Internet and your email account. The combination of all these functions in one device can be overwhelming to anyone over 16. Finding the right one for you can be mind-boggling, time consuming, and expensive.

All-in-one devices have made staying connected very easy. My kids live in New York, and I love having the ability to call or email and get connected quickly. I can snap a picture on my cell phone and send it to my daughter's cell phone in seconds. I've never felt closer to someone 3,000 miles away! This is one of the very special advantages of technology—helping families keep in touch and close even when separated by many miles. Grandparents can be a visible part of their grandchildren's lives and parents stay connected with their kids away at college or when separated by job moves. And one of the greatest benefits of technology is the ability of loved ones to stay connected with family members and friends in the military.

New technology can be very cost prohibitive to purchase when it first hits the market, but consider picking up an older model iPod, digital camera, video camera, or other equipment. Many times someone is ready to move to the next model but still has a perfectly good device in excellent working order to sell. Often you can negotiate and get a terrific price. Keep in mind that although technology changes very quickly, unless you need a particular item to be cutting edge, you can't go wrong buying something gently used.

Here are some of the most valued tech toys, how you can best use them, and what to watch out for.

❏ *iPods and MP3 players:* Great for loading and playing your favorite songs, movies, audiobooks, sermons, and favorite pictures. Excellent for entertainment while traveling. Parents need to monitor child usage. Encourage children to make half their downloads audiobooks.

❏ *Portable DVD players:* Great for viewing DVDs while traveling in the car or on an airplane. May soon be obsolete as many devices are becoming all in one. Again, parents will need to monitor usage.

❏ *Nintendo DS, Sony Playstation, and other video games.* Decide on family night fun by choosing a game that everyone takes turn playing for fun or prizes. Choose teams, have championship battles, and award prizes to the winners—the winning team chooses the snacks for the next game night. Don't forget to play an occasional board game. Be careful to monitor how much time is allowed for video games. Use them as a reward for completing homework or chores. Set a time and usage limit and stick to it.

❑ *Cable/satellite television, DVDs, videos:* Sit down together as a family and choose family friendly television shows and movies that will be viewed together. Schedule them into your week and enjoy with popcorn and soda. Don't turn the TV on for noise or to use as a babysitter. Set aside at least one night a week to keep the television off completely and read together or play an old-fashioned board game that is a family favorite.

❑ *Video or digital video cameras:* Great for recording family history. Keep your camera handy to capture your family's special moments. Send copies to out-of-town relatives so they can keep up on your growing family. Another fun idea is to set up a tripod during special occasions such as Thanksgiving, Christmas, or a birthday celebration and let it run. It will provide many hours of entertainment as the years go by. Family members enjoy watching family movies over and over. It's a great way to keep track of how everyone has changed and grown. Make sure to make back-up copies to be stored in a fireproof safe at an offsite location.

Another great use for your digital equipment is to go through your house and photograph each room and its contents. Store away in case of fire, flood, tornado, hurricane. Make sure to make more than one copy and store at least one offsite. Making insurance claims will be easier if you can show proof of what you really own. It will take time to complete the inventory but will be well worth it.

❑ *Digital cameras:* Great for taking snapshots to print and send via email or over the Internet. Good for scrapbooking endeavors too. The cameras are small and easy to take along to catch those special moments when they happen. There are many different websites that allow sharing photos with family and friends. You can email your pictures to Costco, Wal-Mart, Sam's Club, and other local stores who will print them and have them ready when you get there to pick them up. The price is reasonable and the quality is very good. There are also scrapbooking websites that help you create scrapbooks online and email the finished products. Be careful because you can spend lots of time and money in this area. Set a time limit and budget and stick to it.

Communication Technology

In the area of communication, technology is amazing. Just when I think inventors have reached a pinnacle, something new comes along. By the time this book is published much of what we've written about will be yesterday's news. As computers continue to get faster and faster and smaller in size, really, the sky is the limit as to what we can expect next.

❏ *Electronic mail or email:* This is one of my favorite technological wonders. I (Sheri) am not sure how I could function without it. You can send text messages, include pictures or file attachments, and send messages to more than one person at the same time. You can be creative in your layout or send a very simple note. It is fast and efficient.

But beware! Email can take up a great deal of your time. This is an area where you need to be diligent about how much time you spend sending and reading email. I receive approximately 1,500 emails a week in our office. Many of them are spam (junk mail), and I have to delete them. Another rule of thumb is to answer your emails twice a day—mid morning and early afternoon. If you spend time first thing in the morning, many people haven't had time to check and answer their mail or to send messages that need to go out. Resist the urge to check your email every few minutes unless you're waiting for an important reply. It's easy to get so involved that an hour or two has passed, and you're still at the computer. Set your timer for 15 minutes and work on your email until the timer goes off. Return to it later when you have a few extra minutes.

❏ *Cell phones and text messaging:* Another marvel in modern technology! Before you purchase a cell phone, make sure you check out pricing and packages offered to get the best value for your money. The best deal might be to have you package your home's land line, television cable, Internet service, and cell phone service with one company. When my children moved to New York, I immediately made sure we had a family plan so that we had unlimited minutes for each family member. My personal opinion is that children under the age of 12 don't need a cell phone unless there is a medical condition or special circumstance that warrants it. And even then there are plans available that allow only certain numbers to be dialed from a designated number. You must decide at what age you'll allow cell phones for your children. When they do get their phones, be careful to monitor usage for calls and text messages. Explain the costs and hold them accountable for overages. Teach your children to use good manners when owning a cell phone: turning it off or to silent mode when in the classroom, at church, in a restaurant, or any place where it might disturb others.

Note: Make sure that all cell phone owners in the family have a number labeled "ICE" for "in case of emergency" in their directory. Emergency personnel look for this number when they arrive at an accident so they know who to call.

❏ *The Internet and websites:* There are many ways to communicate via the Internet—chat rooms, blogs, and forums to name a few. You can communicate with a company via their website and email. However, the Internet is a breeding ground for predators, so be vigilant with your children and how much free time they are allowed to be on the Internet. My first recommendation is have only one family computer with Internet access. Place it in the family room where you have constant access to see what your children are viewing. MySpace is very popular with kids today. And there will continually be other new sites that pop up to lure your child in. Children are unaware most times of what can happen by chatting online. They feel safe because they're at home. Set clear boundaries and check often to make sure your kids are following your rules. Warn your children not to give *any* personal information over the Internet. Also be aware of where your kids spend their time when they're not at home, and make sure other parents are aware of your rules.

❏ *Family websites:* Consider making a family website to post pictures and information about your family to be shared with other members. It's a great way to stay in touch, especially when distance separates you from those you love. You can set up audio and video conferencing on your computer—you can see the person you're talking to!

❏ *BlackBerries, Personal Digital Assistants (PDAs), iPhones:* We have really come a long way in managing our time and our ever-present to-do list. Today combined devices make it simple to stay on top of everything that needs to be done each day, from making phone calls to answering emails, from running errands to paying bills. Make sure you purchase the tech device that suits you best and that you will really use. It makes no sense to spend your hard-earned cash on an item you will never turn on or learn how to use to its full capacity. Do your research and find out what will work for you. Watch for special offers from your provider. Many times they will offer a new phone/device free or at a greatly reduced price for extending your contract. Tim and I haven't paid for new cell phones for several years now. We wait until our contract is ready to expire and go online to extend the contract and negotiate to get a new phone free.

Using Technology for Research

Probably one of the greatest strides in technology is the amount of readily available information on the Internet. You can get access to a complete encyclopedia set, dictionary, and thesaurus with just a few clicks of the keyboard. Go to a search engine (Google, Yahoo, AOL), and put in as much information as you can to research a specific area of interest. List key words or phrases and any other information you think will aid in the search process. Give the name of an event, any key people, locations, and categories. If you want help, your local library may assist in locating information on the Internet. There are also classes offered to teach you how to maneuver on the Worldwide Web. Check out your local community college, library, and adult education center.

Recently Emilie called and asked me if I knew the gestation period for eggs to hatch. She was writing a chapter for a new book. She had a pretty good idea but wanted to know for sure. I told her I would see what I could find out. I went to my computer, called up a search engine, and typed in "ask.com" on the address line. When the site came up I typed in my question. Instantly I was given a website that answered my question. I had an answer for Emilie in less than two minutes. Wow! Now that's technology at its best. Just about anything you can think of can be found on the Internet.

- ❏ *Websites:* Bookmark your favorite websites to find them easily the next time you need to. You can also take classes on how to design your own website.

- ❏ *Online shopping:* Online shopping is gaining in popularity every day. Many hard-to-find items can be located easily and purchased without ever leaving the comfort of your home. You can shop at some of your favorite stores online or request coupons for the next time you go to the mall to shop.

- ❏ *Online newsletters and newspapers:* Stay current with the latest news by going online to your local news station or newspaper. And you're saving trees by not buying newsprint!

- ❏ *Health research:* I often hear from others how they have found valuable information on the Internet regarding a health concern for themselves, a family member, or a friend. I'm amazed at how much information you can obtain. However, this is an area where you must be very, very careful. Internet health research doesn't take the place of your personal physician or medicines he or she has prescribed. Feel free to share information you find with your doctor, but don't take what you read to be absolute truth. And be even more careful about ordering medications of any kind over the Internet. There is no way to know you will get what you ordered or what the quality will be. Be very cautious.

❏ *Other types of research available:*

- Personal research—locating a family member or long-lost friend.

- Scientific/technical research—for school or specialized training.

- Financial research—purchasing an automobile, a house, insurance.

- Travel and entertainment—I purchase all our airline tickets, make hotel reservations, and arrange car rentals online. It saves time and money. I even have email reminders sent to me when there is a possible airfare or lodging special I might be interested in. You can research a destination you are interested in to find out everything about a potential vacation location. We have some dear neighbors who are semi-retired and travel extensively around the world. They are able to take several trips a year and book everything online. You can purchase tickets for the opera or theater and even your local movie theater.

Trouble-Shooting and Maintenance

As with anything, there will be times when the very technology we have grown to love causes us frustration, sometimes to the point of despair. Computer viruses, hard drive crashes, and software malfunctions are here to stay. Here are a few tips for eliminating problems before they occur and ways to maintain your equipment so it will last.

1. Find a reputable computer company that offers repair and maintenance. Talk to family, friends, and neighbors. If they know people who are trustworthy and know what they're doing, they'll be happy to recommend them. My nephew, Brad McDermith, is co-owner of a computer company near me. Computer Options has been a lifesaver many times when I really needed help. I recommend them often to family and friends.

2. Identity theft is on the rise. Although the greatest identity theft occurs via our discarded trash, it does happen on the computer via the Internet. Remember to set up passwords for your computer and your Internet access. Also make sure you have firewall protection. This comes with most software security packages.

   a. Don't keep your website user names or passwords on the computer. It would be very easy to have them stolen, or if your computer crashes, you wouldn't have any way to locate them. My friend Lorrie gave me one of the best ideas I have seen used anywhere. Get a small, spiral-bound telephone/address book. These are very inexpensive. List the website names in alphabetical order, and write your user name and password for that site. It's easy to find them again because they are filed alphabetically by website name. Keep the book near your computer but in a safe place. Don't forget to take it when you travel. It's small and compact so it will be easy to pack in your computer case or purse.

   b. Set up security blocks for sites you don't want your children to access. There are programs you can install on the computer that will prevent access to questionable sites.

    c. Viruses are many. The best way to keep them to a minimum is to limit loading a disk or CD from someone else's computer. Keep virus protection programs current and run virus checks on a regular basis. Money for reputable virus protection software is well spent.

    d. Back up your computer and purge files: Back up regularly and at least four times a year set aside time to go through your files and purge old and unnecessary files. This may take quite a while. Once your computer is cleaned, back up again. Discard old back-ups. It's not necessary to keep old back-up disks or CDs.

3. Remember that moderation will keep the amount of time on the computer and using other tech toys to a nice, even balance for the family. Set aside certain times of the day for computer time. During the week keep computer time primarily for homework or research. Let children "earn" time by doing extra chores or as a reward for good behavior or a treat. Monitor your time as well so you set a good example.

4. Cleaning and maintenance of hardware is essential. You will get many years of use from equipment that is taken care of. Here are some quick tips:

    a. Cover all your equipment at the end of the day. Dust is a killer for hardware.

    b. To keep your equipment sanitary and prevent germs from spreading, each morning before you turn on your equipment take a disinfectant towel and wipe down your computer and keyboard and any other electronic equipment. Because we touch them with our hands, they become breeding grounds for germs. This is especially necessary if you share your computer with others. Wipe down all areas where you place your hands: keyboards, printers, telephones, mouse.

    c. Once or twice a month spray your equipment with

"canned air" to release any loose dust. This works especially well for your keyboard. Make sure your computer
is off.

5. Store software and user manuals/warranties where you can
find them. If you find yourself searching for your software
disk or the user manual that came with the computer or
software program, you will enjoy these simple ideas:

a. Purchase an 8½ x 11 three-ring binder and clear sheet
protectors that open at the top. Place the software disk,
user manual or booklet, and any warranty paperwork
in a sheet protector. Put only one set per sheet protector.
You can then file them alphabetically for easy retrieval.
You might want to keep a notebook at each computer
with the software and user manuals that are on that
particular computer. You may need only one notebook
for the entire family. You can also categorize them by
type such as word processing, desktop publishing, photography. This is also a great way to store appliance
user manuals and warranties. You can even attach the
receipt to the user manual in case you need to return it
or prove it is still under warranty.

b. Another storage idea is to take a plastic accordion file
and organize your software and user manuals/war-
ranties. Place one set behind each divider. This works
especially well if you also have some hardware that
came with the computer or software program, such
as cords.

Make sure you add cleaning your hardware to your "Total Mess
to Total Rest" maintenance schedule. You should clean your hardware at least twice a month for occasional use, but once a week if
you use it everyday. Dust builds up inside the case, so clean that
out every six months or once a year. If you take good care of your
"servants," they'll take good care of you.

31

Simple Ideas to Brighten Your Home for Sale

We walk by faith, not by sight.

2 CORINTHIANS 5:7 NASB

There are always a few "For Sale" signs in neighborhoods. For various reasons we're on the move. Most people relocate every five years. Selling a home quickly for the right price can be difficult—and definitely causes stress. When the market is in decline this is especially trying. These simple ideas have proven valuable to owners wanting to sell their homes.

Preparation for Showing

❏ *First impressions are lasting.* The front door greets the prospective buyer. Make sure it is clean and neat. Keep the lawn trimmed and edged, and the yard free of refuse. Be sure snow and ice are removed from walks and steps. If you have the financial resources, a growing trend is to hire a company to "stage" your home for sale. This is especially important for larger, more expensive homes. These professionals know exactly what to do to make your home show well.

❏ *Decorate for a quick sale.* Faded walls and worn woodwork reduce appeal. An investment in new kitchen wallpaper or some paint will pay dividends.

❏ *Let the sun shine in.* Open draperies and curtains and let the buyer see how cheerful your home can be. (Dark rooms are not appealing.)

❏ *Fix that faucet.* Dripping water discolors sinks and suggests faulty plumbing.

❏ *Repairs can make a big difference.* Loose knobs, sticking doors and windows, warped cabinet drawers, and other minor flaws detract from a home's value. Have them fixed.

❏ *Remove clutter from top to bottom.* Display the full value of your attic, basement, and other utility space by removing all unnecessary articles. Brighten a dark, dull basement by painting the walls. It is worth the investment to rent a storage space.

❏ *Put safety first.* Keep stairways clear. Avoid a cluttered appearance and possible injuries.

❏ *Make closets look bigger.* Neat, well-ordered closets show that the space is ample.

❏ *Bathrooms help sell homes, so make these rooms sparkle.* Check and repair caulking in bathtubs and showers.

❏ *Kitchens sell the house to women, garages to men.* It will be worth the time and effort to make sure they both show well. Eliminate counter clutter in the kitchen and have the garage swept and items stored neatly.

❏ *Arrange bedrooms neatly.* Remove excess furniture. Use attractive bedspreads and freshly laundered curtains.

❏ *Turn on all the lights.* Illumination is like a welcome sign. The potential buyer will feel a warm glow when your home is brightly lit for an evening inspection. Light a few scented candles to provide a welcome feeling and nice smells.

❏ *Three's a crowd, so avoid having too many people present during inspections.* The potential buyer will feel like an intruder and will hurry through the house.

❏ *Keep the music mellow.* Turn off the blaring radio or television. Let the salesperson and buyer talk free of loud disturbances.

❏ *Keep pets out of the way—preferably out of the house.*

❏ *Silence is golden.* Be courteous but don't force conversation with the potential buyer. He wants to inspect your house—not pay a social call.

❏ *Never apologize for the appearance of your home.* After all, it has been lived in. Let the trained realtor answer any objections.

❏ *Stay in the background.* The salesperson knows the buyer's requirements and can better emphasize the features of your home when you don't tag along. You will be called if needed.

❏ *Don't put the cart before the horse.* Trying to sell furniture and furnishings to a potential buyer before he or she has purchased the house often loses a sale.

❏ *Let the realtor and buyer discuss price, terms, possession, and other factors.*

Moving Day Countdown

2 to 4 Weeks Ahead

- ❏ Visit your neighborhood moving company and reserve a moving van.
- ❏ Reserve a utility dolly, piano dolly, furniture pads.
- ❏ Purchase or round up packing supplies.
- ❏ Sell or donate unwanted items.
- ❏ Send change-of-address cards to magazines, charge accounts, friends, and relatives. The cards are free at the post office.
- ❏ Collect medical and dental records, eye prescriptions, and pet records.
- ❏ Get copies of school records.
- ❏ Settle all local tax bills.
- ❏ Make arrangements for shipment of pets.
- ❏ Start packing boxes as soon as possible.

1 to 2 Weeks Ahead

- ❏ Have clothing dry-cleaned. Check on items in repair shops.
- ❏ Close and transfer bank accounts and safe-deposit boxes.
- ❏ Notify utilities and telephone companies at both old and new addresses. Set a date for disconnection and hookup.
- ❏ Return borrowed items, and pick up things you have lent.

2 to 7 Days Ahead

- ❏ Discard all flammable items such as paint and gasoline.
- ❏ Inspect and service your car.
- ❏ Line up a babysitter for moving day.
- ❏ Finish packing. Leave out items for moving day.
- ❏ Buy travelers checks.
- ❏ Empty refrigerator and freezer.

1 Day Ahead

- ❏ Clean range. Go through house and pick up trash.
- ❏ Pick up moving van in the afternoon to get a head start the following morning if you're doing the loading.
- ❏ Pick up ice and beverages for moving day.

Moving Day

- ❏ Leave young children with a babysitter. The older children can help load up.
- ❏ Go through the house and pick up any trash. Turn off water and lights. Lock windows and doors.

32

What to Look for Before You Buy a Home

*Unless the Lord builds the house, they labor in vain
who build it; unless the Lord guards the city, the
watchman keeps awake in vain.*

PSALM 127:1 NASB

Purchasing a house is a very emotional experience. We have visualized what our dream home is going to look like: what color it will be, what trees will be in the front yard, and the layout of the landscaping. Before we buy a home, we'll probably have considered if we want automatic sprinklers, an attic with usable space, and a finished basement.

When my (Sheri) husband, Tim, bought his first home at 19, he was more concerned about the price than anything else. Our first home was 720 square feet, had a carport instead of a garage, and the backyard butted up against railroad tracks. We loved it. After living there for a while, it was much easier to know what to look for when we needed to move into our second home.

As you visit various homes, there is more to consider than your dreams. You can do a lot to narrow down the choices by using this chapter. Ask yourself the following questions *before* you put down a deposit.

General Impressions

❏ What do you like best about the home?

❏ What do you like least about the house? Can these disadvantages be corrected?

❏ Will this home be low, medium, or high maintenance? Will your budget allow for proper maintenance?

Space and Circulation

❏ Is there enough bedroom/closet/bathroom space? It's often easier and cheaper to buy a larger home than to add rooms later.

❏ How is the traffic flow through the house?

❏ Is there an easy route to get groceries from the car to the kitchen?

❏ Can people with muddy or sandy feet go directly to a service porch or utility room before going into the living area?

❏ How well are sounds controlled in the house? Can you hear toilets

flush, the dishwasher go through its cycles, or sounds of an entertainment center throughout the home?

❑ Will you be operating a home-based business, and does the space
and zoning allow for that?

Neighborhood and Locale

❑ Visit the neighborhood during different times of the day.

❑ Is the home close to schools, churches, and shopping, with easy
access to freeways or toll roads?

❑ How noisy is it during peak traffic times?

❑ Are there evidences of children the ages of your own in the neighborhood?

❑ Check out the quality of education offered in the neighborhood
school.

❑ What do the homes next door to you and those across the street
look like?

❏ Knock on a neighbor's door and ask how he or she likes the neighborhood.

❏ See where the sun exposure will be during different seasons of the year. This is very important if you live in areas of climatic extremes or if you are a gardener.

Condition

❏ How old is the roof? Are you in a fire hazard area? If so, do you have a fire-retardant roof?

❏ Is the home in a flood zone? If yes, check out flooding history, whether flood insurance is required, and how much the insurance costs.

❏ In what condition is the furnace? Ask to see utility bills from the last 12 months.

❏ If the area gets extremely hot, does the house have central air-conditioning? If not, what would be the cost to have it installed? When was the current air-conditioning and heating installed or replaced?

❏ Is the garage adequate for your needs? Is there an electric garage-door opener? Is there room to hold cars, lawn equipment, ladders, children's bicycles, and snow equipment (if needed)?

❑ Are there any problems with mildew or wetness in the basement? How about termites, material defects, bad septic system, water stains? Request that the seller furnish you with a home inspection certification before the close of escrow.

Since a home is probably the largest purchase you will make in your lifetime, take all the precautions that will give you peace of mind. *Don't rush; take your time.* Make sure it's the right home with no hidden defects that will cause you difficulty later. You want your home to be all that you anticipate it to be.

May the roof above us never fall in and may we good companions beneath it never fall out.

IRISH BLESSING

House Hunting Records

Date _____

Address of home _____ Age _____

Best route to take _____

_____

Owner of home _____ Phone # _____

Salesperson _____

House design _____ Color _____

Square feet _____ Size of lot _____

Asking price $_____ Down payment $ _____ Monthly payment $ _____

Type of utilities _____ Cost per month $ _____

Other costs_____

_____

Garage? ❑ 1 car   ❑ 2 car   ❑ Larger   ❑ Carport

Condition/type of roof _____

Living room: Size _____ Flooring _____

Kitchen: Size _____ Flooring _____

Dining room: Size _____ Flooring _____

Storage space: Adequate? ❑ Yes   ❑ No

Bedrooms: Number _____ Size _____

Number _____ Size _____

Number _____ Size _____

Bathrooms: Number _____ Size _____Colors _____

Number _____ Size _____Colors _____

Fixtures and tile condition _____

Water pressure check _____

Foyer: Size _____ Closet space _____

Family room: Size _____ Flooring _____

Basement: Size _____ ❑ Finished   ❑ Unfinished

Laundry room: Size _____ Flooring _____

Other _____

_____

❑ Central Air   ❑ Fireplace Locations(s) _____

Overall interior condition _____

❑ Patio _____ ❑ Pool _____

❑ Pantry _____

Distance from work: _____ Time_____

Distance from shopping: _____ Time _____

Neighborhood rating _____ Overall rating of home and property _____

Schools: Quality _____ Distance from home _____

Comments_____

_____

Husband's first impression _____

Wife's first impression _____

PART FOUR

More Hours...for Family and Friends

33

Developing Family Traditions

*Where your treasure is,
there your heart will be also.*

MATTHEW 6:21 NIV

I (Emilie) often question ladies about traditions they had in their families while growing up—something that set them apart as belonging to their unique family (a sign, a thumbs-up, a kiss on the nose, a pinch of the cheek, an activity). I found that most people had no such traditions. Some even asked "What's a tradition?" or said "We had no traditions at all, even at Christmastime, birthdays, or anniversaries."

I'm a strong believer in family traditions. It only takes small gestures to bring a family closer. Traditions help families connect and maintain loving relationships.

In a recent 2007 poll, teenagers were asked to list the number one thing that made them happiest. Of all the teenagers polled, 82 percent stated that what made them happiest was time spent with mom and dad! I (Sheri) was pleasantly surprised. So let's work diligently to make great, lasting memories with our children. What they'll remember when they are grown will surprise you. It won't be the expensive toys or fabulous vacations. No, it will be times spent with family. Family is vitally important to children, and we must make sure the family survives.

Being a sentimental person, I love anything that brings family and friends together. Traditions are vitally important to the health of a family. On one of his regular radio broadcasts, Dr. Dobson said, "If you want your children to return home after they are grown for more than just the 'obligatory' visits, you must have established everyday traditions in your family."

Many of the suggested traditions that follow have been used by both the Barnes and Torelli families. Some have been shared with us by women we've met or who have written to us. Select a few that are of interest to you and try them with your family. Bob Barnes' motto is "It's never too late to start a new tradition."

A Butterfly Kiss

Bob Barnes gives his grandchildren a "butterfly kiss" by fluttering his eyelids on the children's cheeks. They love it! Another is a "car-wash kiss." (You can guess what that's like!)

A Special Handshake

Bob always greets a certain male friend and his two grown sons with a special greeting. They shake hands, slip down to a clasp of the fingertips, quickly move into a thumb grip, shift to a knock on the elbow, and finish with a big smile.

Silent Communication

Invent a silent symbol of your family's camaraderie. For example, a thumbs-up, a wink, a tug on the ear. Tim Torelli loves to grab Sheri's hand when he prays, drives the car, and even first thing in the morning before they get out of bed. He squeezes it several times in quick succession. He says he's telling her he loves her!

Kid Fix

Request a "kid fix"—a hefty hug and a big kiss—whenever you feel the need. Let your youngsters know it makes you feel much better.

Once a Day

Tell your children you love them at least once every 24 hours—when you send them off to school, when they come home, when you pray with them at night—anytime!

The Hug Factor

A study was conducted and showed that for the average child to be healthy, he or she requires 10 hugs a day. And not one of you reading this has an average child! So start with 10 and go up from there.

Go Ahead, Try It

Encourage your children to try new things—taste unusual foods, enter contests, write for information on subjects that interest them.

Double Desserts

Once a month surprise your family by announcing double dessert night.

Yogurt Run/PJ Ride

During the summer or when the children don't have school the next day, go into their rooms just before they fall asleep and announce a "yogurt run." They'll think you've flipped out, but they'll always remember those

> *Every house where love abides*
> *And friendship is a guest,*
> *Is surely home, and home sweet home*
> *For there the heart can rest.*
>
> HENRY VAN DYKE

special times when you got them out of bed and went to get some delightful yogurt.

I (Sheri) loved this idea, so when my children were very young I began "PJ rides." We had some rules. They couldn't ask for a PJ

ride, and their behavior had to be good for the day. After dinner and
bath and bedtime routine, I would put them down for bed and go
out of the room for two minutes (no longer or they would fall asleep).
Then I would run back in and yell, "It's time for a PJ ride!" They
would jump out of bed, and we'd get into the car and go for a ride.
Sometimes we would go to McDonalds for an ice cream cone. Other
times we'd get yogurt and then visit their Dad at the fire station or
drive around and sing songs. Years later, after the kids were grown,
one evening they were home visiting with some of their friends. They
started talking about favorite childhood memories. Of all the things
we did with our children, their fondest childhood memories were the
PJ rides with mom and dad. How sweet those memories are!

You Are Special Today

My (Emilie) family has a large red plate inscribed with "You
Are Special Today." We frequently honor a member of the family
or guest who comes to dinner by serving dinner on this plate.
We've even taken it to restaurants, on a picnic, and to a beach
party. We take a photograph of the person, and place the picture
in a photo album that houses pictures of all recipients each time
they're celebrated.

Another feature we've added to this tradition is to go around the
table and have each person tell our honored guest why we think he
or she is special. Then we let our special person tell us why he or she
is special. It's amazing what has happened through this tradition.
For more on this tradition see chapter 37, "Creative Entertaining,"
and the section called "The Red Plate."

Sharing a Secret

You can have a lot of fun by sharing a secret and then keeping up the suspense until Christmas or a birthday comes. It's also
good training to teach the children how to be discreet and keep a
confidence.

What's the Best/Worst Thing That Happened to You Today?

Ask this question toward the end of your meal, and the discussion that follows will keep your family together at the table for a longer time as everyone shares. By allowing your children to share both the good and the bad, you teach them that they will always find security and love at home. It helps to keep communication lines open through those amazing growing years.

Cooking Class

At least once a month set aside a special afternoon where the children are invited into the kitchen to prepare a meal or a portion of a meal. Making desserts is always a winner. Bring out the aprons and chef hats. If they dress like cooks, they will really get involved in the process.

Bravo!

Three cheers for success! Honor your child when he or she does well in an activity, on a test or term report, or by completing a chore. Make it a big deal. You might even cook the person's favorite meal. Don't forget to serve it on the special red plate!

Young Decorator

When sprucing up your children's rooms, allow them to pick the color themes, paints, sheets, curtains, and towels. If that's too risky, give them specific choices (several wallpaper designs, three or four paints, or choices of several bedspreads).

Study Hall

Select a special area at home—a table, the couch, a chair—for your children to review materials to be covered in a test tomorrow. Have them cozy up and get comfortable in their special "study hall." After they've studied for a while, bring out a tray with a treat.

Encourage them by telling them you're proud of them and how hard they're working.

What a Fine Family We Have

Hang family pictures all over the house—individual and group pictures from last summer's vacation, a winter ski trip, and a Christmas group picture. Be sure to put some pictures in the children's rooms too. This gives them a great sense of family identity.

Cowbell

I (Emilie) have an old cowbell that is positioned by my kitchen door. Two minutes before a meal is to be served I go out and ring that bell very firmly. This signals members of the family that the food is ready. They have two minutes to get to the table.

How Pretty!

Let your children wear your old jewelry and dress up when they have playtime.

Sorry

Admit when you're wrong. Your family members know when you've blown it as well as you do. If you admit when you're wrong, you help your children admit when they're wrong.

Pet Names

As the children get older, don't drop their pet names but start using them privately to avoid embarrassing them.

School Projects

Display and use those special clay vases and wooden candle stands that are made and brought home. When my (Sheri) son, Nicholas, was in kindergarten, he made a plastic violet pot with a potted violet plant. The outside of the pot had a clear cover with paper underneath. He drew a sweet picture and proudly wrote his name in his very best writing. A couple of years ago he was home visiting and noticed I still had the plastic pot. He asked why I hadn't thrown it out when the plant died. I told him that if the house caught on fire, it would be one of the things I would be carrying out with me.

I'm Like Dad

Lend your son a tie or something else to wear on special occasions.

I Choose You

Tell your children how much you enjoy being their parents. Kids like to hear they are loved.

Tea Parties and Fireplace Picnics

Of all the things I (Sheri) learned from Emilie, one of my most cherished is the tea party. She taught me to love tea and tea gatherings. She gave me my very first teacup and blesses me often with tea accessories. She also encouraged me to have tea parties with my daughter, Terra. Some of our most treasured memories have been at one of our tea parties. Most of our tea times are very simple—a couple of teacups, a candle, a pretty teapot, a store-bought goodie. I love having fancy tea parties as well, but if I keep them simple, I'm more inclined to do them often. We started when Terra was eight years old. I would set everything up and go wake her up gently. We would gather at the kitchen table, in her bedroom, or sometimes outside for a few minutes of tea and

> [Traditions] help us define who we are; they provide something steady, reliable and safe in a confusing world.
>
> SUSAN LIEBERMAN

conversation. I believe one of the reasons we are close today is from our tea times. It's the first thing she wants to do when she comes home for a visit. I would have tea parties on the first day of school, the last day of school, her birthday, my birthday, and anytime we weren't "connecting." If you have boys, you can have "fireplace picnics. It's the same idea, just with boys. Spread out a large quilt or blanket in front of the fireplace and share mugs of hot chocolate…and don't forget the marshmallows and whipped cream!

34

Team Effort Starts at Home

Make my joy complete by being of the same mind,
maintaining the same love, united in spirit,
intent on one purpose.

PHILIPPIANS 2:2 NASB

Regardless of whether I (Emilie) speak in California, Texas, Florida, or Canada, I always get one question over and over again: "How do I get my husband and children involved?" I've been very blessed over the years. My Bob has always been very supportive. We had five children under our roof when I was only 21 years old. For us to survive, we had to work together. I know this doesn't happen in every family.

Attitudes

The Scriptures teach that we are to live in harmony, to live together in love as though we had only one mind and one spirit (Philippians 2:2). Another key verse is found in Ephesians 5:21: "Honor Christ by submitting to each other." Bob and I used these two verses as a base for our attitudes toward husband–wife relationships, the way we raise our children, how we manage our finances, how we do chores around the home, how we handle changes in our lives, and the type of food we cook and the nutrition we put into our bodies.

Attitude management begins at home. This is the key, regardless if we are college students living in a dorm, single adults living in apartments, married and living in an apartment or small home, or retired and living in a condo. The goal is to have an attitude that allows us to live in love and in harmony with those around us.

Teamwork

Some of the women at my seminars cry out that they are so involved in so many activities they feel all alone. They want to "rent a wife." These women share that they have very little cooperation from their husbands and children.

A spirit of cooperation must exist if we are to survive and thrive in our marriages. Each person must carry his or her part of the load. Aesop, in one of his fables, illustrates this point by having his three sons each bring him a stick. He asks each son to break his stick. With little trouble they quickly snap their sticks in two. After each son has broken his stick, Aesop takes one twig from each son and ties them together. Then he asks each son to break the combined twigs. As hard as they try, not one son could break the bundle of twigs. Aesop points out that this is the way it is when a family joins together. They become stronger when they are united. He encourages his sons to band together and be strong. That's what we must do as families—join together and be strong.

In the "good old days," all the family members had to pitch in to get the chores done around the farm. Through this involvement, they had the opportunity to spend time in conversation and talk about ethics, values, morals, church, Sunday school lessons, and growing up. Parents and children worked often side by side. Now, however, we have to plan to dialogue together.

When our children were small, Bob would help with feeding them, bathing them, dressing them, and reading bedtime stories. This was a great help to me, and it gave the children an opportunity to bond with Dad.

With patio building, laying bricks, planting, landscaping, and installing sprinklers, Bob always had the children underfoot so he could show them how to do the tasks. One time Bob shared with our son, Brad, who was about six, that he was sorry to always have Brad be the "go fer." Brad replied, "That's okay, Dad. That's what little boys are for."

Over the years Dad and the children were big helps in lightening my load. The children rotated and helped with taking out the trash, feeding the animals, cleaning the pool, and sweeping up the leaves on the patio. They were great at emptying the dishwasher, sorting the dirty clothes, doing the wash, cleaning their rooms, and setting and clearing the table.

When our daughter, Jennifer, first started to drive a car at 16, she was thrilled to do our shopping at the market, make bank deposits, and run many of our errands.

Have your family help with errands. For example, if a shirt has to be returned, leave it in plain sight so that anyone going to or near the particular store can return it. To make it easy, attach a note with instructions—credit to charge account, exchange for a different size or color, and so forth.

When company was coming, everyone pitched in to get things ready. The children would even help address our party invitations, apply postage stamps, take the letters to the mailbox, welcome our guests, take their wraps and purses, help with soft drinks, serve the food, and help clean up the dinner dishes. We really valued our time together as a family.

Cooperation and Supportiveness

Even with all the involvement with the children, Bob and I also value our time together as a couple. We realized that our children would grow up fast and leave the nest. We didn't want to one day look at each other and ask, "Who are you?" So we found a workable solution to our unique problems, needs, and circumstances. Sheri and I encourage you to assess your own family's needs, abilities, and desires and come up with a solution to not spending enough time together as a family and as a couple. As a team, you'll learn to distinguish between your wants and your needs. What Bob needed was sometimes more important than what I needed. Sometimes my needs came first. We had to be sensitive to each other's needs at the particular moment.

I receive a lot of letters from mothers and wives who have atypical schedules. They want suggestions on how to adapt to their uniqueness. I don't always answer in detail because families need to work out their own solutions. I do encourage them to gather the family and talk about how they can adapt their schedules to accommodate the requirements of various family members.

If one partner needs to study in the afternoons and evenings because of morning classes, the other mate might have to find something to do to occupy the time and be out of the way during those periods. Many times sleeping schedules are big considerations for the family. Cooperation is the key. If you set up a marriage as a competition rather than cooperation, no one wins. Work out disagreements in a spirit of harmony, and work as a team in managing your home and family.

The Future

Couples need to plan their futures. Visualize your family life five years from now. Goals and plans are not set in concrete, but they do create a starting point. Be flexible. What do you hope to be doing in your family regarding finances, careers, spiritual growth, professions, education, recreation, and physical areas of your life? Long-term goals help you make short-term decisions. When you have defined your goals in life, it makes establishing priorities easier. It also helps you say "no" more quickly to any questionable "opportunities" that come your way.

What obstacles keep you from becoming what you want to be? How can you take any negatives and turn them into positives? Concentrate on your goals rather than on the negatives if you want to succeed. Try alternate plans. Success is a progressive realization of worthwhile goals. In our present-day culture we've lost the virtue of patience. Wait upon the Lord! Strive for patience with yourself and with your family. Teach patience whenever and wherever possible.

Use the salami method to reach your goal. If the size of the project overwhelms you, tackle it one piece at a time. You wouldn't eat a salami whole, would you? You'd cut it into slices. Do the same thing with your big projects and goals.

Family Conferences

As parents Bob and I (Emilie) knew we wanted family involvement in making plans, establishing activities, and dreaming about specific areas concerning the Barnes family. We knew we had to delegate responsibilities, but in order to do that effectively we had to have input from the children. So we set up specific family time on a regular basis. This provided an opportunity for the whole family to review guidelines and rules, discuss future events, and, many times, just have fun.

Of all the activities we did, the family time together proved most valuable in developing and keeping good communication between us. The children knew their input counted when a decision was made. I can remember one occasion when it was time to purchase a new family car. In discussing the particulars, the children asked Dad if we could get a color other than blue. Our last two cars were blue. It was time we changed colors. When we went shopping, blue was not what we looked for.

Another time we moved from one home to another that was out of town. Bob and I had narrowed our selection down to two neighborhoods and two different styles of homes. As we prayed about this decision, our children's input really helped us make a wise decision. These and many more illustrations came about because we were a family who met and planned together.

The length of our meetings varied according to the agenda and the ages of the various children. We tried to make it short and to the point—never too long to bore the children. Sometimes after only 15 minutes we were having refreshments; other times the meeting lasted 30 minutes. On fun nights at the roller skating rink, ice skating rink, horseback riding, a wiener roast, or a beach party, we would not have any formal agenda—just time together as a family. Oh, yes, we would discuss certain items while driving in the car to and from the event. This was a great opportunity to talk in an informal way about values, stress, school, teachers, dates, party invitations, and preparing for tests. These casual moments gave us a lot of insights into our children, and they gave them an opportunity to know Mom and Dad better. Deuteronomy 6:7 gave us a guideline in this style of teaching: "You shall teach them diligently to your sons and shall talk of them when you sit in your house and when you walk by the way and when you lie down and when you rise up" (NASB).

Use every opportunity to teach your children. Casual moments are usually the very best times for children to grasp important concepts that will stay with them all their lives.

We usually made our family conference times family members only events because many times we had items on the agenda that were just for us. However, during the fun nights we would let our children take turns inviting friends as their guests. A lot of close friendships were made during these outings, plus we had an opportunity to build values and caring into the lives of our children's friends.

Be flexible with your plans, but make it a top priority for everyone to be at family meetings. Consistency is most important. If Mom or Dad often isn't there, the children will feel that it's not too important, and they won't be as excited about these "memory moments" and "family building" times.

Management of the Home

I (Emilie) believe the Scriptures are clear that the husband has the responsibility of leadership in the home. I've been very fortunate over the years because Bob has always searched out God's leading in his life. He has read, listened, studied, and talked about how he can be a more effective husband.

I realize a lot of families are struggling in this area. My encouragement to you wives is to let your husbands manage in the home. Yes, you may be able to do it faster and better, but they need to be accepted as the leaders.

Many homes in America don't have a man in the home. The wife must assume the leadership role even if she doesn't want the added responsibility. A home must have leadership to survive.

Jay Adams, in his book *Christian Living in the Home,* gives an excellent explanation of the husband's role as manager of the home:

> A good manager knows how to put other people to work...He will be careful not to neglect or destroy his wife's abilities. Rather, he will use them to the fullest. He does not consider her someone to be dragged along. Rather, he thinks of her as a useful, helpful and wonderful blessing from God...A manager has an eye focused on all that is happening in his home, but he does not do everything himself. Instead he looks at the whole picture and keeps everything under control. He knows everything that is going on, how it is operating, and only when it is necessary to do so, steps in to change and to modify or in some way to help.[1]

Since God gave woman to man to be his helpmate, we must manage together as a team. What are some of the techniques Bob and I used in managing our home that will help you?

Planning—Establish and write out your mission or purpose for life. What do you want to do as an individual and as a family? Let your lives make a statement to your community. Take a look at what's going on and plan for the future. Communicate these plans to everyone in the family. Use the guidelines you establish as a basis for guiding your family. Of course, God's Word is the original and final word for direction, but how are you going to live His words out? Plan a schedule and schedule a plan.

Organization—Once you've thought out your purpose and mission in life, you can establish organizational procedures to reach these goals. Your home, people, equipment, and finances all work to help your family reach the goals and objectives you've set.

Harmony—We are to live calmly and joyfully together. We were not made to fight and use our energies in arguments. A home that is in harmony is much more fun to live in. Love wins out over bickering and fighting. I've found that the woman is usually the harmonizer of a family. Staying married requires the love and devotion of both a man and a woman, but it seems to be the woman who pays close attention to the personal needs and feelings of the people in her home. In harmonious living, the object is to make the other person feel better. It requires paying a lot of attention to the other members of the family. This is a very important concept for each member to know and practice within the family. It is difficult because harmonizing requires a willingness to surrender our egos to the needs of other family members.

Home climate—Treat each member of the family with fairness and respect. Develop an awareness of what every member of the family is doing and give praise. Self-respect is developed in the home and in the extended family. Ephesians 4:29 encourages us to let no corrupt communication come out of our mouths. Our speech is to be "edifying" (to lift or build up). It provides grace to the hearers. As parents, Bob and I insisted that respect be given to each member of the family. Mom and Dad had to exhibit that same respect to each other as well as to all family members.

We also valued creativity, initiative, and a job well done. We praised and rewarded those who did jobs well. That now extends to our grandchildren: Christine, Chad, Bevan, Bradley, and Weston. When they were little we had cute little stickers that said "I Was Caught Being Good." We gave them out when they did something on their own. When, with no direction from us, they decided by themselves that they needed to help out. They were dusting the furniture, helping load the dishwasher, pulling weeds, and picking up leaves off the patio. We made our praise a big deal. They knew they had done a good job! And if one child got a sticker, the other grandchildren wanted the opportunity to get their very own too. In a short time they would all be doing something good. It was a great way to build healthy pride and self-confidence in them. At times we even gave "PaPa Bob" a sticker when he did something good. He liked that too!

Control—Periodic evaluations should be made to make sure the family is staying on target. Mom and Dad can tell quickly if the family is off balance. Many times our children pointed out in our conference times certain areas that we needed to consider as a family. This is why it's important to stay flexible and be willing to change course.

Are you saying "This sure sounds like a lot of work"? Yes, it is. Building a loving, supportive family takes a lot of work. It is a very responsible job, and wimps need not apply. My Bob has expressed the commitment required:

- ❏ All marriages aren't happy; living together is tough.
- ❏ A good marriage is not a gift; it's an achievement by God's grace.
- ❏ Marriage is not for children; it takes guts and maturity.
- ❏ Marriage separates the men from the boys and the women from the girls.
- ❏ Marriage is tested daily by the ability to compromise.
- ❏ The survival of marriage can depend on being smart enough to know what's worth fighting about, making an issue of, or even mentioning.
- ❏ Marriage is giving and, more importantly, forgiving.

❏ With all its ups and downs, marriage is still God's best object lesson of Jesus and the church.

❏ Through submission to one another we can witness to the world that marriage works and is still alive.

❏ Marriage is worth dying for. If we give it proper honor, we will be honored by our children, our families, our neighbors, our friends, and best of all, our Lord.[2]

Now is the time for parents to take charge of their families and redeem them for the Lord. The styles of the sixties, seventies, eighties, and nineties obviously aren't working well. As God-fearing parents, we need to make things happen on purpose. We are to act with conviction and responsibility. Each family has its unique circumstances to consider, but each family can also become a team.

Someone asked Dr. James Dobson what he thought about the future of the family. He answered that, for the most part, women were committed to marriage, family, and children for the long haul. How successful the family of the future will be, he said, depends upon the father and what part he plays in that unit.

Our priorities have to be evaluated and new ones written. Proper organization within the family is a beginning for making your joy complete by being of the same mind, maintaining the same love, remaining united in spirit, focusing on one purpose: to glorify the Lord Jesus Christ.

Our prayers are with you as you create a new beginning. Don't strive for "supermom" status. That is a very tiring and lonely road that leads to burnout, frustration, and disappointment. A team effort starts at home and provides rich blessings of self-respect, healthy self-respect for a job well done, and a feeling of cooperation in all members. As you promote a team spirit you'll notice the whole family's attitude will change for the better. And these changes will most definitely lighten your load as Mom.

35

The Love Basket

*May the Lord bring you into an ever deeper under-
standing of the love of God and of the patience
that comes from Christ.*

2 Thessalonians 3:5

A "Love Basket" can be used for those very special times when
you want to say "I love you" in a different way. Filled with
food for dinner, it can be taken to the beach, a lake or stream, a ball
game, a concert, and to the park. You can even take one in your
car on a love trip. Plan a surprise lunch or dinner in the backyard,
in your bedroom, and under a tree. Be creative and use the basket
to show how much you love and care for the other person. You can
also make these for wedding shower, anniversary, and bridal gifts.

What You'll Need

To make a Love Basket you'll need a basket with a handle, preferably a heavy-duty one—something like a picnic basket without a lid
but having a nice sturdy handle. You'll need a tablecloth. It can be
made from a piece of fabric or a sheet. I (Emilie) generally cut the
tablecloth about 45 inches square. Line the inside of your basket with
this tablecloth, letting it drape over the sides so it looks enticing.

Inside the basket we're going to put two fancy glasses with stems.
It's nice to use glasses with tall stems because they look classy and

special in the basket. We'll also need four napkins. I like to use ones with a small print, or maybe gingham, to make the basket look fun and different. One napkin will be for the lap and the other will be used as a napkin. For now, fluff up the napkins and place inside the top of the glasses so they perk up and look like powder puffs.

Next get a nice tall candleholder and candle. I like to use something tall because it shows over the top of the basket. A bottle of sparkling apple cider is next. This is nonalcoholic but bubbles up very nicely. (You can buy this in the juice department of your market.) You'll want a loaf of French bread, cheese, salami, dill pickles, and any other good food items you both really like. Some fresh and pretty flowers will make the basket look really fun and inviting.

Love Basket Ideas

Now let me share with you some ideas I (Emilie) have for Love Baskets. I've been making Love Baskets for my Bob for more than 40 years. We all sense times when our husbands need a little extra attention. Maybe things have been tough at work, maybe he's depressed over something, or maybe he just needs to know he's needed and loved. Let your man know he's important to you and your life by putting together a Love Basket.

I remember saying to my friends and neighbors, "You know, my Bob needs a Love Basket tomorrow night, and I'd like to do it for him. Would you take the kids for a few hours for me? The next time your husband needs a Love Basket, I'll take your kids for you." I'll tell you, they're happy to do it! And I'm happy to do it for them.

Even though our kids are grown up now, I still prepare Love Baskets for my Bob. One time I called him at work in the morning and said, "Tonight I want to take you out to a special restaurant you've never been to before. It serves your very favorite food." He asked, "Well, where is it?" I replied, "I'm not going to tell you. It's just a special place in town that I'm going to take you to tonight. Can you be home by six o'clock?" Do you know what? He got home at five thirty!

What Bob didn't know was that during the morning I fried his very favorite Southern-fried chicken. I made potato salad, fruit salad, and some yummy rolls. I had the whole dinner prepared in the morning because I didn't want the delicious odors to give away the surprise.

Dinner on the Deck

At that time we lived in a two-story house with a deck off our bedroom that overlooked the city. It had a beautiful view of everything. We'd never had dinner up there, so I took up a card table and a couple of folding chairs. I spread the red-and-white gingham tablecloth on the table and centered the candleholder and a red candle. I put the special red plate on his side of the table. I placed a beautiful Valentine card right on the plate for him. In the bedroom I lit another candle and had music all ready to turn on. It was the most beautiful restaurant in town! And it was just gorgeous that night.

Bob came home and asked, "Well, where are we going?" I replied, "It's a surprise." He asked, "Do I have to change my clothes or anything?" I said, "No, you're perfect just the way you are." So I went into the kitchen and picked up the Love Basket filled with all his favorite foods and covered with a cloth. I handed him the basket and said, "Follow me." Bob knows now, after 40 years, that when the Love Basket comes out, really special things are going to happen. So he followed me eagerly.

Setting goals and planning for those goals with realistic expectations is what makes good things happen.

We went upstairs to where the candle was lit. I quickly started the music. As Bob walked out onto the deck, he saw that beautiful tablecloth with the candle and the red plate and the glasses and the napkins. He opened the Love Basket and took out the fried chicken and all the other special things. That evening we had a beautiful meal together enjoying each other, communicating with each other, and loving each other.

What was I telling Bob by doing this? I was telling him that he was loved, that he was important, and that I cared for him. I didn't have to tell him all I had done that day to prepare for our evening. He knew I took extra care to set the table and make it special. He knew I'd worked hard to create a dinner he would love. Do you know what he felt like? He felt like a king. He knew he was the second priority in my life (after Jesus, of course).

Jenny's Love Basket

Let me tell you a fun experience that my daughter, Jenny, had. She made a breakfast Love Basket for Bill when they were courting. On the morning they were going to Los Angeles for the day for business, Jenny put a Love Basket together. She included flowers, pretty cloth napkins, orange juice, bran muffins, fresh strawberries, and sliced cantaloupe. When Bill came to pick her up at six he couldn't believe his eyes. He'd never seen anything like that before, especially so early in the day.

Later Jenny said, "Mom, it was so great. We got in the car and I did everything. I put the napkin on his lap, and we ate on the freeway and had our Love Basket together." This is a sure way to get a husband—at least it worked for Jenny.

Sheri's Love Basket

When my (Sheri) sister, Teri, and I were both pregnant with our first babies, we decided to make Love Baskets for our hard-working husbands. We were eight months pregnant and it was the middle of July and very hot. We were miserable in the heat. We spent several hours frying chicken and making all the fixings. We created beautiful Love Baskets. When we were done we asked the guys to drive us to the mountains near our home to cool off. Teri and I hid everything in the back as a surprise, and off we went on our adventure. When we found a great place to pull off, we spread out a large quilt and set up a beautiful lunch surprise. We had a wonderful time, knowing our time as couples without children was coming to a close. We discussed becoming parents and how our lives were going to change. It was a great day and made terrific memories!

A Letter of Love

Let me (Emilie) share with you two letters I received from women who attended one of our More Hours in My Day seminars.

Dear Emilie:

I'm still thinking about your seminar and how much food for thought you offered. Everyone had to go away with treasures in thought, word, or deed. From your testimony to your organizing and all the helpful hints, I thank you. And the Love Basket—well, that was the best of them all. Just ask my husband. He got his first one Saturday night. He absolutely loved it—sparkling apple cider, candlelight, and all. He was so thrilled that he says he'll have to thank you personally for that one. It was so much fun! We had ours in our bedroom.

You also helped me so much by one statement you made about seeking and having a quiet and gentle spirit. God used you that night with my husband and answered my prayer for help concerning how to deal with and communicate with my son. I was getting all worked up and frustrated so I was arguing with him. Now I'm firm, gentle, and quiet…and it works. Thank You, Lord, and thank you, Emilie. I thought you'd like to hear that one because I want to encourage you to go on with your ministry as it's blessing lives.

Love,
Rosemary

Dear Emilie:

I've so much wanted to write and share with you. This has been on my heart for a long time.

I've always been a very proud person. So in my relationship with my husband, I would never give my all. I guess I feared he would make fun of me or use me. I was very cold; I never said or did nice things for him.

In your seminar you shared with us about the "Love Basket." It touched my heart. I talked with you after the seminar and shared with you that my husband had cancer. You said you would pray for us. Thank you for your prayers.

I decided to buy a basket and give my husband a "Love Basket." I went all out. I decorated and made a special meal. It was around Valentine's Day so I had a red tablecloth. I bought him a little present. He worked nights and came home at twelve thirty. I told him I would have a surprise for him when he came home. I really decked myself out for him, set my hair, and fixed my makeup. (He liked that...I was usually a slob at home.) When he walked in, he saw the table and candlelight. I greeted him with a kiss. We had a wonderful time. He told me it was the nicest thing I'd ever done for him. I'll cherish that time forever.

My husband died a month later. I pray that if you share this letter with the ladies you speak to, it might touch someone's heart like mine had been touched. Set aside your pride and give to your loved ones.

A friend in Christ,
Denise

36

Plan a Picnic

Why worry about your clothes?
Look at the field lilies!
They don't worry about theirs.

MATTHEW 6:28

What you do today is what you and your family will remember tomorrow. As mothers we want to purposefully plan and build warm memories to create those "special moments" that add to the foundation of a close, functioning family. Over the years I (Emilie) have helped create wonderful memories through family picnics.

Fun-filled recollections of special family times can happen by having a picnic at a park, lake, beach, mountains, desert, backyard, and other favorite areas. Many of our best picnics have been spur-of-the-moment, last-minute decisions based on the weather or a change in our schedule. However, with the hurried lifestyle we all have today, you may want to think ahead and reserve some time on your calendar. (There's a Picnic Planning Checklist at the end of this chapter to help you.)

Don't feel you always have to have excellent weather. Some of our fun times and special memories have occurred when the weather hasn't always been its best: an unexpected rain, high winds, dust storms, or rough waves at the beach.

While it's always nice to plan and prepare ahead, many times the best outings are the "Let's Have a Picnic" picnic—a quick raid on the refrigerator and cupboard and off you go to some pleasant spot under a shady tree. A good tuna sandwich, some pickles, fruit, and an icy drink always taste good outdoors.

I was four years old when my family took a picnic lunch to the desert under a yucca tree. The setting doesn't sound really exciting, but I can still remember the green-and-white checkered tablecloth my mother pulled out and spread on the sand. She took me by the hand, and we picked a few wildflowers for the centerpiece. From an old basket Mom pulled plates, glasses, plasticware, and some delicious food. After lunch we all took a nature walk. My brother and I still talk about that first picnic, and that was 60 years ago. What lasting memories!

As soon as I saw you, I knew an adventure was going to happen.

WINNIE THE POOH

Picnics are loved by everyone around the world and can be planned for any time of the year. Early American picnics were called "frolics" and consisted of games, music, flirtations, and plenty of good food. So why not plan a picnic with another family or several single-adult families and include a theme for the special occasion? Depending upon your geographic location and the time of year, you might consider:

❏ *Mardi Gras Feast*—chicken gumbo, steamed rice, marinated green beans, and New Orleans King Cake

❏ *Abalone Steak Picnic*—fried catfish, hush puppies, tomato slices, and lemon tarts

❏ *New England Clam Bake*—baked clams, Boston baked beans, brown bread, hot cider, and melon slices

❏ *Hawaiian Luau*—glazed chicken wings, rice salad, coconut, fruit, and Hawaiian punch

❏ *Vermont Snow Snack*—navy bean soup, stuffed baked potatoes, hot cocoa, and maple cupcakes

❏ *San Francisco Crab Lunch*—cracked crab, leafy salad, sourdough bread, and chocolate cake

❏ *Indian Summer Brunch*—cucumber salad, squaw bread, and smoked salmon

❏ *Midwest Corn Feed*—barbecued corn, vegetable cheese bake, whole-wheat bread, and apple pie with homemade ice cream

❏ *Pumpkin Patch Picnic*—hot pumpkin soup, apple spice cake, and hot wassail (cider)

❏ *Thanksgiving Dinner*—smoked turkey or roast duck, stuffed acorn squash, and spicy pumpkin bread

❏ *Plantation Buffet*—ham with orange glaze, candied yams, melon balls, pecan pie, and minted iced tea

❏ *Sundae Stop*—a variety of homemade ice cream with 15 different toppings—from nuts to cookie crumbs, from sprinkles to sauces

❏ *Mexican Memories*—taco salad, tortillas, iced lemon-limeade

❏ *All-American Apple Pie Picnic*—fried chicken, biscuits and honey, black-eyed pea salad, cold watermelon, and apple pie with cheese

Keeping Food Cold

After you've made the decision to have a picnic, decided on the theme, selected and prepared the food, you have to decide how to keep the food cold. Here are some guidelines to consider.

❏ The length of time in which food can spoil is relative to the temperature outdoors and the way the food was cooked, chilled, wrapped, and carried. Foods containing mayonnaise, eggs, cream, sour cream, yogurt, and fish are only safe unrefrigerated for up to two hours *if the weather is fairly cool.* If it will be more than two hours before you eat, carry the food in a refrigerated cooler. Cool dishes as quickly as possible after preparing them and leave them in the refrigerator until just before time to leave.

❏ Remember this cardinal rule: *Never take anything on a picnic that could possibly spoil unless you can provide effective portable refrigeration.*

❏ Ice chests or coolers can be chilled with ice cubes, crushed or chipped ice, blocks from ice machines, or water frozen in clean milk cartons or other containers.

❏ Fill plastic bottles (with lids) two-thirds full with water to allow for expansion and freeze them overnight. These frozen containers eliminate the mess of melted ice. Fruit juice in plastic bottles can also be frozen ahead and used in the cooler. Juice will also thaw readily.

❏ Dry ice may be used in coolers. Place it on top of foods because the chilling carbon dioxide, heavier than air, travels downward. Wrap dry ice in several layers of paper; never place it unwrapped in the cooler.

❏ Permanently sealed refrigerator blocks are very handy. They are several degrees colder than ice, can be kept in the freezer between picnics, and don't melt.

❏ Store cold drinks on the bottom with foods on top or in a separate compartment if the cooler is divided.

❏ You can count on heavily insulated metal coolers to keep food sufficiently cold from 24 to 48 hours. Inexpensive Styrofoam coolers work well for much shorter periods, depending on the weather and the amount of ice. Open all ice chests as little as possible after filling. Never allow coolers to stand open. Find a shady place for the cooler during the picnic and cover it with a blanket, beach towels, or a canvas tarpaulin.

❏ It's a good idea to transport mayonnaise in small containers in an ice chest, and then add the mayonnaise to salads or spread on sandwiches at the picnic site.

❑ Whipped cream can be transported in a sealed plastic jar or bowl in the cooler or take a wire whisk to whip the cream at the picnic.

❑ Combine rinsed, dried, torn, and chilled salad greens in a plastic bowl or bag that seals; keep chilled in cooler. Carry dressing in a separate container and toss salad at the last minute. Pack watercress, parsley, mint, grapes, lemon slices, and other garnishes in sealed bags for finishing dishes on-site.

❑ Add cold foods or liquids to thermoses that have been chilled with ice water or placed in the refrigerator for an hour. Food will stay cold from several hours to all day, depending on the weather and how often you open the container.

Packing, Transporting, and Storing Tips

❑ Prepare all food as close to departure time as comfortably possible. Don't cook something earlier unless the item can be frozen successfully.

❑ Whenever possible, pack your hamper or other carryall in reverse order from the way in which you'll use the items at the site: food on the bottom, then serving items and tableware, tablecloth on top.

❑ Always place food containers right side up to prevent spills and breakage. Leaking foods can ruin everything. If tops of containers don't fit securely, reinforce them with a band of masking tape around the lid. Play it very safe and put jars or bowls that might leak inside heavy-duty plastic bags and secure the top of the bag with tape, twist ties, or rubber bands.

❑ Breakable glassware can be wrapped in the tablecloth, napkins, kitchen towels, paper towels, or newspaper. Separate breakable items with plastic containers or soft goods when filling the hamper. Wrap fragile items well and place in a separate container to be held while traveling.

❑ Foods such as pies, tarts, cakes, muffins, mousses, molded salads, and home-baked breads that crumble easily can be carried in the pans in which they were prepared. At time of baking, cakes and bread are turned out to cool, then slipped back into their pans and wrapped in foil for protection en route. Coffee cans are handy to bake in and easy to carry. At the picnic, just open the bottom of the can with a can opener and push out the bread or cake.

❑ Use masking tape to hold spring form pans (with removable bottoms) in place while traveling. Consider taking the frosting separately for simple cakes baked in flat pans. Frost at the picnic site.

❑ Don't leave vacant spots in the picnic hamper or box. If the supplies don't fill the container, add rolled newspaper or paper towels to prevent foods from overturning or bumping together.

Bags

Shopping bags are excellent for holding everything for a simple picnic. In New York it's quite chic to be seen with a famous West Side deli bag packed with food. Save attractive shopping bags for transporting excess items that won't fit into the main picnic basket. Brown-paper market bags make wonderful carryalls. If the item you plan to carry is heavy, double the bags (place one inside the other) to give added strength. Children can decorate these bags to add flair to them, and it's a good activity to channel some of their excess energy. With some care, these bags can be reused several times.

Baskets

Wicker baskets or hampers are traditional picnic carryalls. However, anything goes these days. Import shops sell baskets made in many different shapes, sizes, and price ranges.

Plastic carriers, totes, canvas packs, and duffel bags all make great picnic baskets. Cartons, boxes, and chests can be used too.

Remember: The important part of a picnic is the time spent with your family and friends sharing your love.

Ground Covers and Tablecloths

Choose a blanket, patchwork quilt, bedspread, sheet, comforter, afghan, woolen throw, or any large piece of fabric for a ground cover or tablecloth. Top it, if you like, with a decorative second cloth that fits the mood of the picnic you've planned.

No-iron cotton or synthetic fabric is easy to keep clean and ready for traveling. Other choices are beach towels, bamboo or reed matting, nylon parachute fabric, flannel shirt material, or lengths of any easy-care fabric stitched at each end.

Purchase one or two plastic painter's drop cloths or carry a canvas tarpaulin to put down before you spread the tablecloth if the ground might be damp, dusty, or snow-covered.

Top off the setting with a centerpiece made by your children from resources taken from the area. This might include flowers, shells, wood, nuts, and rocks. You can help them gather these during a nature walk before food time. If your children show a special interest in what they find, follow up at your local library. Your picnic might become the stimulus for a new hobby.

Super Picnic Ideas

❑ *A Cooking Contest:* Let the various members of your family or invited guests bake their favorite recipe. Vote for your favorites and award special ribbons or prizes.

❑ *Winter Picnic Indoors:* Cover tables with red-and-white checkered cloths; set out salads, finger foods, and a basket of breads, plus plastic utensils and paper goods. Enjoy a carefree picnic indoors.

❑ *A Birthday That's Not for Kids Only:* So it's Billy's big day again. This time invite his friends' parents, too. Two parties are

better than one. One parent handles the children, and the
other parent hosts the grown-ups. Switch halfway through.

❑ *The Four-Part Picnic Party:* With a group of four couples, have
hors d'oeuvres at one home, salads at the next, the entrée at
another, and the dessert at the last. Collect recipes and make
cookbooks for everyone.

❑ *The Impromptu Picnic:* Call up some friends in the afternoon
and pick up a party on the way to the picnic area. Stop for
chicken, fast food, drinks, dips, and chips.

❑ *Going Fishing:* All aboard! Rent a boat for the day, and invite
some friends along. Each person can bring his or her own
food or, for a small contribution by each person, one person
can make the food and bring it along. It's a lot of fun even if
only a few fish are caught.

❑ *A Block Party:* Have one section of your neighborhood or one
floor of your apartment complex supply appetizers, have
another bring main dishes, and another bring desserts.

❑ *Potluck Picnic:* Don't forget this favorite old-fashioned way to
get to know neighbors and try out new recipes. Ask people
to bring their best or favorite dishes to this picnic.

Picnic Planning Checklist

In the Refrigerator
- ☑ Beverages
- ☐ Breads/muffins
- ☐ Butter/margarine
- ☐ Cheeses/spreads
- ☐ Eggs
- ☑ Fruit
- ☐ Ketchup/Worchestershire sauce
- ☐ Lemons and limes
- ☐ Meats
- ☐ Milk/cream
- ☐ Mustard/mayonnaise
- ☐ Pickles/olives
- ☑ Relishes
- ☐ Salad makings/sandwich garnishes
- ☑ Sparkling apple cider
- ☐ Vegetables

In the Freezer
- ☐ Breads
- ☐ Cakes/cookies
- ☐ Cheeses
- ☐ Chopped onions/peppers
- ☑ Coffee (decaffeinated)
- ☐ Homemade broths/soups
- ☑ Ice
- ☐ Pie crusts
- ☐ Sandwiches (w/o mayonnaise or lettuce)
- ☐ Vegetables

On the Shelves
- ☑ Beverages
- ☐ Canned brown bread and nut bread
- ☐ Canned fish
- ☐ Canned meats
- ☐ Canned soups and broths
- ☐ Canned vegetables
- ☐ Chips
- ☑ Chocolate chips/candies
- ☐ Cookies
- ☐ Crackers
- ☐ Dried fruits
- ☐ Garlic salt
- ☐ Herbs/spices
- ☐ Marinated artichoke hearts

On the Shelves (continued)
- ☑ Nuts/trail mix snacks
- ☐ Olive oil/salad oil
- ☐ Olives
- ☐ Onions/garlic
- ☑ Peanut butter
- ☐ Pimentos /peppers
- ☐ Powdered milk
- ☐ Salt and pepper
- ☐ Sugar/honey
- ☐ Vinegar

Equipment
- ☑ Athletic equipment
- ☐ Basket, hamper/tote
- ☑ Can/bottle opener
- ☑ Charcoal (self-starting)
- ☐ Coffee creamer
- ☐ Cups: plastic, insulated
- ☐ First-aid kit
- ☑ Flashlight
- ☐ Flatware: plastic or stainless steel
- ☐ Folding stove/hibachi
- ☐ Folding table
- ☐ Fuel/matches
- ☑ Games
- ☐ Glasses: plastic or glass
- ☐ Insect repellant
- ☐ Knives
- ☐ Mess kits: plastic or metal
- ☐ Moist towelettes
- ☐ Napkins: paper or cloth
- ☑ Paper towels
- ☐ Plastic/canvas groundcloth
- ☐ Plastic food containers, wraps, or bags
- ☑ Plates: paper or plastic
- ☐ Portable seating: folding chairs or stools
- ☑ Serving spoons
- ☐ Tablecloth
- ☐ Temporary shelter/shade
- ☐ Thermoses, cooler/ice chest
- ☑ Trash bags
- ☐ Tupperware containers
- ☑ Vase or jar for flowers

37

Creative Entertaining

Don't forget to be kind to strangers,
for some who have done this have
entertained angels without realizing it!

Hebrews 13:2

S omething I (Emilie) discovered years ago was the idea of using sheets as tablecloths and napkins. One of the things that is great about using sheets is you get lots of fabric for a modest amount of money, and they're all wash-and-wear. You can wash them, throw them into the dryer, and put them right back on the table. So throw away the plastic cloth you've wiped off for years and get into sheets!

If you're going to be married or want to buy a new set of dishes, consider a plain set of white or bone dishes. They will go with any tablecloth and whatever else you decorate with. We can't all go out and do that, so we may have to do with what we have. My everyday dishes happen to be brown-and-white calico. I started looking for sheets that would go with them, and it's been a lot of fun! One set I bought in the basement of a department store. The sheets have a little border on the bottom and black and white and brown on the top.

Using What We Have

Now you say, "Well, Emilie, you've got a design border across the bottom of the sheet. Do you cut it off? You often only have one border per sheet." No, I don't cut off the border. I place the sheet so the border shows on the most obvious end of the table. This way, as you walk into my dining room or family room, you see the sheet on the table with the border showing. Nobody has ever come into my house and run around to the other side of the table to see if there's a border over there.

I took the bottom sheet (the fitted sheet), which happened to be a print, and made napkins.

For napkin holders I use small, star-shaped cookie cutters. Or I might use those big fat paper clips available at stationery stores. They come in bright colors and make great little gifts. Add some white daisies on the table, and I have a pretty table setting at very low cost.

Placemats

Placemats are another nice thing to have. You can make them out of quilted fabric. A yard-and-a-half of fabric will make four placemats. Double the quilted fabric and put the two right sides together. Cut each into 14x22 inch pieces and sew all the way around except for about 4 inches at the top. Then reverse it, and tuck in the top where the opening was. Stitch it all the way around two times to get a double stitching. (That makes it stay nice and flat. It's a little heavier on the edges and stays firmly on the table.) These placemats can go in the washing machine, in the dryer, and back on the table.

The Red Plate

One December the Bible-study group I led completed the year with a salad luncheon. We finished early in the month so the women could have time to prepare for the holiday and spend time with their families. The women presented me with one of the best gifts I've ever received. It was a red plate with beautiful white lettering around the outside that said, "You Are Special Today." My heart felt warm and so very special. They were expressing their thanks and love through this unique item. As we shared each other's salads that day, I ate off the special red plate.

I discovered that the plate was hand-glazed of fine ceramic and is like no other plate. No two are exactly alike, even though a company makes them. I was now the owner of an original red plate!

Knowing how I felt when I received the red plate, I wanted to share that same feeling with other people. On Christmas Day that year it was warm and cozy, and the smell of pine and roasting turkey filled our home. Our family of 26 gathered around the buffet table for a time of praise and thanksgiving. Now was the time to present the red plate to a special person.

My Bob and I chose as our honoree a person who came into our lives and family just that year. Our daughter, Jenny, was married that August, and Bill, her new husband, was the most special gift of God to us as a family. I wish you could have seen his eyes and the cute smile that crossed his face when we announced he was the one who got to eat Christmas dinner off the "You Are Special Today" red plate.

More Happiness

Our red plate use didn't end there. As February came along, I planned a special dinner for my husband to celebrate Valentine's Day. I made a Love Basket filled with his favorite foods, and we had dinner on our patio outside our bedroom.

The card table I set up looked delightful with a red-and-white gingham cloth, white eyelet napkins, lit candle, flowers, and at Bob's place the "You Are Special Today" red plate. I knew he was making his choice of who would be his special Valentine, and I wanted to be the one! At the sight of the table with

> *Schedule your "dates" with your husband in your planner just as you would for a client or customer. Your spouse will feel special.*

the plate, all so simple, yet so beautiful, my Bob expressed his love and thanks for making him feel like he was my number one man. This was another way of telling him I loved him and appreciated all he did for our family.

God tells us in His Word that we are to encourage each other and build each other up (1 Thessalonians 5:11). I've also discovered that the red plate was an American tradition the early families used when someone deserved special praise or attention. Now, generations later, let's return to this custom and feed on the positive. I continue to remind my Bible-study women to tell *God* the negatives about their husbands and families, and tell people the positive.

When my son, Brad, turned 21, we had a family dinner to celebrate this special year. As he sat down at his place, there sat the red plate, telling him, "We're proud of you. We're proud that God gave us a son, and now you're a man. Bless you, our son, as you meet life with God's hand on yours."

By then we'd purchased a special pen that writes on ceramic and won't wash off. We listed on the back of the plate the dates and special occasions it was used for. As the years pass we'll always have the remembrance of each special time and date.

Several years ago Bob and I discipled and counseled two special young women. They wanted to do something special for Bob, and as his birthday was drawing near, they invited both of us out for lunch. I took the red plate along, hidden in my tote bag. We asked the waitress to serve Bob his lunch on the "You Are Special Today" plate. Bob was so surprised when the red plate appeared with lunch served on it! The chef was chuckling along with all the other people that day as they watched him receive his food. Did he feel special? You bet!

Building the Good

I'm more excited than ever to accent the positive and build good self-esteem in others with this plate. Our plate is priceless now and becoming a family heirloom that could be handed down from generation to generation, especially with all the occasions and dates listed on the back.

I suggested to a mother, who was in a dilemma as to what to give her son's teacher at the end of the school year, the possibility of collecting 50 cents per child from the class and purchasing a "You Are Special Today" plate (with pen) and having all the children sign and date the back. "Great idea!" she exclaimed, and did so. As she related the opening of the gift, her eyes filled with joy as the teacher read the beautiful lettering "You Are Special Today," the names on the back, and hugged the plate.

In my husband's family there are three sons: Bob, his twin brother, Bill, and younger brother, Ken. Their birthdays all fall in the same month, a day apart. Bob's mother, Gertie, always made a big celebration for their birthdays. I wanted to take the red plate along, again hidden in my tote bag, but I didn't have three plates. So, thinking of a creative way to use the plate, I decided it was natural to use it for Gertie. After our blessing I took Mom Gertie's hands and thanked her for her love and warmth over the years. What a special lady to have given three daughters-in-law such wonderful husbands. We expressed our thanks for her time and love to all our children (her 14 grandchildren). There was no doubt she was the one that day who needed to experience the magic of the red plate.

By now I'm sure you're seeing the excitement of using a plate to speak volumes of love when words aren't enough. Other ideas for the plate include a job promotion, homecoming, when an old friend visits, good report card, new baby, graduation, engagement, Father's Day, anniversary, Mother's Day, winning the big game. You can even use it when someone needs cheered up.

God bless you as you build up the positive in other people!

PART FIVE

More Hours…
for Your Children

38

Children Need to Be Organized Too

Train a child in the way he should go,
and when he is old he will not turn from it.

Proverbs 22:6 NIV

When Brad and Jenny were young there was difficulty because their idea and my (Emilie) idea of organization were different—like the North Pole and South Pole. I had to continually remind myself that this period of life and theirs doesn't last for more than a few years. It would pass soon.

Today there are many times when I walk down the hall and wish I could look into their rooms and find a crooked bedspread. They aren't living at home anymore, and I miss those days of clutter. Happily I can report that both children are grown, and in many areas they've become more organized than I am. They were listening and watching during those tense years. Here are a few ideas that did work at the time, and I'm sure they'll work for you too.

❏ Keep socks sorted by pinning them together with a safety pin or clipping them together with clothespins. Put the child's initials on socks with a black paint pen.

❏ Review the family calendar together. On Sunday evening we went over our large desktop calendar to see where we were all going to be during the coming week. Were there any transportation or babysitting needs—any church activities, birthday parties, holidays? Was homework ready for Monday at school? Were any gifts needed for the week? This let us touch bases and make sure we were all on the same schedule.

❏ Have one area where the children place all their school items when they come home. I used colored bins by the front door where each child would put his/her gym clothes, homework, schoolbooks. After they do their homework, have them return their school materials to this place. This saves a lot of last-minute hunting for items before running off to school.

❏ Have a dress-up box available for those spontaneous plays your children perform on days they're inside because of weather. Today I use these old clothes for the grandchildren when they come over.

❏ Have a box of games, toys, and coloring books to take with you on long trips. Also bring along an old sheet and spread it on the backseat and floor. Let all the debris fall on the sheet. When you get to your destination, all you have to do is pull out the sheet, shake it on the ground, and put it back into the car. No more worrying or nagging about crumbs.

> *While we try to teach our children all about life, our children teach us what life is about.*
>
> ANGELA SCHWINDT

❏ Some areas or rooms can be off-limits, if you desire. I have a very valuable collection of china cups and saucers. The grandchildren know those shelves are off-limits, but also that one day, when they're older, they will be able to pick up the dishes.

❏ Color-code your children's items. Jenny knew the yellow towels were hers, and Brad knew his were blue. This color system can be used in many other areas of the home.

❏ Make sure each child has a place to hang clothes and store belongings. This place doesn't have to be an expensive dresser or organizer. Many times plastic bins and wooden crates work fine.

❏ Put the masterpieces of your young artists on the refrigerator, bulletin board, or in a folder designated for that child's age or grade in school. Some of the extra artwork can be used to wrap grandparents' gifts.

❏ Clean out a bedroom before the arrival of new items. Before birthdays, Christmas, and the change of seasons, go through the bedroom with the child, helping clean out old items, broken toys, and clothes that are too small. Be sure to use the three-bag system: 1) Give Away/Recycle, 2) Put Away, and 3) Throw Away. (Reread the chapter "Total Mess to Total Rest.") Give items to friends, neighbors, or church groups.

❏ Children need shelves, hooks, and bins for their toys and possessions. Let them help decide where these items should be placed in their rooms.

❏ Put books and games on lower shelves in the playroom. Paint, clay, scissors, crayons, and anything you don't want kids to play with unsupervised go on the upper, out-of-reach shelves.

❏ Each bedroom needs a bulletin board to hold pictures, awards, certificates, postcards, and special items.

❏ Each child needs to have a study center. Make sure there is plenty of light, basic supplies of pencils, pens, paper, paper clips, a stapler, ruler, hole punch, and rubber bands. If you don't have room, put all these items into a color-coded plastic bin so each child has his or her own supplies that can be carried to an area where homework is done.

❏ Have a list of emergency numbers by the telephone. When going out for the evening, review with the children and their babysitter where you are going, the phone number, and the approximate time you'll be home.

39

Safety Tips for Schoolchildren

*Better the little that the righteous have than the
wealth of many wicked; for the power
of the wicked will be broken, but the LORD
upholds the righteous.*

PSALM 37:16-17 NIV

As our children were growing up, I (Emilie) never was concerned about their safety as they went from home to school and then back to home. We had neighborhood schools, everyone knew each other, and it was a kinder world. But over the years a lot has changed and caused us to be more and more conscious of safety for children in all situations.

These school transportation safety tips could save your children's lives.

Here Comes the Yellow Bus

With more and more children taking the bus to school, teach your children to:

- ❑ remain seated and keep the aisles clear.
- ❑ not throw objects.
- ❑ not make loud noises or distract the driver.
- ❑ keep arms, head, and legs inside the bus.

❏ wait for the bus to stop before exiting.

❏ make sure they get on the correct bus.

❏ help new riders so they feel welcomed to the new school.

Riding Bicycles to School

If your children ride bikes to school, make sure they are at least eight years old and teach them to:

❏ choose a safe route, which may not be the same as a safe walking route. Young bicyclists should stay away from busy streets.

❏ wear a helmet each time they ride their bicycles.

❏ keep their bicycles in good working order. Fix any parts that aren't working properly. Keep the correct air pressure in the tires.

❏ avoid night bicycle riding. Darkness drastically increases the chances of having an injury even if the bikes are equipped with lights and reflectors.

❏ insist on only one rider per bicycle unless it is built for multiple riders.

❏ store the bicycles in an enclosed area away from traffic.

In Your Car

❏ Make sure all children use seat belts.

❏ Remove any heavy or loose objects that could become airborne if you were in an accident.

❏ Let children out of your car on the sidewalk on the school side of the street. Avoid having them cross a street to get to school.

❏ Pick children up at a safe place away from the congested area of cars.

❑ If carpooling, take added safety precautions. You are carrying your kids and someone else's most-prized possessions.

A Good Walk Will Do Them Good

❑ Walking is great exercise, and children have good, young, strong legs.

❑ Choose the safest route for your child before the first day of school. Opt for the most direct route with the fewest street crossings. Let the child go on a couple dry runs on his or her own before that first day.

❑ Have your children take the same route to and from school each day.

❑ Warn your children to not be distracted by strangers and to not go up to any strangers who might ask them for directions or information. It's better for children to be rude in this area and remain safe.

❑ Teach your children about all traffic markings. Explain the different color of lights and all signs. Even though the lights flash green, teach your children to look both ways before stepping out in the street. Remind them to be patient and wait for lights to change—even if no cars are coming. Let them know it's okay to wait even if others don't.

❑ Instruct your children to always use pedestrian crosswalks when crossing a street or to cross at corners when there aren't crosswalks.

❑ Warn your children to not cross a street between parked cars or behind buses.

❑ Emphasize to your children to look left, right, and then left again before crossing the street.

Calling for Help

Post these numbers near your telephone. (See chapter 6 for a handy Important Numbers chart.)

- ❑ Emergency medical services (9-1-1)
- ❑ Fire and police departments (9-1-1)
- ❑ Ambulance and nearest hospital
- ❑ Physician
- ❑ Pharmacist
- ❑ Poison control center
- ❑ Gas company
- ❑ Electric company (customer service and 24-hour service numbers)
- ❑ Water company
- ❑ Dependable neighbors' numbers
- ❑ Any work numbers for you or your husband

Establish a message center in your home. It needn't be elaborate—it can be on the refrigerator or on a bulletin board or door. Encourage everyone to use the message center to list plans, needs for the next trip to the grocery store, and—especially important—all telephone messages. Keep the message center current; throw away outdated notes.

40

Resolutions for Good Parenting

*When times are good, be happy; but when times
are bad, consider: God has made the one
as well as the other.*

ECCLESIASTES 7:14 NIV

There are two times of the year when we usually write down resolutions: New Year's Day and the beginning of school for our children. Here are some suggestions.

❏ Don't let children watch TV, play video games, or spend too much time on the computer on school nights (at least not until *all* their homework is completed). These activities waste a lot of creative time.

❏ Don't let feelings of inadequacy creep up on you if your children aren't doing well in certain subjects or even the whole grade. The primary responsibility is on the child; however, you do need to support and encourage the learning process.

❏ Homework is for your children. This is a difficult resolution. Provide an adequate study area with proper light and space. Let them know you are available to help when absolutely needed. Their responsibility is to do their homework on a timely basis. While they are studying, protect them from distractions such as loud noises, interruptions, TV, telephone calls, and visitors. Assist your children's schoolteachers by making sure the work is done on time.

❏ Don't bail your children out when they leave their lunch and books at home—or when they leave their books at school. They'll soon get the idea that it's their responsibility.

❏ Don't do large projects for your children. It's okay to help, but it's their responsibility to research and complete it.

People were bringing little children to Jesus to have him touch them, but the disciples rebuked them. When Jesus saw this, he was indignant. He said to them, "Let the little children come to me, and do not hinder them, for the kingdom of God belongs to such as these. I tell you the truth, anyone who will not receive the kingdom of God like a little child will never enter it." And he took the children in his arms, put his hands on them and blessed them.

MARK 10:13-16 NIV

❏ Support your child's teacher. It's so important that your child realizes you support his or her teacher. If you have a difference of opinion with the teacher, set up an appointment to discuss it without your children present.

❏ Let your children solve their own social problems unless the situation is extraordinary. (With the increase in violence in our schools, this may not always be an easy resolution to keep.) Children need to learn to work out their differences.

❏ Teach the 3 Rs at home (respect, responsibility, resourcefulness), and let the teacher teach his or hers (reading, 'riting, and 'rithmetic). Send children to school who are ready to learn.

❏ Don't push your children into your areas of interest. Wait until they express a desire to participate. Children today are overscheduled with outside activities. Don't drain the children's energy or your free time.

❏ Let your children grow and excel in the gifts God has given them. Most children can't be good in all subjects or be interested in all outside activities. Let them succeed in their strengths.

❏ Let your children know you're on their team. Show a positive interest in their school activities. Teachers can do a better job of instructing your children if they know you're interested in your children's learning. Teachers cry out, "Where are the interested parents?"

41

Jobs Children Can Do

Children are a gift from God; they are his reward.

PSALM 127:3

Delegating responsibility to children is such an important aspect of motherhood, and you can start when your children are fairly young. A three year old can dress himself, put his pajamas away, brush his hair, brush his teeth, and make his bed. Two and three year olds can fold clothes, empty the dishwasher (they may need some help; begin by having them unload plastic things), clear dishes off the table, empty wastebaskets, and pick up toys before bedtime (plastic baskets are excellent for toys). Make it fun for them; create games out of the jobs.

Training Our Children

Proverbs 22:6 (NASB) says, "Train up a child in the way he should go, even when he is old he will not depart from it." As Christian parents we want to train our children and direct them so they develop good habits and social skills. When they become adults we don't want them to be domestic invalids.

Five year olds can set the table, clean the bathrooms, and straighten drawers and closets. As you go through your home, take your little ones with you and show them what you're doing. Often children don't even realize there's toothpaste on the mirror. They haven't been taught to notice or been told to wipe it up. They think it just somehow disappears.

More things children can do are clean up after the pet, feed the cat, walk the dog, dust the furniture. They may do a sloppy job of dusting, but don't go back and do it over right away. Wait until tomorrow. Let them move the dust around so they see the responsibilities you're fulfilling. Many of you work outside your home and then do a full-time job at home. Delegate some responsibilities to your children—for their sakes and yours!

Seven and Up

Seven year olds can empty the garbage, sweep walks, help in the kitchen after dinner, and prepare lunches for school. (If a child makes his own lunch, he's less likely to complain about it!) They can help clean out the car. (Then they'll realize they have to clean up the messes they make in the car when you're driving them around. You'll find that when their friends get in the car, your children will say, "We don't drop things in our car.")

Do you know what you call those who use towels and never wash them, eat meals and never do the dishes, sit in rooms they never clean, and are entertained till they drop? If you...answered, "A houseguest," you're wrong because I have just described my kids.

ERMA BOMBECK

A seven year old can learn to iron. When our daughter, Jenny, was eight years old she was doing all the laundry in our home, from washing it to putting it in the dryer (or hanging it up) to folding it. These are things children can learn to do, and it even helps their physical coordination. An eight year old can wash bathroom mirrors, wash the windows, wash the floors in small areas, and polish shoes.

As the children grow older they can be given more and more responsibilities, such as washing the car, mowing the lawn, making dessert, painting, and cleaning the refrigerator.

When our children were growing up, we delegated to each of them one night a week when they completely prepared dinner. Food could be their choice with what was on hand or what was on the Menu Planner, but they were to make the meal. If you do this, you'll find out how creative your children are! One family I (Emilie) know had one child cook and one child clean up. But often the cook was very messy so there was a lot of complaining. Eventually they had the same child cook and clean up. This worked great.

Teaching Children

Deuteronomy 6:5-7 (NASB) says, "You shall love the LORD your God with all your heart and with all your soul and with all your might. These words, which I am commanding you today, shall be on your heart. You shall teach them diligently to your sons and shall talk of them when you sit in your house and when you walk by the way and when you lie down and when you rise up." We need to be instructing our children in all areas: teach them when we're in the kitchen, teach them about God's creation when we're bicycling together, teach them while we're making a lunch or preparing a picnic, teach them as we're at the park and the beach. We're to teach them many things as we build our homes around God and our families, and as we organize and reveal our creativity.

As we allow our children to do some of the work for us, they begin to realize they are vital parts of the family. Families who work together and play together also love together, pray together, and worship God together. Let's raise children who are balanced people, who will become creative, responsible adults with wonderful homes of their own!

Jobs for Your Children
Three year olds

- ❏ Get dressed, put pajamas away
- ❏ Brush hair
- ❏ Brush teeth
- ❏ Make bed

❏ Fold clothes and small items

❏ Empty dishwasher (will need help)

❏ Clear meal dishes

❏ Empty wastebaskets

❏ Pick up toys before bed

Five year olds

❏ Set table

❏ Clean bathroom sink

❏ Help clean and straighten drawers and closets

❏ Clean up after pet

❏ Feed pet

❏ Walk dog

❏ Dust furniture in a room

❏ Vacuum a room

❏ Help put groceries away

Seven year olds

❏ Empty garbage

❏ Sweep walks

❏ Help in kitchen after dinner

❏ Help make lunch for school

❏ Do schoolwork

❏ Clean out car

❏ Take music lessons

❏ Iron flat items

Eight year olds.

❏ Wash bathroom mirrors

❏ Wash windows

❏ Wash floors in small area

❏ Polish shoes

❏ Shred mail

As your children grow, more responsibility can be given to them.

❏ Wash car

❏ Mow lawn

❏ Make dessert

❏ Paint

❏ Clean refrigerator

❏ Do yard work

❏ Iron

❏ Fix a simple meal

❏ Do grocery shopping

When my (Sheri) daughter, Terra, was 15 years old, she could cook an entire turkey dinner. She wanted to learn to cook, and I was delighted to teach her. I knew it would come in handy someday. The first year my adult children lived in New York, they couldn't come home for Thanksgiving. Terra cooked Thanksgiving dinner with little input from me, and their guests raved about the meal.

Children need to know they are valuable to the family and that they are needed for the family to function properly. Kids will have a positive attitude toward themselves when they are around people who believe in their worth. Let them help and feel needed; let them do important jobs. The outcome of the job isn't as important as helping your children develop skills and confidence. Whenever we appreciate their contributions, no matter how small—and tell them!—we are helping them see themselves as capable, productive people.

Helpful Hints

❏ *From a creative mother:* After many nights of interrupted sleep, I finally hit on a solution that keeps my five year old in her own bed—at least most nights. I labeled one bowl "Mama's Bed Buttons" and another "Christine's Bed Buttons" and put 25 small buttons in each. For every night Christine stays in bed, I owe her one button. She pays me a button if she gets in bed with me. When her bowl is filled, we do something special—a roller-skating trip, a movie, an outing of her choice. Now she only comes to my bed if she really feels she needs to.

❏ One most-appreciated gift a neighbor gave me (Emilie) after the birth of my first baby was a freshly baked apple pie with a card attached worth eight hours of free babysitting. The pie hit the spot since I was tired of eating hospital food, and it was reassuring to know there was someone available close by to babysit if needed.

❏ Once a year have a babysitter swap party. Each attendee must bring the names and telephone numbers of three reliable sitters.

❏ A tasty variation on the standard peanut-butter-and-jelly sandwich: Make the sandwich as usual, but just before serving, butter the outside of the bread, and brown the sandwich in a hot skillet.

❏ When sewing buttons on children's clothing, use elastic thread. It makes buttoning much easier for little fingers.

❏ When you buy your children a fruit or soft drink, cut the straw off short so it is easier to hold and handle. There is less chance of a child spilling or dropping the drink too.

Children and Money

For the man who uses well what he is given shall
be given more, and he shall have abundance.

MATTHEW 25:29

We live in a world where adults often find themselves in financial trouble. Where and how do we learn about money? We usually learn by trial and error. Few families take the time to teach their children how to be smart with money. In light of today's finances we need to teach children at an early age about money and what it can do for them.

Children who know how to handle money effectively will be ahead in this mystery game of life. Learning to deal with money properly fosters discipline, good work habits, and self-respect. Here are several ways you can help your children.[1]

1. *Start with an allowance.* Most experts advise that an allowance should not be tied directly to a child's daily chores. Children should help around the home not because they get paid for it, but because they share responsibilities as members of a family. However, you might pay children for doing extra jobs at home. This may develop their initiative. We know of parents who give stickers to their children when the children do a chore they haven't been asked to do. At the children's discretion, they may redeem the stickers for 25 cents each. This has been a great motivator for initiative and for teaching teamwork in the family.

An allowance is a vital tool for showing children how to budget, save, and make their own decisions. Children remember and learn from mistakes when their own money is lost or spent foolishly.

How large of an allowance you give your children depends on your financial status and beliefs. A fair budget allows for entertainment, snacks, lunch money, bus fare, and school supplies. Add some extra money for giving to church and saving. Be willing to hold your children responsible for living within their budget. Some weeks they may have to go without when they run out of money.

2. *Model the proper use of credit.* In today's society we see the results of individuals and couples using bad judgment regarding credit. Explain to children why it's necessary to use credit and the importance of developing a good credit history by paying their loans back on a timely basis. You can make this a great teaching tool. Their first loan might be from you to them for a special purchase. Go through all the mechanics that a bank would: Have them fill out a credit application and sign a paper with all the information stated. Teach them about interest, installment payments, balloon payments, late-payment costs, and so forth. Guide them to be responsible about paying on time.

3. *Teach your children how to save.* In today's instant society, it's hard to teach this lesson. At times we should deny our children certain material things so they have a reason to save. As they get older they will want bicycles, stereos, a car, a big trip. This will help them relate to establishing the habit of saving for major purchases.

One of the first ways to begin teaching the concept of savings is to give the children a piggy bank. Spare change or extra earnings go into the piggy bank, and when the bank gets full they can open an account at a local bank.

When they're older, establish a passbook account at a local bank so they can go to the bank and deposit money in their account. Another option is to load a prepaid credit card so they can understand how credit cards work and understand how important it is to watch the balance.

Children who learn how to handle money better appreciate what they've worked to acquire.

4. *Show them how to be wise in their spending.* Take your children with you when you shop. Discuss cost comparisons and quality and quantity. They will soon see that with a little effort they can save a lot of money. Show them in a tangible way about value shopping. When they want to purchase a larger item for themselves, go to several stores and write down the most expensive price and the least amount for the same item. Let them choose which one they want to purchase, and pay them the difference between what they chose and the most expensive. This way they can really see the savings.

Clothing is an area where a lot of lessons on wise spending can be made. After a while children realize that designer clothes cost a lot more because of that label or patch. Jenny, Emilie's daughter, soon learned that outlet stores were great bargains for saving dollars. To this day she looks for bargains by comparison shopping.

5. *Let children work part-time.* There are many excellent part-time jobs waiting for your child. Fast-food outlets, markets, malls, yard work, and babysitting are some options that give valuable work experience to your children. Some entrepreneurial youngsters even begin a thriving business around their skills and interest. These part-time jobs are real confidence boosters. Just remember to help them keep a proper balance between work, home, church, and school. A limit of 10 to 15 hours per week might be a good work guideline.

6. *Let them help you with your expenses.* Encourage your children to help you budget the family finances and pay for expenses. This gives them experience in real-life money problems. Children's ideas are generally good when it comes to suggestions about how we can better utilize the family finances. This will also give them a better understanding of why your family can't afford certain luxuries.

7. *Give them experience in handling adult expenses.* As your children get older, they need to experience real-life costs. Since children live at home, they don't always share in true-to-life expenses. Let

them experience paying for their own telephone, car, and clothing expenses. Depending upon the situation, help in paying a portion of the utility and household bills would be a valuable experience for children who have left school and are still living at home.

8. *Give to the Lord.* Parents and children should talk about where things come from. Even very young children should be aware that all things are given by God, and He is just letting us borrow them for a time. Children can understand that we are to return back to God a portion of what He has so abundantly given to us. This principle can be experienced either through their Sunday school giving or church offerings. When special projects at church come up, you might want to review the need with your children so they can decide if they want to give extra monies above what they normally give to their church. Early training in this area lays a solid foundation for becoming a giver in life.

Your children will learn about money from you, so be a good model. As they get older, they will imitate what you do. If you have good habits, they will reflect that; if you struggle with finances, chances are so will they.

One valuable lesson to teach is that money doesn't reflect love. A hug, a smile, a kiss, and time spent together is much more valuable.

Money never made a man happy yet, nor will it. There is nothing in its nature to produce happiness. The more a man has, the more he wants. That was a true proverb of the wise man, rely upon it: "Better is little with the fear of the Lord, than great treasure, and trouble therewith."

BENJAMIN FRANKLIN

Children's Budget Worksheet

Name _____

Activity Period _____

Income	Weekly	Monthly
Allowance	$_____	$_____
Gifts	$_____	$_____
Outside work	$_____	$_____
Other	$_____	$_____
Total Income	$_____	$_____

Expenses

	Weekly	Monthly
Saving (10%)	$_____	$_____
Giving		
Tithe (10%)	$_____	$_____
Gifts	$_____	$_____
Other	$_____	
Spending		
Clothes	$_____	$_____
Food	$_____	$_____
Music	$_____	$_____
Hobbies	$_____	$_____
Entertainment	$_____	$_____
School	$_____	$_____
Other	$_____	$_____
Total Expenses	$_____	$_____
*Extra monies left over	$_____ +	$_____ +
*Short monies	$_____ –	$_____ –

* With extra money ask, "Where should this money go?" With a shortage of money ask, "What am I going to adjust or eliminate?"

A Daily Plan
▪ Notes ▪

A Daily Plan

*Be beautiful inside, in your hearts, with the
lasting charm of a gentle and quiet spirit
that is so precious to God.*

1 PETER 3:4

Sample Daily Routine

A. Start your day the night before.

> *She is energetic, a hard worker, and watches for bargains.
> She works far into the night!*
> PROVERBS 31:17-18

❏ Gather, sort, and wash laundry.

❏ Set the breakfast table.

❏ Lay out vitamins in individual cups.

❏ Set up coffeepot for the morning.

❏ Make a to-do list of what must be done the next day.

B. Get up early.

> *She gets up before dawn to prepare breakfast for her household
> and plans the day's work for her servant girls.*
> PROVERBS 31:15

❑ Make the bed.

❑ Put on a decent robe or attractive clothes.

❑ Do at least a light makeup job and hair combing.

❑ Put in the first load of wash.

C. Advance to the kitchen.

> *She watches carefully all that goes on throughout*
> *her household and is never lazy.*
> PROVERBS 31:27

❑ Rejoice that the table is set and attractive.

❑ Cook breakfast and put out butter, milk, etc.

❑ Call everyone to the table with a two-minute warning.

❑ Serve everyone at once and sit down yourself. (Don't be a short-order cook.)

❑ Remind everyone to take vitamins.

❑ Review each person's day, noting where you are needed.

❑ Have everyone scrape their dishes and take them to the sink.

❑ Put all dishes in the sink to soak in hot water.

❑ Quickly put away perishables.

D. Say farewell to the family.

> *When she speaks, her words are wise,*
> *and kindness is the rule for everything she says.*
> PROVERBS 31:26

❑ See if your husband needs help from you.

❑ Check each child's room *with* him or her.

❑ See that the bed is made and clothes are hung up or in the wash.

❑ Check the bathroom for dirty clothes and for cleanliness.

- ❑ Check to see that each child has a lunch, money, books, homework, gym clothes, etc.

- ❑ Compliment them on how well they have done something.

- ❑ Send them off with a loving hug.

- ❑ Be a smiling mother, not a screaming shrew.

- ❑ *Remember:* "It's not what you expect, but what you inspect."

E. Back to work.

> *She is energetic, a hard worker.*
> PROVERBS 31:17

- ❑ Put clothes in dryer and start a second load of wash.

- ❑ Do the dishes.

- ❑ Do advance dinner preparation—brown hamburger for a casserole, cook rest of bacon for future use, make a dessert, prepare Jell-O, etc.

- ❑ Clean up counters.

- ❑ Water houseplants.

- ❑ Do general housecleaning for 15 minutes a day in an area of your home.

- ❑ Rejoice that your basic housework is done and it's still early!

F. Prepare the home for the evening.

> *She watches carefully all that goes on throughout her household and is never lazy. Her children stand and bless her; so does her husband. He praises her with these words: "There are many fine women in the world, but you are the best of them all!"*
> PROVERBS 31:27-29

❏ Light a fire and candles (seasonal).

❏ Prepare munchies if dinner is a bit late: energy mix, raisins and nuts, sour cream and cottage cheese dip with carrot sticks, cucumber, zucchini, and cauliflower.

❏ Set the table with a centerpiece.

❏ Prepare yourself: freshen your makeup, check your outfit, check your hair, put on perfume.

❏ Start thinking toward a quiet and gentle spirit.

❏ Organize the children as best as you can.

❏ Be ready for your husband's arrival.

❏ Always meet him at the door with a hug, kiss, and smile.

❏ Let him have 15 minutes of quiet to unwind with the paper or the mail.

❏ Do not share any negatives with him until after dinner.

❏ Enjoy your family.

NOTES

Chapter 3—Family Mission Statements and Goals
1. Some material in this chapter is adapted from Bob and Emilie Barnes, *The 15-Minute Money Manager* (Eugene, OR: Harvest House Publishers, 1993), pp. 13-27.
2. Charles J. Givens, *Financial Self-Defense* (New York: Simon and Schuster, 1990), p. 17.
3. Adapted from Ibid., pp. 23-24.
4. Adapted from Barnes, *15-Minute Money Manager*, pp. 47-49.

Chapter 5—Your To-Do List
1. Some material in this chapter is adapted from Bob and Emilie Barnes, *The 15-Minute Money Manager* (Eugene, OR: Harvest House Publishers, 1993), pp. 36-38.

Chapter 13—The Organization Test
1. Adapted from Emilie Barnes and Sheri Torelli, *Your Simple Guide to a Home-Based Business* (Eugene, OR: Harvest House Publishers, 1999), pp. 17-23.

Chapter 16—Miracles in Minutes
1. Adapted from Emilie Barnes and Sheri Torelli, *Your Simple Guide to a Home-Based Business* (Eugene, OR: Harvest House Publishers, 1999), pp. 141-47.

Chapter 34—Team Effort Starts at Home
1. Jay Adams, *Christian Living in the Home* (Grand Rapids, MI: Baker Book House, 1972), pp. 91-92.
2. Bob and Emilie Barnes, *Growing a Great Marriage* (Eugene, OR: Harvest House Publishers, 1988), p. 27.

Chapter 42—Children and Money
1. Adapted from Bob and Emilie Barnes, *The 15-Minute Money Manager* (Eugene, OR: Harvest House Publishers, 1993), ch. 40.

To contact Emilie Barnes or Sheri Torelli, to find out more about More Hours in My Day time management and organization seminars, or to buy More Hours in My Day products, such as forms and boxes, go to:

www.EmilieBarnes.com

or
write to

More Hours in My Day
2150 Whitestone Dr.
Riverside, CA 92506

or call

951-682-4714

Harvest House Books by Bob & Emilie Barnes

Bob & Emilie Barnes

*15-Minute Devotions
for Couples*

Be My Refuge, Lord

*A Little Book of Manners
for Boys*

*Minute Meditations
for Couples*

Bob Barnes

*15 Minutes Alone
with God for Men*

*500 Handy Hints for
Every Husband*

Men Under Construction

*What Makes a Man
Feel Loved*

Emilie Barnes

The 15-Minute Organizer

15 Minutes Alone with God

*15 Minutes of Peace
with God*

*15 Minutes with God
for Grandma*

101 Ways to Love Your Grandkids

*500 Time-Saving Hints
for Women*

Cleaning Up the Clutter

*Emilie's Creative
Home Organizer*

*Everything I Know
I Learned in My Garden*

*Everything I Know
I Learned over Tea*

Friendship Teas to Go

Garden Moment Getaways

A Grandma Is a Gift from God

Heal My Heart, Lord

Home Warming

If Teacups Could Talk

I Need Your Strength, Lord

An Invitation to Tea

Join Me for Tea

A Journey Through Cancer

*Keep It Simple
for Busy Women*

Let's Have a Tea Party!

A Little Book of Manners

A Little Hero in the Making

A Little Princess in the Making

The Little Teacup that Talked

Meet Me Where I Am, Lord

Minute Meditations for Busy Moms

*Minute Meditations for Healing
and Hope*

More Faith in My Day

More Hours in My Day

Quick-Fix Home Organizer

*Quiet Moments for
a Busy Mom's Soul*

A Quiet Refuge

Safe in the Father's Hands

*Simple Secrets to
a Beautiful Home*

Survival for Busy Moms

A Tea to Comfort Your Soul

*The Twelve Teas®
of Celebration*

*The Twelve Teas®
of Friendship*

The Twelve Teas® of Inspiration

What Makes a Woman Feel Loved

Youniquely Woman

More Great Harvest House Books by Emilie Barnes

MEET ME WHERE I AM, LORD

Devotions for Women

In these short but thought-provoking meditations created especially for busy women, you can experience the lasting refreshment of God's presence meeting you... right where you are. Emilie Barnes offers...

- devotions to inspire and encourage
- practical suggestions for infusing life with faith
- closing prayers to place concerns in God's hands
- Bible verses for wisdom and comfort
- space to write reflections

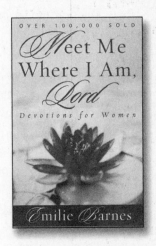

MORE FAITH IN MY DAY

10-Minute Meditations for Women from Proverbs

Emilie invites you to take a moment away from daily demands to rejuvenate your heart and mind with wisdom from Proverbs. More Faith in My Day offers the Bible's insights to your heart through features like...

- devotions inspired by Proverbs' teachings of goodness, love, work, family
- "Today's Wisdom" to enrich personal faith life
- ideas to turn God's abundant knowledge into action
- prayers for moments of meditation and connection

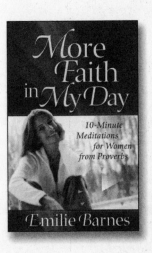

HOME WARMING

Secrets to Making Your House a Welcoming Place

Bestselling author Emilie Barnes shares her gift of gracious hospitality with those longing to express kindness and joy in their home's décor, personality, and style.

Artist Susan Rios' paintings of charming living spaces invite readers to relax, take in the ambience, and glean from Emilie's passion for creating a home with a heart.

- Treat strangers like friends, friends like family, and everyone like royalty.
- Let your living room become the home's hearth, a place of warm conversation.
- Make spaces that welcome everyone from little children to the elderly.

This beautiful collection of friendly advice and practical ideas inspires every woman's personal touch and is a radiant gift for weddings, showers, and housewarmings.

YOUNIQUELY WOMAN

Becoming Who God Designed You to Be

by Kay Arthur, Emilie Barnes, Donna Otto

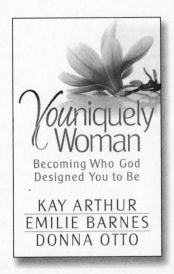

Have you ever longed for a wiser, seasoned woman to take you lovingly under her wing and help you find your way in this confusing world? Here is your answer. Bestselling authors and speakers Kay Arthur, Emilie Barnes, and Donna Otto have been great friends for years, and now they've come together to share—with warmth, humor, and compassion—the wisdom and life experience they've gained in their years of following God and being wives and mothers.

Offering straight talk on their mistakes and what they wish they'd known and put into action when they were younger, these dynamic women share specific ways you can make your life richer and more fulfilling, including how to:

- live intentionally and follow the path God has for you as a woman
- develop and carry out a biblically based vision for your home, marriage, and children
- nurture your own spiritual life and the spiritual life of your children

Kay, Emilie, and Donna have helped many women move toward all that God designed them to be—now let them help you.